Understanding Religion through Artificial Intelligence

Scientific Studies of Religion: Inquiry and Explanation

Series editors: Luther H. Martin, Donald Wiebe, William W. McCorkle Jr., D. Jason Slone, and Radek Kundt

Scientific Studies of Religion: Inquiry and Explanation publishes cutting-edge research in the new and growing field of scientific studies in religion. Its aim is to publish empirical, experimental, historical, and ethnographic research on religious thought, behavior, and institutional structures. The series works with a broad notion of scientific that includes innovative work on understanding religion(s), both past and present. With an emphasis on the cognitive science of religion, the series includes complementary approaches to the study of religion, such as psychology and computer modeling of religious data. Titles seek to provide explanatory accounts for the religious behaviors under review, both past and present.

The Attraction of Religion, edited by D. Jason Slone and James A. Van Slyke
The Cognitive Science of Religion, edited by D. Jason Slone and William W. McCorkle Jr.
Contemporary Evolutionary Theories of Culture and the Study of Religion, Radek Kundt
Death Anxiety and Religious Belief, Jonathan Jong and Jamin Halberstadt
The Impact of Ritual on Child Cognition, Veronika Rybanska
Language, Cognition, and Biblical Exegesis, edited by Ronit Nikolsky, Istvan Czachesz, Frederick S. Tappenden & Tamas Biro
The Learned Practice of Religion in the Modern University, Donald Wiebe
The Mind of Mithraists, Luther H. Martin
Naturalism and Protectionism in the Study of Religions, Juraj Franek
New Patterns for Comparative Religion, William E. Paden
Philosophical Foundations of the Cognitive Science of Religion, Robert N. McCauley with E. Thomas Lawson
Religion Explained?, edited by Luther H. Martin and Donald Wiebe
Religion in Science Fiction, Steven Hrotic
Religious Evolution and the Axial Age, Stephen K. Sanderson
The Roman Mithras Cult, Olympia Panagiotidou with Roger Beck
Solving the Evolutionary Puzzle of Human Cooperation, Glenn Barenthin

Understanding Religion through Artificial Intelligence

Bonding and Belief

Justin E. Lane

BLOOMSBURY ACADEMIC
LONDON • NEW YORK • OXFORD • NEW DELHI • SYDNEY

BLOOMSBURY ACADEMIC
Bloomsbury Publishing Plc
50 Bedford Square, London, WC1B 3DP, UK
1385 Broadway, New York, NY 10018, USA
29 Earlsfort Terrace, Dublin 2, Ireland

BLOOMSBURY, BLOOMSBURY ACADEMIC and the Diana logo are trademarks
of Bloomsbury Publishing Plc

First published in Great Britain 2021
Paperback edition published 2023

Copyright © Justin E. Lane, 2021

Justin E. Lane has asserted his right under the Copyright, Designs and
Patents Act, 1988, to be identified as Author of this work.

For legal purposes the Acknowledgments on p. ix constitute an extension
of this copyright page.

All rights reserved. No part of this publication may be reproduced or transmitted
in any form or by any means, electronic or mechanical, including photocopying,
recording, or any information storage or retrieval system, without prior
permission in writing from the publishers.

Bloomsbury Publishing Plc does not have any control over, or responsibility for, any
third-party websites referred to or in this book. All internet addresses given in this
book were correct at the time of going to press. The author and publisher regret
any inconvenience caused if addresses have changed or sites have ceased
to exist, but can accept no responsibility for any such changes.

A catalogue record for this book is available from the British Library.

Library of Congress Control Number: 2021933610.

ISBN: HB: 978-1-3501-0355-9
PB: 978-1-3502-4131-2
ePDF: 978-1-3501-0356-6
eBook: 978-1-3501-0357-3

Series: Scientific Studies of Religion: Inquiry and Explanation

Typeset by Deanta Global Publishing Services, Chennai, India

To find out more about our authors and books visit www.bloomsbury.com and
sign up for our newsletters

Contents

List of Illustrations		vi
Foreword		vii
Acknowledgments		ix
1	Introduction	1
2	Religions, Old and New	31
3	Bonding and Belief	55
4	Identity and Extremism	77
5	Artificial Intelligence and Religions in Silico	105
6	From AI in Silico, to AI in Situ: Creating AI Gurus, Bird's Eye Views of Christianity, and Using MAAI to Study Social Stability	133
7	Schisms and Sacred Values	163
8	The Future of Religion	175
Notes		199
References		209
Index		240

Illustrations

Figures

1.1	An example of a simple artificial neural network	6
3.1	Proposed relationships of the IIS	60
3.2	Network-based representation of a personal schema	70
3.3	Visual depiction of schemas with conceptual ties	72
4.1	An example of a semantic network map constructed from a participant's semi-structured interview during the initial pilot study	101
4.2	Results of SEM	103
5.1	Motivation plot for typical run of the model presented in Whitehouse et al. (2012)	109
5.2	Run of IIS model with similar settings to Whitehouse et al. (2012)	128
5.3	A conversion to a new religious movement within the simulation	130
6.1	Visualized output of the Rescorla-Wagner model	139
6.2	Results from analyzing the strength and frequency of key terms drawn from sermons in a census region	151
7.1	A depiction of how the IIS explains some social schisms	166

Tables

5.1	Variables and Settings for DMR1 Model as Published by Whitehouse et al. (2012b)	107
5.2	Settings for DMR1 Parameter Sweep Experiment	110
5.3	Parameter Settings for DMR1 Replication	127
5.4	Means for Social Identity by Group Size	132

Foreword

Get set for an invigorating ride to the frontiers of the cognitive science of religion by a scholar who is not afraid to seek new pathways in unexplored territory and who is even willing to point to new places to build striking abodes. The role of intrepid explorer fits Justin Lane well. He has already accumulated an impressive number of publications on subjects of intense interest, for example, predicting religious extremism, explaining the conditions of religious violence, the role that anxiety plays in religious behavior, modeling terror management theory, identify fusion, and semantic networks. Need I go on?

Those of you who read the Foreword before turning to the Introduction or, if you are in a hurry, Chapter 1, most probably do so because you want to taste the flavor of the book before you are ready to delve into its contents. Be ready, then, to be surprised because Lane wants you to face up to science at its most adventurous when dealing with puzzling but important phenomena, namely religious thought and behavior.

All scientific investigation involves employing theoretical spectacles to bring obscure data into focus. Lane is willing to show us what the "magic" of artificial intelligence (AI) can bring to light in very unexpected ways. So here we have before us *Understanding Religion through Artificial Intelligence: Bonding and Belief*. If both the pope and Elon Musk signal both the possibilities and dangers of the work that algorithms on big data can accomplish, then it is surely worthwhile to give an expert in AI a hearing as he shows you what new knowledge can be gained by modeling various forms of religiosity and also warning us of what ethical dangers lurk when data mining is employed for bad ends. Many people will indeed be surprised that AI can not only predict patterns of religious extremism but write convincing sermons!

It is not as if cognitive scientists had not already turned their attention to religion as a subject worthy of investigation. The move from interpretation to explanation had already begun to gather steam in the last decade of the twentieth century with a number of groundbreaking works such as Dan Sperber's *Rethinking Symbolism*, Stewart Guthrie's *Faces in the Clouds*, Lawson and McCauley's *Rethinking Religion: Connecting Religion and Culture*, Pascal Boyer's *The Naturalness of Religious Ideas*, and Harvey Whitehouse's *Modes of*

Religiosity. These works had begun to attract the attention of a new generation of students in psychology, anthropology, philosophy, religious studies, history, and even evolutionary biology who were eager to participate in the cognitive revolution. They brought with them not only a profound interest in theoretical and methodological issues that connected cognition and culture but a conviction that empirical and experimental studies were next on the docket. *Religion Explained? The Cognitive Science of Religion After Twenty-Five Years* tells an important part of the story of the development of the cognitive science of religion when scholars from various disciplines decided to work together by leaning and speaking the same language that had emerged. But science is always a work in progress, its discoveries always provisional. There is always more to learn, more to discover, new methods to apply. Justin Lane brings to this quickly developing field, or dare we say discipline of inquiry, the tools of artificial intelligence. In reading this work you will learn how the practitioners of AI go about figuring out what is happening when people engage in attention-grabbing forms of behavior. You will also discover what kinds of behavior will emerge when certain conditions prevail, for example, extreme forms of religious violence. You will also find out why simulating certain processes provides a means of understanding instances such as identity fusion and bonding.

The overall project that has captured Lane's attention is how computational modeling can provide us with a deeper understanding of how groups maintain social cohesion. This is a serious issue that is relevant for political scientists and their influence on makers of policy, sociologists and their concern for constructive and destructive social arrangements, psychologists and their concern for issues of identity, historians and their focus on group conflict and peaceful resolutions. It is also of interest to the general public in times of peace and strife.

Every chapter in this book points to new ways of explaining and therefore understanding old subjects in new ways. I was particularly impressed with his chapter on ritual, an obvious favorite of mine. Lane goes beyond how rituals are formally represented to their effect on social cohesion.

The cognitive science of religion has proven its staying power as it attracts new students to its laboratories. This book is a welcome and impressive addition to an already burgeoning corpus of investigations into religious thought and behavior.

E. Thomas Lawson

Acknowledgments

As with any work of this type, there is a list of people who deserve a great deal of thanks, not all of which are able to be mentioned here. First, in working with my doctoral supervisor, Prof. Harvey Whitehouse, I have learned many valuable lessons that I will carry with me. I have been fortunate to have many academic mentors, including Bill Paden, Luther Martin, and Tom Lawson: you have been great mentors and I have been honored to work with you in the past, and more so to have continued to work with you after my time as your student had passed. If not for your guidance, I would not have had the chance to undertake this research in the first place.

Ken Kahn, Wesley Wildman, LeRon Shults, and Saikou Diallo: you have been invaluable resources, mentors, and friends as I honed my skills developing and redeveloping the models that have come from the work discussed here—I look forward to working with all of you in the future. I would also like to thank Joe Allen, Rob Singler, and John Balch: you helped clarify many of these thoughts through debates that I look forward to continuing.

To the many connections I made in Singapore: Clarence, Kimal, Mario, Penny Tok, and Paul Reddish, and the many friends I made at church: without your help and support I can say this research could not have been as successful. Also, thanks to Jenny Ng at Barker Road Methodist Church and Rev. Tan. Your wisdom and knowledge of the history of the church is a priceless resource to us all. Rev. Poon and the YAM, your openness to me and my research made the church feel like a home away from home for me on many occasions.

Furthermore, while many of my colleagues around the world have been valuable during this process a few warrant specific note. Lee McCorkle and Dimitris Xygalatas, your mentorship and encouragement over the years have been priceless. Similarly, my friends in Brno, Aleš Chalupa, Tomáš Hampejs, Radek Kundt, and of course Kat Štastna, I only hope to be able to return your support and kindness in the future. To my colleagues at Oxford, I often cannot say enough. Srin Madapalli and Tamer Azer, your conversations inspired me on more than one occasion to never forget the options we have and the paths that we make available for ourselves. Also, my colleagues at ICEA cannot go overlooked, particularly Dan Mullins, for your friendship and guidance in helping me to navigate the Oxford system; and Chris Kavanagh, and Jonathan Jong: a great deal can be learned about academic politics from those you trust. This work also wouldn't have been completed if it weren't for Cathal, Mick, and Veronika, who brought great craic to me and the 'sheaf when we needed it most.

Lastly, and most importantly, my family, to whom this work is dedicated, deserves the greatest thanks. You have been there for me throughout all my travels and when trying to meet every goal, even if I did not return the favor; particularly my mother, Suzie, to whom I feel I owe so much for her sacrifices, and my grandparents, Lt. Col. James A. Fife and Janet Fife, for opening my mind to so many new ideas with thoughtful conversation. Lastly, my wife, Veronika, and my son Adam: you have my deepest thanks. Your love and patience have allowed me to embrace the aspects of living that mean the most to me.

1

Introduction

01001001 01101110 00100000 01110100 01101000 01100101 00100000
01100010 01100101 01100111 01101001 01101110 01101110 01101001
01101110 01100111 00100000 01000111 01101111 01100100 00100000
01100011 01110010 01100101 01100001 01110100 01100101 01100100
00100000 01110100 01101000 01100101 00100000 01101000 01100101
01100001 01110110 01100101 01101110 00100000 01100001 01101110
01100100 00100000 01110100 01101000 01100101 00100000 01100101
01100001 01110010 01110100 01101000 00101110

—Genesis 1:1

The next day I drove to the town from which I had left the country. I knew where the bus station was located. I had a plan to get to the train station at 10 and leave from there. I waited patiently with a smile on my face as I waited for the bus. When the bus pulled in, I climbed up on the stairs and walked down a couple feet and the driver stopped the bus along the way to listen to my prayer.

At that moment, I felt the answer to the question I had asked myself. He wanted me to see the light of God within me and to give myself an opportunity to receive His love unconditionally. And that is when I knew that God loved me unconditionally.

I asked God to love me and to give me that opportunity to receive His love.

—AIwaken (the AI guru), 2019

In September 2019, Pope Francis said that artificial intelligence (AI) systems "raise increasingly significant implications in all areas of human activity" (Reuters, 2019). Similar phrases have been echoed by many others, including the entrepreneur Elon Musk, who regularly warns of the dangers of AI systems. At the time, neither one of them was aware of the fact that new AI systems have been created that can not only predict patterns of religious extremism and violence but also write sermons like the one you see in this chapter's epigraph. While I aim to discuss the obvious ethical issues that may have already come to mind surrounding the idea of AI that appears religious, much less AI that appears to mimic religious extremism, by the end of this book, I think it best to start with a bit of foundation concerning how we can view religion in a way that can support grounded scientific research and then move to how we can discuss AI in a realistic sense to avoid hyperbolic pronouncements about an AI apocalypse.

Setting off to discuss religion, in any venue, puts one in the middle of such a complex topic that the discussion is usually fruitless from the beginning because the basic assumptions about "religion" can vary wildly. Therefore, bringing AI into this already complex discussion could—on the face of it—appear to be an idea doomed to fail. My belief is that this is not so. Rather, I believe that the use of AI and other disciplines from computer science can help us clarify many of the issues; and this belief is shared by a growing number of experts in both religious studies and the computational sciences (data science, AI, engineering, modeling and simulation, cognitive science, etc.). My goal in this book is not to make anyone a new expert in either religious studies or AI, but rather to provide more fundamental discussions of each subject and to use the foundation of cognitive science to create a bridge linking two of today's most important subjects. The result of this, I hope, is the presentation of a new framework that can create an interdisciplinary framework that fits well within current trends in the field but pushes them further by leveraging the power of computer science.

1.1 The Scientific Study of Religion

Religion has many components, such as rituals, gods, rites of passage and holy texts. Just about any component that you can conceive of already has books, journals, and conferences that have been dedicated to the subject. For millennia, questions about religion have been answered theologically. It was not until the late 1800s that there was a serious push toward a secular study of religion (Müller, 1882), however unsuccessful it may have been in hindsight. Even among the relatively recent "secular" study of religion, the approach to religious phenomena has—almost exclusively—been nonscientific in its methods. This is not to say that science did not inform these approaches. One of the earliest classics in religious studies was written by William James (James, 1902), one of the founders of modern psychology. However, there is a difference between utilizing theories that are informed by scientific trends to interpret aspects of religions (as was done by James, Freud, Jung, and others) and testing theories about aspects of religion scientifically.

This pattern of nonscientific research into the study of religion may have its roots in the historical beginnings of the field, as religion—as a way of knowing things about reality—is rooted in different forms and degrees of revelation. That is to say, it has been perfectly legitimate in theology to gain new knowledge through revelation. Religious studies, even in its secular form, follows this tradition in the form of "thinking" about religion by using interpretive paradigms that do not need to be tested empirically to be considered useful by the field. The secular approach to religion has, however, removed some of its theological assumptions and moved its "offices" from places of worship to big cushy armchairs in rooms with many books; typically located in the halls of Western universities. Science, in contrast, bases its threshold for generating new knowledge on the scientific method. To simplify it, this is a circular method where ideas (or hypotheses) are stated, data is gathered about the idea, the data is analyzed to see if the idea generally holds up, and then the results can lead to the revision of the original idea and some new knowledge.

Given the differences between how knowledge is created in the domains of religion and science, it is of little wonder why these two systems have been considered "at odds" in the minds of so many since the Renaissance. Today, many suggest that science "disproves" religion. My perspective is that this sort of statement shows a poor understanding of both science and religion. As I mentioned above, science is not a body of knowledge, but a way of discovering knowledge. As such, science is not an immutable set of beliefs or knowledge, nor is it defined by it. Religions, as I will discuss later, are often demarcated by their beliefs and the behaviors in a way that science is not. In this way, science and religion may have different beliefs, but in both cases, the beliefs are subject to change—albeit by different mechanisms. The idea that science "disproves" religion is further from the mark than many realize for another reason: science—which assumes naturalism—addresses aspects of our natural world and things related to that which we can measure, while religion does not. When a religion makes a claim about the supernatural world, it is by definition outside of the domain of science—that is to say, the natural world; so science can offer a competing, empirically rooted alternative explanation to the idea that thunder and lightning are caused by Thor. However, science cannot measure or test that which would be required to negate the religious interpretation: to demonstrate that Thor, or any other deity, does not exist.

1.2 Artificial Intelligence

In today's world, AI is treated with almost as much enchantment as the gods of yesteryear. It appears to have superhuman capabilities that are nearly unexplainable, and there appears to be an increasing number of people who link AI to the end of humanity or its ultimate salvation and immortality, not unlike a religious doomsday. In reality, the AI systems we have today are very artificial and rather unintelligent. Most AI systems today are specialized to complete a single very specific task, and when applied to other tasks that they weren't designed for, even within a similar domain, they perform rather poorly. In most cases, an AI system cannot even handle new tasks because of how it was designed. For example, an AI system designed to discern positive or negative emotion in a text will throw an error if you ask it to discern the positive or negative emotion portrayed in an image. It simply cannot handle the image because the system was only trained to address text data. This inability for AI in its current state to generalize is a serious problem for the field and an obvious hurdle that AI needs to overcome in order for it to become our new overlords. This is not to say that there aren't very bright people working to create generalizable AI systems that could—for example—process symbols with emotional information associated to them from multiple sources, and that they aren't making strides toward that goal—they are. However, when it comes to many of the aspects that we think of when we consider the human experience, AI is not addressing them.

1.2.1 Machine Learning

Today, the term "AI" is synonymous with what is called machine learning. Machine learning is a type of AI that is inspired by how our brain learns. Neuropsychologists have long noticed that our brain, which is comprised of cells called neurons, works by creating connections between neurons and then activating these patterns of neurons. In early research into neurons, it was found that a neuron either fires or it does not. When it does, an electro-chemical signal is triggered across two or more neurons, activating them in our brain. What was found is that those neurons that are activated together repeatedly begin to create links that can facilitate easier activation in the future. These networks of neurons, through the information transmitted over them by our sensory facilities over time, can result in neural patterns that allow us to learn different patterns and perform different tasks.

Today, even the most advanced machine learning systems, such as those employed by companies like Google, IBM, and OpenAI utilize algorithms that are inspired by this neurophysiological analogy. The way that they create computational systems that work like our mind is by creating what are called artificial neural networks. While their name is somewhat self-explanatory as to what these systems are (neural inspired computational systems), how exactly these systems work is far less understood by many.

One way that we can begin to understand machine learning is through a simple example. Let's take a simple lab-mouse. This mouse lives its life in a cozy little cage in a lab. In its cage, there are two levers: one red and one blue. One day, the mouse puts its weight on the blue lever, causing it to trigger a mechanism that drops a tasty blue pellet into its cage. After eating the pellet, it goes back to that lever, and pushes again, causing yet another blue pellet to be dropped. As the mouse plays with other toys, wheels, and things in its cage, it realizes that the other objects do not provide the tasty blue pellets, but when the blue lever is pushed, the blue pellet is provided. One day, it pushes a red lever, which provides it with a red pill that is not tasty, but also opens the door to the cage. The mouse however gets hungry, and because it has learned that the blue lever provides the tasty food, it returns to its cage and pushes its blue lever, receiving its reliable treat.

Effectively, machine learning algorithms mimic the exact same process. More technically, you can imagine a dataset that has a table with two columns. In one column, it says "blue lever" and "red lever." In the other column it says, "tasty food" and "nasty food." As we know from the example earlier, we know that the cage is set up so that the blue lever releases tasty food, while the red lever releases nasty food and opens the door. Machine learning algorithms can utilize networks of nodes and links, where each link has a weighted value connecting the nodes. The nodes can then be selected to "fire" or not depending on the data input to the system. The system can be trained by repeatedly exposing the network to data over time, just like the mouse was exposed to the food repeatedly over time. And in this way, the system can learn the associations between its input and an expected output over time.

Just as repeated exposures between the lever and food can be learned, so can its co-occurrence between the lever and the status of the door. In this way there are two potential inputs (blue lever, red lever), and four potential outputs: two for the food (tasty blue pellet, nasty red pellet) and two for the door (door closed, door opened). We can code the relationships between the levers and the status of the door as either 1 or 0, for present or not. That is to say, if there is a relationship between the blue lever and the tasty blue pellet, it can be represented as a 1. But, when there is no relationship, such as that between the blue lever and the nasty red pellet, or open door, it can be represented as a 0. One way of visualizing how this network looks, and how we can mathematically represent it is shown in Figure 1.1.

Naturally, AI systems are often more complex than this. There are several ways of representing networks, changing the way in which they learn, how they can work, if they output discrete outputs (as in categorization) or not (as in regressions), how the system is trained, how it optimizes the learned associations in the system, etc. New forms of machine learning, such as deep learning, take these facets even further by effectively stacking multiple neural network systems on top of another, creating multiple layers of neural networks that can have different properties for learning (and even for forgetting). These networks are more state-of-the-art systems and can even outperform humans in domains such as image recognition and even playing games like *Go* and *StarCraft*. Nevertheless, basic approaches using reinforcement learning in the traditional sense of machine learning and as integrated into more constrained MAAI approaches are discussed later in Chapters 6 and 7. Among the topics discussed, a presentation of a new machine learning system to create religious leaders (and possible extremists) is presented in Chapter 6.

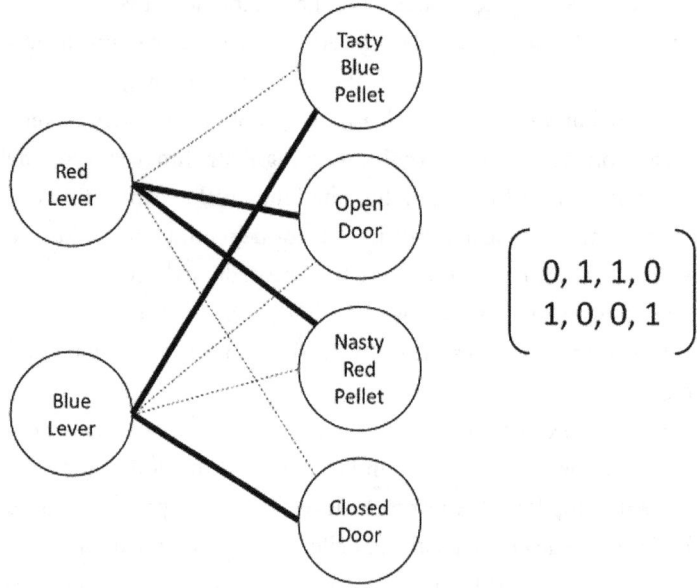

Figure 1.1 An example of a simple artificial neural network.

1.2.2 Encyclopedic AI

Even though machine learning is—by far—the most common approach in AI, it is not the only possible form. Other approaches to AI attempt to create computer systems that are told the answers to every question (rather than having the system learn answers itself); in these ways, the systems are attempting to create computational encyclopedias, where questions and answers are stored and retrieved as needed. This approach has largely been abandoned because it is not only burdensome to create, but it is also outperformed by machine learning systems in almost every domain.

1.2.3 Ontologies

Other AI systems have attempted to use more complex interactions to study the relationships between human language and behaviors. These systems rely heavily on what are called "ontologies." Ontologies generally are ways of organizing information about a specific idea (or representation). Usually, an ontology is limited in its focus to a particular domain, and this limiting of scope can allow for the ontology to be very rich in information because it isn't trying to capture everything, but only specific domain-relevant knowledge about a topic and the ways representations are used within that domain. Ontologies typically have formal ways of defining categories, properties, and relations between (and within) representations. For example, a representation about a person could be that a person has an age, a gender, a name, an ethnicity, a religion, or a nationality. The rules for each of those categories would also be defined: age must be a number, gender could be a word (to define it categorically) or a number (if looking to place gender on a spectrum from 0 to 1 for example), name would be a word, and ethnicity, religion and nationality would all be words as well (or sets of words for multi-ethnic people). In the past, ontologies have been difficult and time consuming to create because humans need to code the rules and relationships that define the ontology. In later chapters, I will describe new ways of automatically creating a kind of ontology (a semantic network) from text data (drawn from online sources and transcriptions of field interviews) that can be a powerful tool for research into culture and religion.

1.2.4 Multi-Agent AI (MAAI)

Naturally, there are potential applications for all of the kinds of AI that have been previously developed for studying different aspects of religion. However, when considering that here we wish to study the relationship between bonding and belief in religions, it brings to mind a critical aspect of human religiosity is not a part of the earlier approaches: human sociality. Machine learning has made many impressive advances in the past few years alone, which has led to renewed discussions concerning how AI is quickly reaching a human-like kind of intelligence, for better and for worse. However, machine learning still neglects one of the most important factors of human intelligence, social intelligence. The simple fact of the vast majority of human experience, critical aspects of human intelligence, and learning, is premised upon the evolutionary fact that we are social creatures: AI is not . . . yet. As such, we cannot really have a human-like AI unless we also have a social (and I would add cultural) AI.

There is, however, a form of AI that does attempt to address human sociality. This AI, called multi-agent AI (or MAAI), seeks to create psychologically realistic computational systems that are able to be implemented in agent-based computer models where the agents in the model represent people (Lane, 2013). When I first introduced this idea to the study of religion, it was directly inspired by the work of others in the area of AI and social simulation, specifically the arguments put forward by researchers like Ron Sun (2001, 2006) and Joshua Epstein (1999, 2006; Epstein & Axtell, 1996). What sets MAAI apart from other kinds of AI today is that it does not focus solely on machine learning. Rather, it aims to instantiate psychologically realistic algorithms that approximate the mechanisms of human cognitive processes. So, whereas AI today goes about simulating human psychology in a generally roundabout fashion (if at all) rooted in machine learning, MAAI takes a more directed approach rooted in cognitive psychology.

A key difference between machine learning and MAAI can be observed in the application of artificial neural networks, which attempt to replicate the neurophysiological makeup of the human mind. Whereas artificial neural networks are great for a wide range of learning applications, and they can often learn to approximate the same output as a human (given enough input and proper structure and training), the algorithm itself is largely blind. Artificial neural networks can often approximate very complex algorithms, and the ability for artificial neural networks to approximate such a wide range of complex associations has led some to consider neural networks as universal function approximators. The universal approximation theorem states that artificial neural networks (at least feedforward networks) with a hidden layer consisting of a finite number of neurons can approximate continuous functions (Hornik, 1991).[1] This has led to their widespread adoption as a tool for solving many complex problems. However, there is a serious question to be raised here: in the space of human psychological functions, and in particular, that subset that is relevant to governing complex social reasoning and interaction, how many of those cognitive functions can be sufficiently modeled as mathematical functions? This is largely an open question. However, adding for example, basic logic statements (such as conditional logic statements like p→q "if p, then q") require additional functionality that are more complex than just the replication of a specific mathematical function; that is to say, machine learning may be able to determine complex relationships between variables, but it requires additional functionality to actually make decisions based on the discerned relationships (a statement that iterates in complexity for each observation-decision function that needs to be defined in the system). When discussing the theorem of universal approximation, feedforward networks are typically discussing functions that would represent a regression-like problem, which is different from discussing how well artificial neural networks can approximate any decision. This is not to say that they are not—in principle—be able to do so. On the contrary, it is possible to view social decisions (go to a party/do not go to a party) as classification problems, which could allow for us to replicate many key decision mechanisms if we represent them mathematically as problems solvable for regressions that address binary data.

For example, in a classic experimental paradigm used by psychologists to measure inhibitory control called the go/no-go task, participants have to decide to do something quickly and sometimes signals are given to not do that thing (so you either decide to "go" or not). From this, psychologists can calculate the number of errors and the speed with which they are made. Similar systems, given enough training data could easily outperform a human on this task. Indeed, it is easily conceivable that an AI system could complete almost any go/no-go task with near immediacy and without error. But there are two issues with the fact that it would not be human-like at all. First, the system would be premised on that specific task. Until new rules were learned for a new task, performance on any other inhibitory control task would be sub-optimal even if it were possible (and it likely would not be depending on how the initial system was implemented to interact with the task—keep in mind, AI designed for language can't solve math today). If that reason is not damming enough, there is a secondary issue, which is that we have errors in our inhibitory control, which can be linked to key evolutionary problems, which can be beneficial for survival in certain contexts. For example, inhibitory control is manipulated by ritual behavior even in young children cross-culturally, but too much inhibitory control can be damaging to development and survival (Rybanska, 2020; Rybanska, Mckay, Jong, & Whitehouse, 2018). In addition, inhibitory control has been found to support creativity throughout the lifespan (Cassotti, Agogue, Camarda, Houde, & Borst, 2016). However, it appears that it is not perfect inhibitory control that allows for creativity. Rather, there needs to be enough relaxation in inhibitory control to allow for spontaneity, while also allowing for an individual to concentrate on the newly generated idea. Therefore, even the kind of creative cognitive thinking that we take for granted on a daily basis would require multiple systems (and possible subsystems of those systems) to function at a basic level, even within a constrained domain, and machine learning today is unable to account for or generate this kind of behavior. This suggests two things: (1) that there is more going on in human intelligence than can currently be captured by AI and (2) that AI is nowhere close to being able to dominate its human creators.

On the other hand, the MAAI approach is more "method agnostic." It approaches the "software of the mind" as a suite of modular functions. These functions can be modeled using mathematical functions, artificial neural networks, as if-then conditional logic, as Bayesian systems, or all of them simultaneously addressing different domains or abilities as the literature would suggest is most appropriate.

By the end of this book, I hope that the reader will not only have a better idea about how we can approach religion in a way that is productive and scientifically valid, but also how AI can fit into this critical research project. Of course, the subjects of religion and AI are both too large to be covered in the space we have here, and providing an exhaustive account of how these two fields could be synthesized is beyond the scope of this book. However, there are a few clear intersections where new breakthroughs in AI provide a fascinating opportunity to facilitate great leaps in our understanding about certain aspects of human religiosity.

1.3 Defining the Links: Religion as a Cybernetic Assemblage

Now that we have a brief overview of AI, we should also briefly unpack what is meant by the term "religion" and how we can build a framework for such a complex social phenomena that would allow us to potentially engage directly in computational models of religion. To do that, I'll first address some issues around the idea of defining religion and then discuss how we can view social systems (with a particular focus on religions) as cybernetic assemblages that can address the ways in which religions (and other complex social systems) act as complex adaptive systems, but does so in a way that can facilitate clear and careful theorizing about the complex mechanisms that individuals possess that give rise to the array of social phenomena we observe in the world's religious landscape. This approach, whereby complex social systems are viewed as dynamic assemblages, I refer to as cultural cybernetics.

All books such as this often discuss how this is a slippery term or a "thorny" issue, and some scholars don't even bother to operationalize the term "religion." Instead, many opt for a more heuristic approach to the study, hearkening to US Supreme Court Justice Potter Stewart's "I know it when I see it" approach to pornographic obscenity in Jacobellis v. Ohio (Stewart, 1963). While this may work for some, I fear that failing to operationalize what we are talking about when dealing with subjects as poorly defined, variant, socially important, and emotionally charged as religion can be more damaging than useful.

One of the things that a multi-agent AI approach such as the one outlined in this book can provide the field is a slight reframing that deals with a problem of mereology[2] that is rarely discussed. Effectively, the scientific study of religion today has several issues, the most pressing of which, I believe, is a mereological one. To put it simply, religions are made up of groups of people, but the group—as an entity—does not exist. We discuss "Christianity" as if it were some physical *thing* out in the world that we can study. However, many philosophers of science have long discussed a distinction between what are called natural kinds. A common way to define a "natural kind" is that "it corresponds to a grouping that reflects the structure of the natural world rather than the interests and actions of human beings" (Bird & Tobin, 2017). A natural kind can be studied for its physical properties. It has properties such as mass, dimensions, and can physically interact and is affected by physical laws such as gravity. Religions are not natural kinds. What for example is the "mass" of Paganism (assuming for the moment that it would be a viable single category)? How would one even calculate such a thing? We could perhaps take all of the constituent parts that we believe are important for our definition of Paganism as a religion (i.e., the people, books, temples, holy sites, etc.) and then calculate their mass, but then have we calculated the mass of Paganism? Or have we just calculated the mass of several things that we believe constitute an abstract category or thing that we have assembled artificially? Naturally, the foregoing questions come off as absurd when put so directly, but they serve to show that religions are defined as things that reflect "the interests and actions of human beings." Therefore, it's best that we understand religions for what they are: academic abstractions. They are often useful academic abstractions, however, and therein lies the importance of the debate.

How we define something affects how we can study it. In the study of religion, we often look at religions as groups of people. Obviously, this is not entirely misguided, as any one person believing in supernatural agents that control their life is a fascinating subject for clinical psychology, it is only if a group of people believe in the same supernatural agent that it becomes a subject within the purview of "religious studies."

Similarly, the way in which we define religion as a category or subject of study is often problematic. Some scholars have moved beyond the "I know it when I see it" approach and offered definitions that are based on heuristics or the idea that religion can be defined as a constellation of features. However, this is not so informative as it may first appear. If we say that something has twelve features, but we only observe six of those features, is it still the thing we wish to study? Is it half of what we want to study? Do we only want to then focus on the features that are present? How do we define that which does not possess all the required features? And what do we do in cases where what we want to study is changing and may cease to have one of the features or begin to add another feature?

Historically, the study of religion has been a Western endeavor, and a relatively recent endeavor at that. While for all of human history we have been enacting behaviors that appear to be linked to belief in supernatural agents, religion has not always looked as it is today, and this affects how we study the subject itself. Early on, all of what we would now call "religious studies" was comprised of theologians and other related clergy, and theologians may have—at times—interacted with people or materials from different religious traditions than their own. When religious studies began to take form as a subject of study separate from theology after the enlightenment (particularly in the late 1800s), it had not been separated from its theological roots; even today, some discuss how the field still harbors latent theological tendencies (Martin & Wiebe, 2012; Wiebe, 1991, 1999).

The study of religion has always been preoccupied with typologies—likely because of the group-like nature of religion. As time has facilitated greater exposure between the religions, the typologies have become more descriptive. Early on, religions were effectively Judeo-Christian or pagan. Then, Islam was moved from a quasi-pagan delineation of "Mohammedan" religion to be included with Christianity and Judaism as "religions of the book" on the one hand and pagan traditions on the other hand. Then, as more exposure between East and West led to cultural and knowledge exchange in the 1800s, religions became framed as "world religions" and Paganism and the world religions included the original "religions of the book" and added to them Buddhism and Hinduism (it is also interesting to note that this inclusion of Eastern traditions was done on the one hand with a quasi-theological agenda on the part of Theosophists as well as a conception, which lasts to this day, that Eastern religious traditions aren't in fact "religions," but philosophies; see Albanese, 2008). This broad narrative of how we have typologized religion should not be so surprising. It mimics how ethnic and racial stereotypes develop as well: once we discern that there are differences, we start with an us and them dichotomy, then as we learn more about other groups we broaden our group definitions with more nuance and demarcations; however, doing so tells us more about how we view those groups than it does about those groups on their own right (similar things have also been found in how we frame ethnicities in the context of conflicts; see Brubaker, 2002). And this is one of the dangers of heuristic definitions in scientific research. Good scientific research can be extremely useful, but bad scientific research, or pseudo-scientific research parading as science, can be dangerous because the findings appear to have the merits of scientific knowledge, when in fact they are as problematic—and useful—as personal revelations. Working with a complex subject like religion, without defining the subject itself effectively results in research that produces a general system of revelations that are presumably relevant to a subject, but lack directionality and focus in a way that can be easily addressed by adopting a useful—if imperfect—definition of its subject.

To help appropriately address the issue of defining the object of study in a way that embraces the complexity of the subject but offers useful structure for theorizing, I think it is useful to view religion as a cybernetic assemblage. An assemblage is a collection of things, generally speaking.[3] In recent work, the philosopher Manuel DeLanda has outlined a definition of an assemblage that extends to understand complex (possibly emergent) phenomena such as social systems. Specifically, he focuses on the idea that several heterogeneous things can interact in specific ways to give rise to new "things" that can be a subject of study, such as a culture or religion, which is made up of its people, behaviors, languages, places, artifacts, etc. (DeLanda, 2006).

Generally, I am sympathetic to DeLanda's intent, but wish to extend and amend the concept. Specifically, assemblages are typically conceived of as being comprised of parts where their relations are contingent, and not necessary, and the interactions are not typically framed as mechanistically causal. This treads dangerously close to a heuristic "I know it when I see it" approach to defining and formalizing a social system. By treating the relations between the constituent parts of an assemblage as necessary we can better define it as a complex social system. In addition, by formalizing those relationships as mechanistically causal and specifying the conditions under which those interactions would have a specific effect, the system is formalized in a way that is more strictly related to an information processing framework than DeLanda and others may be willing to accept. As such, in the way that I intend to use the term, an assemblage is a collection of heterogeneous entities with defined relations (as rules of interaction) and the necessary and sufficient conditions[4] for that system to produce the higher-level phenomena of interest. From this perspective, you can say that a social system is made up of components and their interactions (people and their interactions with one another, people and their interactions with aspects of the environment, aspects of the environment and their interactions with one another, the effect of the environment on people, the effect of people on the environment, the effect of individual cognitive mechanisms on the people's interactions with both other people and the environment, etc.) and that these interactions can be defined in relation to one another and contextualized. This is not to say that the "constellation" of "traits" that some scholars have used in the past is not a useful approach. Rather, it is to say that we can better define when and how traits of the constellation appear, coappear, or do not appear in religious systems and what arrangement we can expect based on how the underlying components of the system interact with themselves and their environment. In this way, our theorizing doesn't rely on features (or traits) to "emerge"; rather what we could consider traits of the social system are *generated* from the underlying mechanisms of the system (ala Epstein, 1999; Lane, 2017a; we will return to this idea of "emergence" later on).

The assemblage approach also has utility in that it can capture variance along multiple dimensions as well. Whatever a scholar of religion might use as their definition, religious groups in the real world will almost certainly have several different dimensions on which they vary; for example, the number of rituals, the frequency of each ritual, the intensity or emotional arousal associated with each ritual, the number of people in the group, the number of gods in the group, the commitment of the members to the group, and so on. Among those variables that comprise the religious system (i.e., assemblage) any of them could interact with any number of other variables. When viewing a religion as a cybernetic assemblage, the *system* is defined by those variables and their interactions, which, in turn should provide the necessary and sufficient conditions to observe the variance in the different dimensions that we can observe about that religion. As the underlying interactions change in response to external environmental factors (such as other groups in the environment or perhaps even a change in the physical environment), the dimensions will shift and change in response. In this way, religions can be viewed as complex adaptive systems, without having to assume random variation and selection are key mechanisms driving the behaviors and cognitive outputs of individuals.

This is not so unlike the "Evoked Culture" approach, which generally states that cultural variance can be explained by the way in which different evolved cognitive mechanisms interact (or are evoked) by inputs from their environment (Barkow, Cosmides, & Tooby, 1992). One of the differences is that in viewing the social system as a cybernetic assemblage, it explicitly aims to define the interactions between evolved cognitive mechanisms, and does not require that they operate with specific unique inputs into any one module (that is to say, information encapsulation is not necessecarily required; cf. Fodor, 1985). This relaxes some of the assumption concerning the idea that our behaviors are governed by evolved modules in that we do not need to assume modularity or implicate it with specific packets of information that would activate the module. Rather, we can understand that cognitive mechanism vary in the extent to which they are domain general or domain specific and that in some instances, domain specific modules are bootstrapped by their ability to utilize and employ domain general mechanisms as well.

Within an assemblage, we can imagine the different components that are important to the social system as nodes in a network, with links that define under what conditions their interactions occur and what those interactions (and their outcomes) should be. Naturally, there can be more than one link between two nodes in such as system. In this way, we can visually imagine a network existing within a complex (computational) space, shifting and morphing as its constituent parts change in reaction to themselves, their interactions, and their environment. This framework of entities and rules is a thread that will follow through the cybernetic approach that uses multi-agent AI to study social systems.

One issue that may arise when viewing complex systems as assemblages is that the assemblage can include a near-infinite number of variables and interaction rules at lower levels of causation within the system. For example, in religious and cultural systems, you can define the interactions of individuals with their environment, buildings, artifacts, and texts. You can further define the interactions of the evolved cognitive facilities of their minds and perceptual mechanisms that each individual utilizes to interact with environments, buildings, artifacts, and texts. You can even further specify the ways in which neurobiological structures give rise to those facilities and mechanisms—and further to the chemical properties of the neurotransmitters and synaptic reactions that facilitate the neurobiological processes—and so on. Many times, lower (and higher) level processes such as these are considered externalities and ignored or simplified through mathematical assumptions such as averages or distributions for the sake of convenience. However, there is an additional concept that can clarify how we can define complex social systems (both as assemblages and as a target of study), that concept is a singularity. In mathematics, a singularity is a point where some object is not well defined, or the object ceases to be differentiable or readily analyzable. When defining a cybernetic assemblage for a complex social system, those interactions with the constituent parts produce variations that instantiate what can be treated as traits or properties of the system. If there is some subset of the systems parts that do not actually produce any variation, or any variation in the constituent parts that constitute that variable itself, then that variable can be taken as a singularity, since any variance in that constituent part would not constitute any meaningful change in the system as a whole.

The idea of a singularity, and its ability to help us define a scope of study can also be linked to the idea of information processing itself. "Information," as a term, is pervasive in our culture today; some even refer to our current period as the "information age." However, information is rarely defined despite how common it is. Many may be shocked to find out that there is no standard definition of information, but multiple definitions depending on your field of study. Information often exists almost as a fundamental unit that doesn't need to be defined in many cases, it just "is." One of the most common definitions of information, particularly in the small literature addressing information as it pertains to culture and religion, is that of Gregory Bateson (e.g., 1972, p. 229) who defines a unit of information as "a difference which makes a difference." This disarmingly vague notion can be extremely powerful upon further reflection. For example, if no change exists, even from a perceptual standpoint, no information is being processed. Take, for example, two humans in a car. If those two humans do not move, it is not that they can't be perceived, their visual presence can be perceived by us, but without any movement, there isn't any new information that would trigger any required processing. In complex systems, if the system is no longer undergoing any changes, and is in complete stasis, then it isn't producing any new information. This observation fits with the more technical definition of information provided by Claude Shannon, whose theory of communication was not only the basis for one of the most widely utilized definitions of information, it is the basis of the information age's key communications technologies from telegraphs to cellular phones and the internet (Gleick, 2012). In Shannon's definition of information, information can be measured through entropy—or predictability. Effectively, it is looking to understand the probability of observing some bit (or information) as a measure of uncertainty.

$$H(X) = -\sum_{i=0}^{N-1} p_i \log_b p_i \quad (1)$$

Generally speaking, this equation estimates the probability of seeing a bit of information given the probabilities of all the bits that could be observed.

When using this calculation to estimate the entropy of a string of letters (or a word or a text), it demonstrates the point: the entropy of "Shannon," is 2.128; the entropy of "cybernetics" is 3.096; the entropy of the genetic sequence "ATCGTAGTGAC" is 1.981; and the entropy of "aaaaaaaaa" is 0. Notice that in the final string, there is no change, there are no differences that make a difference, and so, if you calculate the entropy of that string, it equals 0. In this way, we can say that if there are no differences that make a difference, then the entropy is 0, there is no significant information held there. We can apply similar thinking to the idea of a cybernetic assemblage and a singularity. If there is no variation of the constituent parts of a singularity that would themselves produce a difference then there is no meaningful information there to be processed and—as such—that singularity can be assumed to be a static force in the system and there isn't a requirement to reduce that part of the assemblage to any constituent parts.

Viewing complex social systems as cybernetic assemblages offers a foundation that brings the study of complex social systems (e.g., religions) closer to being able to offer predictions in the sense more commonly reserved for the natural sciences since it defines the interactive mechanisms and suggests that the interacting parts and their effects can constitute necessary and sufficient conditions that could be specifically stated. In the natural sciences, laws govern the mechanistic operations that produce clear and reliable predictions. In the social sciences, approaching complex social systems as cybernetic assemblages can provide the structure and definition needed to offer more clear mechanisms that can be bounded to create a reliable (i.e., probabilistic) range of outputs that act as predictions; in lieu of calculations based on constant variables.

The approach outlined here focuses on the information processing systems that set religion apart from other forms of human social and cultural behavior and allows us to define religion more specifically: *religions are the set of beliefs held—and behaviors enacted—in reference to supernatural agents by people who share a common set of social ties and are able to exchange information between one another*. This general definition can be the guiding boundary for what we consider to be important to include in a cybernetic assemblage that describes a religious system (or, as offered in the subsequent chapters, parts of a cybernetic assemblage that describes a religious system).

Some readers acquainted with the scientific study of religion might notice that this definition of religion is inspired by a standard definition used in the cognitive science of religion, first presented by Lawson and McCauley, who state that they "construe a religious system as a symbolic-cultural system of ritual acts accompanied by an extensive and largely shared conceptual scheme that includes culturally postulated superhuman agents" (Lawson & McCauley, 1990, p. 5); this definition is itself an adaptation of Spiro's earlier definition of religion as "an institution consisting of culturally patterned interaction with culturally postulated superhuman beings" (1966, p. 96). Like Lawson and McCauley, I choose to "concentrate on 'religious systems' rather than 'religious traditions'" (Lawson & McCauley, 1990, p. 5; although I will use the terms interchangably).

One critical addition to the definition that I have proposed to that of Lawson & McCauley is the clause concerning "people who share a common set of social ties and are able to exchange information among each other." This addition is there to further define a religion by those who participate together in its practices. One could argue that we can interpret the Lawson and McCauley definition to imply a similar boundary, however, I aim to make it more explicit for the sake of clarity. For a moment, let us indulge the idea that there could be two groups of people on two islands who have never spoken to one another. Let us further assume that these two groups have the exact same beliefs and practices (derived from those beliefs) at a single point in time. Does it make sense to consider these two groups part of the same religion? I would argue that it is not. Just because two groups have found that their practices are similar at one point in time does not guarantee that they have the same history—or the same potential futures. It is possible that the two groups are so similar because of the same environmental conditions. But it is unlikely that they will maintain this similarity for much longer as the individuals within those groups come to share information about their beliefs over time. This could cause one of the groups to drift and—because there is no communication between the groups—the consensus between the groups would certainly degrade. This shows one example where clarity can be found in viewing religions as cybernetic assemblages, rather than sets or constellations of traits themselves.

Studies of human social networks in real life as well as online (such as Twitter, Facebook, and Reddit) have shown that humans connect in social groups in such a way that supports very efficient sharing of information across our social ties. This would also affect the development of our two fictional groups under a difference scenario. Specifically, if there are plausible links that could connect two groups with one another in a sufficient and relevant way, it could facilitate a mutual exchange of information among the members of the group in such a way that beliefs could spread throughout the group like a virus spreads throughout an office or school.

This analogy with epidemiology—of beliefs spreading like a virus—is one that we should also take the time early on to unpack. While the analogy might be a useful way of describing how beliefs spread in a social group, it falls short of providing the best explanation for how and why we believe what we do, and how beliefs can come to stabilize in a religion. Religion is not simply supported by the spread of beliefs. If it were, we would be hard pressed to come up with rational explications as to why so many religions share the common features that they do (beliefs in afterlife, ghosts, gods, fairies, extra-terrestrials, etc.) despite being isolated by their historical time period and geographic distance. While the specific content of any one religion is mandated by the information that we are exposed to, we also should step back and look at the psychological tendencies (e.g., heuristics and biases) of the human mind that help us to conceive new religious beliefs and aid in fundamental aspects of our engagement with religious beliefs. By analogy, we can view religions as liquids in different shaped glasses. Some are big, some are small, some have different colors or flavors, but these liquids are all held by their glasses, which have their own properties that allow for us to retain the liquid in a specific form. The construction of some glasses does not hold liquids well, just like some arrangements of psychological features do not efficiently support stable religious systems. So for the purposes of how religion is treated here, our evolved psychological and cognitive capacities are taken as primary causal factors, while our ability to share information through social learning is secondary by the fact that the very ability for us to process religious information that is shared socially is rooted first and foremost in the existence of the appropriate evolved cognitive mechanisms.

The cultural cybernetic approach to religion shifts our focus from how many have approached religion in the past. While most studies of religion focus on the beliefs of a group (in the usual guise of religious studies as well as with the subset of approaches utilizing a scientific—or quasi-scientific—or even pseudo-scientific approach; see Bunge, 2011 for a discussion of the basis of much of evolutionary psychology and cultural evolution as pseudo-scientific), the cultural cybernetic approach builds upon a foundation of human cognition. This foundation allows us to take a strict cognitive approach that can facilitate both comparison between groups—since we start from a similar foundation about the cognitive mechanisms shared by all homo sapiens as a species wide feature—as well as analyses comparing the differences between groups—as the output of those mechanisms vary in accordance with unique biological and social environments (i.e., ecologies) in which the mechanisms operate.

Naturally, this shift toward a shamelessly cognitive one is nuanced, done both for its convenience and its function. It is convenient to study religions in a way that can facilitate a study of both similarities and differences. It allows us to be comparative and study the overarching themes that occur around the globe, but it also allows us to study the deep contextual aspects of individual traditions. However, this shift also creates a connection with the larger scientific literature on human cognition and—eventually—neurobiology. Addressing the cognitive level of analysis, which is arguably the "highest" level of study available today that we might reasonably suggest shares uniform features across the human species, may very well be the best level at which we can explain pan-human phenomena such as religion and culture. Trying to explain the aspects of any one religion often leads us into circles of further description and contextualization while missing out on the ability to compare the features of one religion with that of another. But going down to a neurobiological level appears to be too low—as it can't yet facilitate any understanding of the beliefs and behaviors that make human religiosity such a rich and fascinating phenomenon to study. Ideally, in the future, the neurobiological level of explanation could provide more utility when better correspondences can explain the missing links between neurobiological formations and cognitive functions (the hardware-to-software relationship of the brain-mind if you will).

In addition, framing a study of religion within a cognitive approach allows us to work directly within an information processing paradigm from top to bottom. In the past, many scholars have used a hodgepodge of theories to explain religion from many disciplines, and they pick and choose examples and theories that fit their preconceptions, without much care as to counterexamples and the extent to which the very foundational assumptions of their own theories are axiomatically incompatible. I have no doubt that the information processing approach that is presented here has flaws and will continue to do so. Debating the merits and doing so in the spirit of scientific progress so that we can better our own research should be the very nature of academic debates; and if this work is able to push forward debates about the nature of a cognitive approach to religion, then it would have succeeded in at least one regard. However, using information processing approaches and the tools that are offered through it, such as computer modeling has at least one key merit in this regard: forced clarity. Typically, theorizing about religion is done through writing. People write what they think about religion, its aspects, its connections, its causes, etc. From there some hypotheses are derived, people argue about the nature of the variables, the appropriateness of any way we could measure these things, etc. In much of the study of religion (based in the humanities and social sciences) the theories are often interpretive in nature, so they are not even interested in—or benefited by—debates about measurement and empirical tractability of a claim. In these instances, a theory is read by a scholar—with debatable clarity and quite possibly a great deal of interpretation on their own part leading them away from the original intended meaning of the theory—in order to be applied to a single instance or observation of some religious phenomenon. Debates can therefore become lost in the weeds, with scholars debating the original intent of a theory, the best way to define the scope of the theory, the appropriateness of its use, etc. These debates are intellectually engaging, perhaps, but detract from our ability to apply our knowledge about religion, in a day and age when religions have extreme geopolitical and security implications (for example). Theories, however, do not exist in just one form. The theories that have enjoyed a great deal of debate in the English-speaking academy for example, are often not even originally written in English. Let us take Durkheim as an example. Durkheim is one of the founders of sociology and his influence on the study of culture and religion cannot be easily overstated. From high school textbooks to the halls of Oxford, Durkheim's work entitled "The Elementary Forms of Religious Life" (1915) is quoted and used to understand many social aspects of religion. For many who study the text, its translation is fortunate, since they could not understand the publication in the original French; rather, they work with the Durkheim in translation, hoping that they have a version that is of high quality and appropriately captures the aspects of the theory that they need when it was translated. Using a computer model of a social theory is similar, in that, instead of translating a theory from French, German, or English, to our own local vernacular, we translate a theory from a human language into Java, C++, Python, or some other computer programming language.

This shift in theoretical codification does not just offer a new medium. The formalization of a theory in a computer programming language also requires that strict definitions of variables and their linkages be codified in a clear and logical manner. This clarity allows for theories to be debated and investigated with greater precision as the variable definitions and their connections are more constrained in their interpretation and less prone to being obfuscated by polysemy. Computer programming languages are often fickle in ways that force logic and consistency, much to the frustration of those beginning to learn how to work with them. For example, programming languages handle several kinds of data types, such as: Boolean variables (storing true/false values), char or string variables (storing characters or words), integer—or int—variables (storing integer values, e.g., 1, 2, 3, . . . 42), and double (storing floating point decimal numbers, e.g., 1.618, 5.1115, or 3.14). When instructing a computer to perform some function or operation, the kind of data and its sizes (usually) need to be clearly defined. There are ways to convert between the datatypes, but you cannot do so without explicitly stating that you are doing so in the program. In this way, if a theory is addressing some phenomenon by describing interactions at the level of the individual person, it is clear that it applies only to a single person. If the theory is extended to deal with multiple people, then the program must specify this. The same goes for all interactions between the variables that represent beliefs, behaviors, environments, etc. In this way, theories that can be interpreted as addressing an individual, or multiple individuals, can be clarified in how they're being used in ways that are less clear in non-computational formulations of a theory.

In addition to clarity when codifying a theory for others, the effort that goes into formalizing a theory as a computational model also has epistemological benefits. If nothing else, because of the constraints and requirements of computer programming languages, formalizing a theory can provide clarity about a theory and its hypotheses. This is just as much the case for interpretive theories as it is for explanatory theories, and is one way in which computer modeling can serve as a way of bridging disciplinary boundaries, particularly those that exist between the sciences and humanities in a way that can bring together both qualitative and quantitative, interpretive and explanatory, approaches.[5]

Using an information processing approach as a basis for theorizing in this way allows us to have more continuity between certain aspects of a theory and the way it is recorded with the ways we could potentially test the theory empirically. Assuming an information processing paradigm as the basis for our theorizing about the cognitive and social mechanisms that make up a cybernetic assemblage, we can aim to leverage continuity between what we program into our computers, and the ways in which we think about and measure the same thing in the real world. In this way, theorizing in an information processing paradigm can help us to create correspondence between the *in situ* (in the real world) and *in silico* (in silicon) versions of what we are studying. Given the complexities of religion and AI mentioned in the beginning of the chapter, we need all the help we can get to study the many features of religion that we are interested in. Naturally, these features are many, and using an information processing approach does not so much trim the number of features available for us to study as it does refocus how we approach those features. Aspects of religion such as prayer, meditation, altered states of consciousness, ritual, spirituality, the afterlife, God, salvation and faith, reincarnation, taboos and prohibitions, shamanism, sacrifice, prosociality, holy wars, terrorism and extremism, embodiment, pilgrimage, and others are all still on the table, it is up to us to focus on these features of human religiosity and use the tools available to see if we can create a better understanding of the complex links between these features that, when combined, are taken by us to represent something close to what we heuristically mean when we say the word "religion."

By working within a paradigm that allows us to generate the group-level religious phenomena from the interactions of sub-individual (i.e., cognitive) systems, individuals (i.e., individuals and their social networks/groups), and their environments, MAAI allows us to produce what has been reduced. While psychological studies (rightly) utilize reduction to get a clearer picture on a subset of variables, this approach will not allow us to rebuild our picture of religion, it will only give us piecemeal insight into a larger phenomenon. MAAI systems allow for us to take the insights from these studies and instantiate those empirically discerned mechanisms that link variables within a computational system, formalizing those links into a simulation that represents a theory of interaction in its own right. In this way, MAAI can be a powerful tool for studying social systems because it can take empirical findings and reintroduce the complexity of the real-world system, which is controlled for in laboratory settings. Computational modeling approaches such as MAAI fit well with a theoretical approach that views social systems as cybernetic assemblages because it can formalize the assemblage and its components computationally; allowing researchers to harness the dynamism of complex adaptive social systems within an evolutionary framework without having to rely on overly stochastic theories of selection that are not tractable (such as many of those subsumed in the framework of cultural evolution).

However, reintroducing complexity is a double-edged sword. Despite the prima face promise of highly complex AI models for helping us to unravel the thorny theoretical and empirical issues of studying complex social systems like religion, the more complex we make our models, the harder they are to validate; which is to say, it is hard to know what's going on inside of complex AI models. The multi-agent AI approach shares this issue of interpretability with all complex computer models.

This issue of interpretability can—to an extent—be addressed by incorporating research at multiple levels into the construction of a model from the beginning. As discussed earlier, there is a wealth of historical and psychological data about religious phenomena. Using the historical data to validate the output of a model under a variety of conditions can help us to demonstrate that there is correspondence between what our model outputs and what we observe in the real world (i.e., the relationship between the thing being simulated *in silico* and *in situ*). I refer to this correspondence between the output of a model and real-world data as *output correspondence*, which is the most common approach toward validating computer simulations. However, when we incorporate psychological studies, we have an additional opportunity. Specifically, in the cybernetic approach to religion discussed throughout this book, human cognition is taken as the causal mechanisms that mediate environmental, interpersonal, and inter-cognitive effects, as well as the causal mechanism whereby we get group-level effects from individuals (and their interactions) that others would call emergent (Lane, 2018c). In this way, psychological studies can serve to validate the mechanisms of the model, which is to say, psychological studies can be used to create correspondence between the mechanisms that produce social phenomena in the real world and the mechanisms we build into our models. This correspondence between the mechanisms of a model and real-world studies is called *mechanistic correspondence*, and is more rare in the development and validation of computer simulations, but its further incorporation can serve as a backbone for the development of MAAI, as MAAI's focus on psychologically realistic agents can focus on mechanistic correspondence in order to create valid—and realistic—human agents for testing in a variety of applications, not just religion.

Mechanistic correspondence can help us to be sure that even in the face of complexity, our model is an acceptable (i.e., valid) representation of the real-world system that we are aiming to study (e.g., religion) by validating key causal mechanisms, not only the output patterns of the model. This key matter of correspondence also fits well within the framework of viewing complex social systems as cybernetic assemblages. Recall that our approach here views religions as complex systems of interacting parts. In the research discussed here of course, those parts are largely limited to the individual agents (or people) in the religious system and their beliefs. The links that define the interactions are the behaviors enacted between these agents and the cognitive mechanisms within the agents that store, retrieve, manipulate, and utilize the agents' beliefs about their sociocultural and biological environments. In this way, the assemblage of a religious system can be defined using complex dynamic social networks representing the social fabric of the religion and complex and dynamic semantic networks (or belief networks) representing the schemas of beliefs that the individuals hold. The assemblage is further defined in MAAI systems by specifying the rules of interactions between the constituent parts and how these networks facilitate interactions and changes within the system, this is described further in the later chapters.

1.3.1 Bonding and Belief

One of the key features of religion that has overarching repercussions for society today is the ability for religions to bind people together in social groups around a core set of beliefs. In fact, early writings on the nature of the word "religion" itself have argued that the Latin origins of the word comes from the words meaning "to re-bind" (Hoyt, 1912). It is here, at this intersection of belief and bonding that I propose that we can use modern information processing tools to make great strides in our ability to understand how religion affects or daily lives, as well as the effect it has had throughout human history.

1.3.2 Social Cohesion

In order to understand the nature of the relationship between religion, bonding, and belief, it is important to keep a few things in mind. For example, until about ten thousand years ago, a short period of time on an evolutionary time scale, human societies comprised small bands of mobile hunter-gatherers. Since then, civilizations have arisen encompassing hundreds of millions of people. In order for these groups to endure and compete successfully with other groups, the group requires at least some level of social cohesion. While we know a great deal from the archaeological record about the rise of large complex societies (Barker, 2009; Hayden, 2009; Mithen, 2006; Zeder, 2011), less is known about the psychological mechanisms involved in generating and sustaining social cohesion in large groups. The term "social cohesion" is used in many ways by different fields (e.g., see discussions in Friedkin, 2004; McLeod & Von Treuer, 2013), however here I use social cohesion to refer to the bonds between members of a social group as well as their bonds to the group as a whole, which is rooted in varying levels of consensus in large groups as explained in the following chapters.

Many groups, such as nationalities, ethnicities, and religions seem to maintain cohesion over hundreds and sometimes thousands of years, even in the midst of great changes both internally and externally. Examples include the world religions (e.g., Buddhism, Hinduism, and the Judeo-Christian traditions) that have their origins in the Axial Age (Baumard, Hyafil, Morris, & Boyer, 2014; Bellah, 2011; Christian, 2005; Shults, Wildman, Lane, Lynch, & Diallo, 2018), which are forms of *doctrinal religions*—that is—traditions involving the worship of supernatural agents[6] that emphasize the importance of adherence to a commonly shared set of beliefs or doctrine. While religious beliefs are not the only kind of doctrine, they have been prominent throughout human history. Doctrinal religions have had significant historical and contemporary impacts. For example, the spread of Christianity has reshaped the geopolitical landscape of the Western world while the rise of religious extremism has been a major motivating force in shaping public policy in recent years (Toft, Philpott, & Shah, 2011). In spite of the fact that the size of these groups makes it impossible to know every other member, individual members feel a sense of shared identity and belonging. Because the groups are so large that nobody could know all of the other members, these groups are in many ways imagined communities (Anderson, 2006). Imagined communities do not exist in many real or tangible ways to any individual member, but the overall abstraction of the group is very real to them. My aim in the coming chapters is to introduce how the use of modern computational tools and AI can explain why such groups maintain social cohesion.

Within any complex social group, we do not need to assume that all people in all religions bond in the same way. Indeed, in the next few chapters, I will discuss some theories that discuss how bonding functions very differently in large-scale religions than in small-scale religions. However, as a religion is an abstract group of people and not a single cognitive entity (or agent) in its own right, I want to focus on the individuals that make up that group. This is because the individuals that are instilled with the cognitive mechanisms that process information about the group hold the roots of motivation and emotion that bind an individual to the group.

Having the ability to explain, and possibly predict, social cohesion of such groups can have a large impact in many aspects of social and political life. For example, understanding social cohesion in religious organizations can help to predict extremism, terrorism, and humanitarian responses to natural disasters.

There are also ways in which the social cohesion of large groups affects our political and financial systems. For example, the Arab Spring, which saw the political realignment of many powerful and economically central Middle Eastern nations had a vast impact on industries including, finance, tourism, shipping and logistics, intelligence and defense, and—perhaps obviously—oil. Having better tools for studying such groups, given the vast impact they have on our modern world, allows not only for better predictions, and therefore planning and policy, but also for understanding.

1.3.3 From Individuals to Groups

Focusing on the individuals as a networked collection, rather than on the group as a singularity, is not done because a "group" is not a useful thing to analyze. Rather, when looking at complex social groups scientifically, taking the group as a level of analysis has problems and the way a group is defined can often reveal more about a researcher's assumptions about the group than any real underlying patterns or distributions of the constituents of the group themselves (Brubaker, 2002). The heterogeneity of human social groups is fundamentally important, as not all members of a group have the same connections, have the same personalities, interests, or identities, and nor do they all serve the same roles. For example, in many religions the leaders are of paramount importance and exhibit traits not unlike alphas in other species (Lane, 2009). When that leader dies, its effect on the religious group is not the same as if another member of the group were to die. This suggests that not only are people demographically and psychologically heterogeneous within the group, but also that individuals are functionally heterogeneous within the social system. We can take as an analogy how you can study a glass of water. In a glass of water, H_2O molecules are doing many different things but removing or varying the properties of any one molecule does not affect the properties of the glass of water itself. In this way, the glass of water can be taken as a singularity when viewed from a higher level. Human social groups are different. Removing any one person can (and often does) have a unique effect, so we cannot assume that the group is a singularity or singular point that is the most useful singular entity of study. To explain complex behaviors such as group cohesion, we should understand that the group is an artifact of our own cognitive mechanisms but is not as useful in an explanation as studying the individuals that make up that group.

From this perspective, "religions" do not exist as singular entities (singularities as discussed earlier). Religions do not *do* anything. However, the people who view themselves as part of a religion exist and do things; and in that is the key, *the people who view themselves* as part of a religion are critical, as they are the point of self-definition for which we can construct the groups that we discuss in a more abstract academic way. So, the question then becomes, how is it that we come to view ourselves as part of a group? Or, put in other words, how do we align ourselves with a group?

1.3.4 Group Alignment

To answer this question, we can build upon the work of psychologists. Here, I will discuss two forms of group alignment that are prominent in the psychological literature, fusion, and social identification, before discussing how they can fit within an overall paradigm of information processing.

Fusion is best described as an intense feeling of oneness with a group. Fusion theory suggests what we can call a synergistic relationship between personal and social identities (Swann, Jetten, Gómez, Whitehouse, & Bastian, 2012). *Personal identities* are the beliefs, values, attitudes, and knowledge that individuals have that make them unique; examples include preferring certain types of literature, having certain personality traits, or having a belief in guardian angels. *Social identities* are the social categories that one aligns with as part of how we see ourselves.[7] Fusion theory suggests that the feeling of connectedness to a group is magnified in fused individuals because of a porous boundary between their self and their group (Swann et al., 2012). In this way, fused people feel a "oneness" with their group that can make it hard to distinguish between one's self and the group that they're fused to. This intense bond is proposed to be extended to the individual members of the group as well (Swann, Buhrmester et al., 2014; Swann et al., 2012). In principle, for fused individuals, when their social identity is made salient, their personal identity is salient as well (and vice versa). This synergistic relationship has been related to an increased propensity to endorse extreme pro-group behaviors such as self-sacrifice and attacks against an out-group (Swann, Buhrmester et al., 2014). Studies have also found that fused individuals are more likely to donate money and time to their in-group in times of crisis (Buhrmester, Fraser, Lanman, Whitehouse, & Swann, 2014). Field research with fused individuals in conflict zones has also found that fused individuals are also more likely to be found on the frontlines of armed conflicts than individuals who are not fused, who generally play more supportive roles outside of open combat (Whitehouse, McQuinn, Buhrmester, & Swann, 2014).

Fusion is thought to be quite different from social identification[8] (Swann et al., 2012). *Social identification* is a form of group alignment where someone feels they are part of a social category, referred to as a categorical tie (Swann et al., 2012; Whitehouse & Lanman, 2014) because they share beliefs, attitudes, and values that define that group with other individuals (Billig & Tajfel, 1973; Hogg & Abrams, 1988). Social identification posits an antagonistic relationship between personal and social identities (as opposed to the synergistic relationship proposed by fusion). As such, when one's social identity is salient, one's personal identity is suppressed (and vice versa). Individuals can identify with a group in order to maintain a positive self-image, as opposed to fused individuals who are unable to separate their personal identity from their social identity. For example, when a group is being praised, an identified individual can identify more strongly with the group. However, when a group that an individual identifies with is being chastised, an identified—but not fused—individual can separate themselves from the group and rely on their own personal identity to maintain a positive self-image (Swann et al., 2012). On the other hand, a fused individual takes his group being chastised personally, since they view themselves and their social group as one and as such, an attack on the group is akin to an attack on them personally.

These two forms of identification affect nearly everyone. We can all think of individuals that we know where we would have an intense emotional reaction if they were attacked or harmed, and we would likely respond as if we ourselves are being attacked. For many of us, these people are family or close friends. Nearly every parent would do anything for their child and has no qualms about admitting that they would physically harm anyone who would wish to harm their child or children and many would endorse corporal (even capital) punishment for anyone who would attack them. It is not uncommon to also have close friends, those whom we consider extended family in their own right, for whom we would sacrifice a great deal. These individuals are all people with whom we have a direct social relationship. This form of fusion—fusion to those with whom we have a direct social relationship—is called local fusion. Fusion to a large social group, like a world religion or nationality, is called *extended fusion*, and this form of group alignment is relatively rare in comparison to social identification. However, there are many social institutions that are reliant on individuals to sacrifice their own time or resources, and even their lives, for a larger group. The world over, our countries keep standing armies, many of which—like that of United States—go through long and grueling training programs that appear to fuse those individuals not only to one another, but to their country. Indeed, while further research is needed to investigate the extent to which individuals are fused to the country before volunteering for a job that very well may cost them their lives to support or defend their country, those individuals who join volunteer armies such as the United States' have signed their name on the "dotted line" (literally and figuratively) to make the ultimate sacrifice for their group—despite the fact that they have never, and will never, meet the overwhelming majority of their fellow citizens.

Fusion to large religions can also take a darker form, in the form of religious terrorism. While terrorism will be addressed later in the book as well, it is worth pausing to consider that many of those in religious extremist groups, from Christian new religious movements like Jonestown and Waco, to Islamic terrorist groups like Al Qaeda and the Islamic State, and Buddhist cults like Aum Shinrikyo, to UFO cults like Heaven's Gate, all shared an intense commitment to a group that suggests that the members are fused.

In the next chapter, the discussion will delve further into these two kinds of social identification, and how they work and what empirical evidence exists for (and against) some of the theoretical claims. From this, we will begin to formulate an information processing approach to social cohesion that aims to incorporate the key parts of these theoretical approaches to group cohesion and then integrate an approach to group consensus that can address both group cohesion and consensus simultaneously to create a more holistic theory of social cohesion.

2

Religions, Old and New

Religious beliefs and behaviors appear to be unique to homo sapiens. While other nonhuman primates, like our close relatives chimpanzees and bonobos, appear to have some of the same psychological tools that religion relies on, such as social norms and communication, there is no evidence that they have the ability to think about abstract ideas such as gods and spirits, and thus lack any sense of a supernatural entity. There is evidence that Neanderthals, who died out approximately 40,000 years ago buried their dead (Rendu et al., 2014) and appear to have decorated some bodies with flowers (Pomeroy et al., 2020), which suggests that there was at least ritual behaviors, and perhaps a sense of afterlife, suggesting that they may have had beliefs about supernatural agents (their dead ancestors), and thus may have had religion as well. While this is promising, it is also complicated. Elephants also appear mourn the death of one of their own, and even appear caress the remains of the deceased. However, analyses of their behavior has revealed that they do not appear to have a preference for the remains of specific elephants (McComb, Baker, & Moss, 2006), suggesting that they mourn death, but might not have the sense of continuity of the "self" after death that would suggest afterlife beliefs or beliefs in anything "supernatural." Chimpanzees, one of our closest relatives in the animal kingdom, have also been documented performing different ritual behaviors where there are repeated performances, apparently unconnected to a natural outcome related to status or resources, that include a patterned approach and ten to fifteen-minute "dance" near the foot of waterfalls and similar dances have been observed at the onset of heavy wind or rain (Goodall, 2005). Other groups of chimpanzees in West Africa have been noted to throw rocks at trees and to fill holes in trees, which has been noted as "the first record of repeated observations of individual chimpanzees exhibiting stone tool use for a purpose other than extractive foraging at what appear to be targeted trees" (Kühl et al., 2016). This results in collections of small mounds of rocks near specific trees that aren't unlike some of the "shrine" sites created for religious purposes in West Africa (Lentz & Sturm, 2001). Even though this evidence strongly resembles what we would be familiar with as ritual, the authors of the studies note that the behavior is very individualistic. In this way, it does not share some of the cooperative aspects of ritual such as negotiation between individual agents with different roles to bring about a specific ritual outcome that is the hallmark of human rituals (e.g., Lawson & McCauley, 1990 go to great lengths to describe how individuals with different roles are critical to the formation of human ritual systems). As such, today, homo sapiens appear to be alone in the animal kingdom, with their wide array of socially held and enacted beliefs and behaviors, attached to a realm other than our own.

Some of our earliest records of human sociality are burials from nearly 100,000 years ago (Bar-Yosef Mayer, Vandermeersch, & Bar-Yosef, 2009; e.g., Bar-Yosef, 2001). At these burial sites, it appears that we gave special treatment to the dead, such as adding colors, ornaments, and burying the dead with things that they might want to have if they were living. Archaeologists have made sense of this as evidence for belief in an afterlife where humans might have the same needs and wants in death as they did in life.

At that point in human history, humans lived in small groups where we would be related to everyone else in the group to some degree. It wasn't until about 10,000 years ago that larger-scale human civilizations began to arise, and our way of life shifted from living in small bands of hunter-gatherers, with group sizes limited to a few hundred at most, to tribes that combined many familial bands (Dunbar, Gamble, & Gowlett, 2014); this is often referred to as the agricultural transition or the Neolithic transition. With this transition came an interesting shift in our ability to specialize our skills into unique jobs where we fill a specific role within our group. This specialist concentration appeared to allow for experts in trades, material good's production, and even religion to arise (Dávid-Barrett & Carney, 2015). While some scholars have suggested that religion was a primary causal factor in this shift (Bulbulia et al., 2013; Norenzayan, 2013; Whitehouse & Hodder, 2010), new evidence suggests that religions shifted in response to our economies (Baumard & Boyer, 2013; Baumard et al., 2014), and this debate is very much ongoing currently.[1] In any case, the evidence is clear that from about 10,000 years ago, at the time when humans began to professionally domesticate plants and livestock, many cultural groups began to grow, and their way of life drastically changed.

2.1 Divergent Modes of Religiosity

With this shift in civilization from small-scale groups to larger social groups, new forms of religiosity also began to arise as we shifted from small-scale religions where almost everyone we interacted with were related to us, to larger-scale religions where we were not bound by kinship, but by beliefs. This dichotomy between small-scale religions (sometimes referred to as "tribal" or "local" religions) and larger "world religions" has been noted many times throughout history and is often used to describe religions or as a basis for taxonomy (a system used to classify religions).

In the early 1990s, a new theory, the theory of Divergent Modes of Religiosity (also known as the DMR or "Modes Theory"; Whitehouse, 1995, 2000, 2004), aimed to explain why these two forms of religion are so prevalent. The DMR theory is going to be a starting point for our entry into the relationship between bonding and belief because it is one of the only theories to have attempted to include aspects of consensus and group alignment into a framework that uses behaviors and psychology to explain religious patterns of social cohesion.

The DMR theory proposes that cognitive mechanisms that develop in all humans can explain patterns of observed religious behaviors (Whitehouse, 2004, pp. 21–2). It describes six psychological and six sociopolitical features that should generally be observed together in a religious system, and these constellations of features represent attractor points in the complex space of all possible forms of religiosity. As these two spaces are attractor spaces, it is permissible to find other variants, but they should be short lived (more on this in a moment), and—importantly—the DMR theory suggests that these modes are built upon variables that comprise mutually reinforcing systems, which is why the two modes are *divergent*. Each mode is reliant on one of two types of rituals to encode information in our memories.

The DMR theory proposes that different kinds of rituals produce different types and intensities of social cohesion. The theory suggests that rare and emotionally intense rituals can bind the members of smaller, more localized religions to one another by means of mutually shared experiences that are often emotionally or physically stressful or painful (i.e., dysphoric). These experiences result in intense social cohesion among small groups of individuals, such as the small bands of mobile hunter-gatherers of ancient prehistory (Whitehouse & Hodder, 2010). The DMR theory states that rare but emotionally intense rituals are the basis of what it refers to as the *imagistic mode* of religiosity. In the imagistic mode, individuals derive personal meaning through personal reflection in lieu of any available standard orthodoxy with which to interpret the experience; as such, high levels of consensus are not expected.

The DMR theory also proposes a different way of creating and bonding very large groups, of the kind associated with the rise of Axial Age and world religions, called the *doctrinal mode* of religiosity. According to the DMR theory, the doctrinal mode relies on frequent (i.e., daily or weekly) collective rituals to help spread an orthodox doctrine by providing occasions for leaders to present beliefs to the group, making them more likely to be accurately stored in memory. Frequent rituals also provide occasions for leaders to correct unorthodox beliefs. This creates a situation for individuals to align themselves to a group based on a stable set of socially learned beliefs and practices.

One of the DMR theory's key observations is that rituals generally come in one of two forms: (1) high frequency of performance with low emotional intensity and (2) low frequency of performance with high emotional intensity (Atkinson & Whitehouse, 2011). The DMR theory proposes that these two ritual types are effective because they activate different memory systems, which facilitate different patterns of social cohesion and memory for religious beliefs. Each of these two ritual forms effectively encodes information in our long-term memory, where it can be stored and recalled for later use. *Long-term memory* is memory that is retained and available for use over longer periods of time (from minutes to decades) than short-term memory, which is memory that is only available for a brief period and is forgotten unless it is rehearsed.[2]

Rituals in doctrinal traditions are proposed to be high frequency with low emotional intensity and should elicit semantic memory. *Semantic memory* "refers to knowledge about people, objects, actions, relations, self, and culture acquired through experience" (Binder, Desai, Graves, & Conant, 2009, p. 2767). Information encoded in semantic memory extends beyond schoolbook knowledge and includes beliefs and practices valued by our social groups. Decades of empirical research suggest that semantic memories form through multiple exposures to the same information (e.g., Aldridge & Crisp, 1982; Gardiner, Gawlik, & Richardson-Klavehn, 1994; McFarlane & Humphreys, 2012; Wixted, 1991). As the semantic memory system does not encode where you were when you learned something or from whom you learned information, semantic memories appear decontextualized (i.e., they are unattached to any specific social relationships or physical context). In this sense, the information held by one person is just as valid as that of another. Within the framework of the DMR theory, this is stated to result in depersonalized information that is not associated with any one person (Whitehouse, 2004). In addition, the DMR theory proposes that revelation in the doctrinal mode is the result of instruction and logical integration and any personal idiosyncrasies should be corrected during the frequent ritual events that typify doctrinal religions. This should produce stable schemas of information that are socially shared among potentially large number of individuals.

The DMR theory notes that semantic memory can efficiently create and maintain complex schemas of information that are shared between the members of a group. These complex schemas can be transmitted by leaders or texts and, over long periods of time with frequent repetitions, result in complex narratives and teachings being integrated into a set orthodoxy. Because semantic memory encodes information such as socially shared norms and beliefs, frequent ritual attendance can encode social information that individuals can use to align themselves to groups by means of social identification (Whitehouse & Lanman, 2014). As noted in Chapter 1, social identification is a form of group alignment where individuals feel that they are part of a social category (i.e., group) because they have shared social schemas holding the beliefs, attitudes, and values that define that group.[3] Whitehouse and Lanman suggest that this form of group alignment can be understood as a perceived *categorical tie* or tie between the individual and a social category (cf. Brewer & Gardner, 1996).

Rituals in imagistic traditions are proposed to be rarer and more emotionally intense (particularly dysphoric) than rituals in doctrinal traditions and elicit a type of episodic memory called a flashbulb memory. *Episodic memory* is the information we retain for a specific event. This includes everything from what one does on any particular day to great milestones in one's life. Empirical evidence suggests that if an event is particularly emotionally intense, such as being a victim of a crime or witnessing a tragic event, it can result in a flashbulb memory (Conway, Skitka, Hemmerich, & Kershaw, 2009; Curci & Luminet, 2009; Kvavilashvili, Mirani, Schlagman, Foley, & Kornbrot, 2009). *Flashbulb memories* are like images, where one can imagine the context of the memory (such as who they were with during an event) but not specific details of the memory (such as exactly what any one person said during an event). Flashbulb memories encode information almost like pictures and can be recalled in detail years after the event. They create a record in our mind of details such as who was present at the event, what it looked like, and where it took place. In theory, flashbulb memories should not facilitate memories for what was said during the event because a single presentation of information would not be enough to encode the information in semantic memory. Indeed, some research shows that flashbulb memories are not good at encoding information about what was said during emotionally intense rituals, such as those involving fire-walking (Xygalatas, 2012; Xygalatas et al., 2013). Therefore, individuals cannot rely on teachings during an event that resulted in a flashbulb memory to draw meaning from the experience in the same way that someone might from a doctrinal ritual. The DMR theory posits that, because emotionally intense experiences are not encoded with information regarding the meaning for a ritual experience, individuals will reflect upon the experience to make sense of it. This is different from the DMR theory's proposition for the doctrinal mode, which suggests that reflection is suppressed because frequent rituals encode the meaning of ritual experiences as provided by the group's leadership. In the imagistic mode, reflection is typically assumed to be personal and untutored, which can lead to idiosyncratic beliefs becoming diffused throughout the group (Whitehouse, 2004, p. 72). If these idiosyncratic beliefs are not diffused throughout the group, they could potentially decrease within-group consensus overall (repercussion of this are discussed more in Chapter 7).

Because of the intensity of events that create episodic memories, the events can potentially become defining aspects of how we see our personal self. However, they can also affect how we align ourselves socially. The DMR theory proposes that flashbulb memories about who was at an intense event facilitate intense life-long bonds between co-participants. These intense bonds between the individual members of a group are called *relational ties* (cf. Brewer & Gardner, 1996). Whitehouse and Lanman (2014), along with other fusion theorists (e.g., Gómez, Brooks et al., 2011; Swann & Buhrmester, 2015; Swann et al., 2012), suggest that relational ties are the basis of fusion (discussed in more detail later).

The psychological features of each mode are also proposed to have unique sociopolitical correlates. The DMR theory states that doctrinal religions are typically larger than imagistic religions. Doctrinal religions spread quickly because they are bound by how widespread the group's beliefs can become. They often use texts and religious experts in complex hierarchies that can authoritatively police beliefs to ensure the stability of the doctrine. Religious authorities can utilize the frequent ritual gatherings as occasions to both spread orthodox doctrine and correct any deviations. This results in high levels of within-group consensus. Additionally, because the group boundary is defined by holding a set of beliefs, doctrinal religions are considered to be inclusive of individuals who may not have previously participated in the group's rituals.

The imagistic mode has a different set of sociopolitical features. The DMR theory states that the sizes of groups operating in the imagistic mode are smaller than in the doctrinal mode as practical considerations constrain the number of participants that can participate in a ritual. For example, high costs of performing a ritual (in terms of resource expenditure per person) can limit the number of people who can participate. The DMR theory argues that, because group membership in the imagistic mode is premised upon having undergone an infrequent (and costly) ritual, the groups are more exclusive and do not spread as quickly as doctrinal religions; they only grow as fast as individuals can participate in its key ritual(s). In addition, the DMR theory posits that imagistic groups do not need active leadership or a complex hierarchy to reinforce orthodoxy because there is no set doctrine to police (recall that beliefs in the imagistic mode are more reliant on independent reflection than teachings); this results in low within-group consensus among the members of the group.

The relationships proposed by the DMR theory appear to be a useful heuristic for understanding how religious experiences can affect the two components of social cohesion. On the face of it, doctrinal religious groups are reliant on frequent rituals with low emotional intensity: Christianity, Islam, and Judaism all perform weekly low-arousal rituals. However, there are many examples of atypical rituals that present problems for the DMR theory's explanation of social cohesion in doctrinal religions.

2.1.1 Atypical Ritual Forms in Doctrinal Religions

In the historical and ethnographic record, doctrinal religions, such as Christianity and Islam, include rare but highly arousing ritual experiences in addition to their weekly low-arousal rituals. For example, Sunni and Shi'a Islam, which have over 1 billion combined members (Pew Research Center, 2009b, p. 8), mandate that adherents complete a pilgrimage to Mecca (the Hajj), which typically happens once in a lifetime. Catholicism, a religion with over 1 billion members (Pew Research Center, 2011, p. 23), mandates rituals such as baptism, confirmation, and marriage—which only happen once in a lifetime. Other rare and emotionally intense religious experiences are more common today than they were fifty years ago in some areas. For example, a survey of Americans in 1962 found that 22 percent of respondents reported having a mystical experience; this has steadily increased to 49 percent by 2009 (Pew Research Center, 2009a). In addition, having emotionally intense religious or spiritual experiences is defining for many Pentecostal and Charismatic Christian communities (Luhrmann, 2012; D. E. Miller & Yamamori, 2007; Pew Research Center, 2006). Of the many examples of emotionally intense experiences in doctrinal traditions, we will focus on those that occur within contemporary Christian communities, particularly those in Pentecostal and Charismatic Christian communities. As discussed in this section, the DMR theory needs to be amended in order to provide an explanation for social cohesion in doctrinal religions that incorporate emotionally arousing experiences. Key to this amendment are the relationships between frequency of in-group ritual attendance, emotional intensity, memory, and group alignment.

The DMR theory suggests that emotionally intense rituals in the doctrinal mode should not have the same effects as emotionally intense rituals in the imagistic mode. One reason the DMR theory suggests this is because highly arousing experiences in doctrinal religions often happen to individuals (not as part of a group) and the experiences are not systematically integrated into the group's tradition. There are many examples of individual spiritual experiences in doctrinal religions that are not shared with a wider community, such as the kind of mystical and revelatory experiences documented by William James in his text *The Varieties of Religious Experience* (1902) or more recently discussed by Anne Taves in her book *Revelatory Events* (Taves, 2016). Within studies of the DMR theory, similar examples have been discussed regarding medieval Christian monasteries (Clark, 2004) and evangelical Christian groups (Malley, 2004).

However, earlier presentations of the DMR theory by Whitehouse have discussed instances of imagistic features in Melanesian doctrinal religions that are not limited to individual experiences (e.g., Whitehouse, 2000, Chapter 6). Whitehouse suggests that interactions between the two modes typically come in the form of doctrinal religions that have temporary imagistic practices. Whitehouse argues that brief periods where emotionally intense rituals are found in doctrinal religions serve to periodically reinvigorate communities that have lost motivation for high-frequency ritual practices with low emotionality. In addition to noting that these imagistic practices typically only last for a few months, the imagistic practices should result in bonding localized communities (Whitehouse, 2000, p. 135)—not entire doctrinal traditions. As such, the high intensity, fusion style bonding more common in imagistic traditions should rarely affect an entire doctrinal religion; furthermore, when it does appear to affect and entire doctrinal religion, it appears as such because multiple local communities realize they have all shared the same experience post hoc; examples include the Paliau Movement and Pomio Kivung in Papua New Guinea (Whitehouse, 2000, Chapter 6).

Brian Malley's account of emotionally intense experiences in the Creekside Baptist Church shares some similarities to the account of Melanesian religions presented by Whitehouse and is relevant to the example of Pentecostal and Charismatic Christianity. Generally, individuals in Creekside Baptist Church report having emotionally intense experiences individually—typically during a time of hardship. Malley notes that individuals are later encouraged to frequently recount their experiences publicly to the church (called testifying), which is a common practice in many evangelical churches. Malley considers this to vicariously increase the motivation of other members of the church, suggesting that "the reinforcement is individual, but the institution benefits" (Malley, 2004, p. 86). This account from a contemporary American evangelical church parallels the Melanesian account presented by Whitehouse in that intense experiences are not happening as part of the overall tradition. Rather they are happening to an individual in private or in small groups. Individuals come to perceive these experiences to be collective after they are encouraged to share their personal experience.

In addition to individual emotionally intense experiences, doctrinal religions can also have emotionally intense ritual experiences, such as those observed in Charismatic and Pentecostal churches or in many new religious movements and schism groups. Intense experiences are common in new religious movements (oftentimes referred to as "cults"). For example, we can take the Branch Davidians (a splinter group of Seventh Day Adventism), which became famous for their standoff against American police and the Bureau of Alcohol Tobacco and Firearms after a controversial raid on their religious compound that resulted in the deaths of eighty-six people (twenty-one of which were only children). In this group, their leader, David Koresh (born Vernon Howell), was known to regularly hold lengthy and intense sermons on biblical interpretation, often running into the early morning hours. He was also known for demanding strict adherence to his "New Light" teachings, which demanded chastity from all men but himself and the decree—he said it was a revelation from God—that he could take any woman as his wife and should have twenty-four children, who would rule over the world after the return of Christ; at the time of the standoff, he had at least twelve children with multiple wives (Tabor & Gallagher, 1997). This appears to echo groups like the People's Temple, which met a tragic end in their socialist-inspired agricultural compound commonly known as "Jonestown," when nearly 1,000 people committed a ritual suicide. This ritual suicide had been rehearsed multiple times before in rituals called "white nights." The first white night ritual rehearsals occurred before the community moved to Jonestown, but while at Jonestown, the ritual became more defined and prominent (Reiterman, 1982). The final "white night," which resulted in the end of Jonestown, was motivated as a response to the leader—Jim Jones—coming under pressure from US federal investigations. This led to Congressman Leo Ryan visiting Jonestown. While there, Congressman Ryan appeared to have a positive assessment of the group and offered to take several members back with him. At which point, Jones ordered the assassination of the congressman, and then, while giving a final sermon, his followers (including the children) were presented with a cyanide-laced drink; those unable to drink it themselves (such as young children) were given the mixture via syringe. Ritually, Jonestown—like the Branch Davidians—performed long rituals, often wearing on into the morning hours where people could suffer from exhaustion (Layton, 1999). The People's Temple also regularly staged miracles such as faith healings with high levels of emotional arousal (originally to recruit people at their public gatherings). Behind the scenes, many members reported examples of ritualized physical abuse, which was framed as penance for disobedience to rules, faith, and—often—Jim Jones himself (Layton, 1999; Wessinger, 2000).

The pattern of high-arousal rituals in doctrinal religions is not unique to Melanesian groups and Christian schism movements. Groups as variant as the Buddhist group Aum Shinrikyo, which released sarin bombs into the Tokyo subway in 1995 in an attempt to spur on the end of days, are also reported to have regularly performed intense ritualized actions such as initiations and rituals involving hallucinogens (Kaplan & Marshall, 1996) or drinking the leader's blood (BBC News, 2018). Intense and frequent rituals were also present in the new age UFO cult, Heaven's Gate, who became famous for its ritual suicide in 1997 so that the members could join the "evolutionary level above human" by traveling to a spaceship that was hidden behind the Hale-Bopp comet. The group ritualized nearly every aspect of their life and demanded a strict asceticism, and even led to the castration of many of the male members (DiAngelo, 2007).

It could be argued that these examples are extremes, and that they should not be taken as representative of some interesting aspect of religion as a category. To that point, there are two things to consider. First, every religion was, at one point, a new religious movement, and many accounts of early Christianity point to a highly arousing form of Christianity that included aesthetic practices as well as more dysphoric experiences such as fasting and even full immersion baptism (Eisenman, 1998; also see Martin, 2005); so greater engagement with new religious movements is not only looking at the fringe of religions. When looking at religions as dynamic things, new religious movements aren't the fringe, they're the beginnings. That so many new religious movements appear to show this trend is worthy of further investigation. Second, most religions are relatively unsuccessful. Most religions practiced today are the kind of groups that we could refer to as new religious movements or cults. While many people can probably name five or ten religious groups off the top of their head, these groups are typically the larger or more successful groups. The sizes of religions follow what is called a "power-law" distribution, where there are only very few large religions, and the sizes of religions get exponentially smaller. This creates a distribution where there are very few extremely large religions, and a very large number of extremely small ones.[4] For example, if we think of how many religions there are in America today, we typically think of Christianity (Protestant and Catholic), Judaism, Islam, Buddhism, and Hinduism. A few astute people might also mention Mormonism (which is comparable to Islam in membership in the United States), Scientology, or list different denominations of Protestantism as religions. However, Melton's Encyclopedia of American Religions added 200 new entries in its most recent edition, bringing its coverage to 2,800 religions in the United States alone (Melton, 2009). From this perspective, most religions aren't successful, large, or well known. Most religions are what would likely be called "cults" in common parlance.

However, what is problematic about the previous examples is that they are so often unsuccessful. In this way, it would almost suggest that, as Whitehouse and the DMR theory suggest, these groups are doomed to fail because they do not fit the pattern. However, the rise and success of modern Charismatic and Pentecostal churches calls that conclusion into question and may even suggest that there are other factors in the failures of so many new religious movements, such as the inability to move beyond the death of a charismatic leader (Lane, 2009), or factors contributing to tensions between the group and its cultural environment (Stark, 1996; Stark & Bainbridge, 1987).

In Charismatic and Pentecostal churches, regular Sunday services often have dancing, loud music, and flashing lights that serve as a backdrop to intense experiences for some of their members. The intensity of these experiences is evidenced by observations of glossolalia (speaking in tongues) or worshippers being *slain in the spirit*, which is when a worshiper falls to the floor during worship, often appearing to lose consciousness. This is interpreted as the result of the worshipper being filled by, or overcome with, the presence of the Holy Spirit, which is one of the three entities in the Christian Holy Trinity along with God and the Son (in reference to Jesus). These experiences should not be dismissed as rare or anomalous within Christianity. Pentecostal and Charismatic Christianity currently comprises over half a billion people, roughly a quarter of all the world's Christians (Pew Research Center, 2011). However, it is important to note that it is not always the case that every individual is having an emotionally intense experience on a weekly basis. While the rituals at Pentecostal and Charismatic Christian churches typically facilitate the possibility of these experiences for the congregation, any one individual member might only experience being slain in the spirit once in their lifetime, making it a tricky issue to address using theories that rely on the assumption that any one ritual has the same effect on all participants.

The DMR theory makes multiple predictions about such emotionally intense rituals in doctrinal traditions. However, it does not appear that Pentecostal and Charismatic Christianity fit the predictions of the DMR theory. In what follows, I outline the DMR theory's predictions for such rituals and how Pentecostal and Charismatic Christian traditions do not fit these predictions before turning to the ways in which we can extend the DMR theory to better understand the role of emotionally intense ritual practices in doctrinal religions.

The DMR theory makes five predictions regarding why emotionally intense rituals should be short lived (i.e., the ritual will fail to be transmitted) in doctrinal religions: (1) Emotionally intense rituals that are not frequently repeated should ultimately result in a tradition that resembles the imagistic mode. (2) Emotionally intense rituals that are frequently repeated should suffer from poor verbal transmission, as their high levels of emotional intensity are supposed to impede semantic memory formation. As such, the performance frequency of the ritual will be reduced, and they will begin to operate within the imagistic mode. (3) The rituals will begin to accommodate lower levels of emotional intensity and the poorly transmitted ritual can survive without modal effects. (4) The ritual can go extinct due to poor verbal transmission. (5) The DMR theory also states that if the ritual is frequently performed, emotional intensity can be lowered, at which point the ritual will conform to the standard attractor position of the doctrinal mode (see Whitehouse, 2004, fig. 9.1).

Pentecostal and Charismatic Christian churches seem to be doctrinal traditions with imagistic features, but they do not appear to fit the DMR theory's predictions (although many of the new religious movements noted earlier do fit some of these predictions). The rituals of Pentecostal and Charismatic Christians are weekly, so they would not qualify as infrequent. However, it is not uncommon for Pentecostal and Charismatic Christians to have rare emotionally intense experiences within frequently performed rituals. In addition to being slain in the spirit, one experience that is common to Pentecostal and Charismatic Christians is being *born again*. The experience is typically described as positive and very transformative. This experience typically happens once and is considered by Christians to be a form of "spiritual rebirth" (Luhrmann, 2012). Being born again is surprisingly common. Indeed, the 2004 General Social Survey, which collected data on a nationally representative sample from the United States found that 32.8 percent of respondents claimed to have had a born again experience (Davis & Smith,

2004; T. W. Smith, 2006). Burgess reports that 51 percent of all individuals who are born again consider themselves to be Charismatic Christians and that charismatic churches make up almost a quarter of all Protestant churches (Burgess, 2005). However, Pentecostal and Charismatic Churches do not appear to be imagistic religions because of their size, frequent (weekly) rituals, hierarchy, focus on orthodoxy, and inclusivity toward outsiders as evidenced by their positive outlook toward evangelism.

Concerning the second prediction, the data does not suggest that individuals in Pentecostal and Charismatic traditions are attending less frequently. In fact, a cross-cultural survey by the Pew Research Center found that a higher percentage of Pentecostal and Charismatic Christians claim to attend weekly services than Christians from other denominations in nine of the ten countries surveyed (Pew Research Center, 2006, p. 20). If the prediction is interpreted as addressing the frequency with which the tradition will perform the ritual (regardless of who attends) there have been no large-scale shifts noted in the literature. Pentecostal and Charismatic Christian churches are still reliant on weekly rituals.

Additionally, it does not seem that Pentecostal and Charismatic Christian churches have adjusted their emotional intensity levels to conform to the attractor arrangement of doctrinal religions (high frequency and low emotional intensity). Nevertheless, the predicted negative effect on verbal transmission is difficult—if not impossible—to estimate from the available ethnographic or historical accounts and there is not much empirical data on the subject. This question is discussed again later in Chapter 4.

The fourth prediction is that the tradition will go extinct. This does not seem to be the case for Pentecostal and Charismatic Christianity either. The Pentecostal movement began in the American Midwest in 1901 when students in the Bethel Bible School (Topeka, Kansas) began having ecstatic experiences and speaking in tongues. By the 1960s, individuals having intense experiences speaking in tongues or being slain in the spirit were reported in Roman Catholic and Protestant churches as well; known originally as the "Charismatic Revival" (D. E. Miller & Yamamori, 2007). The fact that these practices have been continually occurring for over a century and include multiple generations of adherents seems to violate the DMR theory's prediction.

The fifth prediction is that emotional intensity levels associated with the ritual can be lowered. However, it appears that the emotional intensity levels in Pentecostal and Charismatic communities have been maintained. A 2006 survey by the Pew Research Center found that a majority of Pentecostals and Charismatics in ten countries attend services where there is speaking in tongues, spiritual faith healings, or exorcisms (Pew Research Center, 2006), suggesting that the practices that defined the community decades ago are still prevalent today.

The finding that so many Pentecostal and Charismatic Christians in the world are attending rituals with high levels of emotional intensity also suggests that there are critical differences between the Creekside Baptist Church and Melanesian religions and Pentecostal and Charismatic Christianity. Specifically, unlike the Creekside Baptist Church and Melanesian traditions, modern Pentecostal and Charismatic practices are not relegated to individual experiences that happen in isolation. These intense experiences are occurring in settings where the experience is shared with a large congregation (potential effects of this are discussed further in Section 2.3).

Additionally, Pentecostal and Charismatic Christian churches do not seem to be collections of localized communities that only come to perceive that they share an experience upon later reflection. Unlike the reports from Melanesian religions and the Creekside Baptist Church, individuals in Pentecostal and Charismatic churches are not having these experiences in isolation or small communities. In some cases, they are having these experiences in congregations that sometimes have tens of thousands of individuals (known as mega-churches). The size of mega-church congregations precludes the possibility that members could all be bonded by means of episodic memories for mutually shared experiences with specific individuals, as is the case in the imagistic mode. In addition, Pentecostal and Charismatic churches of all sizes seem to share a core set of beliefs and practices from which they draw their identification. For example, many churches even invite pastors from other churches to preach on Sundays and members attend large retreat events, such as the Hillsong retreat which draws 30,000 individuals annually from churches all over the world (Koziol, 2015) and invites leaders from multiple churches preach at the event.

In order to better understand the nuances of group alignment that could be relevant to these practices, we can turn to the psychological factor that allows us to bond with one another to begin with: group alignment. This can allow us to better understand how we align with a group and what cognitive mechanisms we might employ to bond to one another based on the beliefs shared in doctrinal religions. From this, we can then set out to build a new AI architecture that could be instantiated into a computer system and tested to better understand, and explain, religion (discussed in Chapters 3 and 4).

2.2 Group Alignment

Social identity theory and fusion theory each proposes different ways in which personal and social identities interact that have distinct consequences for group alignment in doctrinal religions. These are each outlined in the following sections as a more nuanced understanding of these group alignment processes can help elucidate the issues addressed by the current research.

2.2.1 Social Identification

Social identity theory proposes that people can represent groups as social categories by representing groups as prototypes, or "context-specific fuzzy sets that define and prescribe attitudes, feelings, and behaviors that characterize one group and distinguish it from other groups" (Hogg, 2001, p. 6).

Social identity theory posits the *principle of functional antagonism* (Turner, Reynolds, Haslam, & Veenstra, 2006), which states that when personal identity is elicited, social identity is suppressed and vice versa. Social identity theory states that individuals can have multiple social identities and identify with different groups in different contexts or highlight their unique personal identity to maintain a positive self-image (see Ashmore, Deaux, & McLaughlin-Volpe, 2004; Mccauley, 2006; Settles, 2004). So, while an individual can dissociate their personal and social identities (as described by the principle of functional antagonism), they align with groups that share their beliefs. In this way, there is congruence between a person's beliefs and the set of beliefs defining the social category to which they align. However, these beliefs are held in such a way that the person can functionally separate their self-image from the beliefs of their group if the beliefs associated with that group no longer support a positive self-image. As such, in contexts where a person's social group is criticized publicly, an individual can still maintain a positive self-image. The process whereby one dissociates oneself from a social group in order to maintain a positive self-image is called *disidentification* (Bhattacharya & Elsbach, 2002; Elsbach & Bhattacharya, 2001; Jans, Postmes, & Van der Zee, 2011). An example of disidentification would be someone who is socially identified with a group that is publicly criticized (e.g., gun rights organizations in the United States, such as the National Rifle Association—or NRA). If the spokesperson for the NRA says something insensitive after a public tragedy such as a school shooting, rather than defending the group, individual members might insist that they are different from the group because their own personal beliefs (i.e., personal identity) do not align with that statement. On the other hand, in times of personal uncertainty, identifying with a social group can provide a sense of certainty by tying one's own fate to that of their group (Buhrmester et al., 2012; Ellemers, Spears, & Doosje, 2002).

Social psychologists have shown that individuals can identify quite easily with groups. For example, psychologists have shown that using "minimal groups," created simply by assigning individuals to a "blue group" or "red group" and making this group socially salient, is sufficient to induce in-group favoritism and out-group derogation (Otten, 2016). Empirical evidence from the social identity literature supports the idea that individuals can have multiple identities (e.g., Brewer & Pierce, 2005; Mccauley, 2006; Settles, 2004; Steffens, Jetten, Haslam, Cruwys, & Haslam, 2016; Turner-Zwinkels, Postmes, & Van Zomeren, 2015); however, this book only focuses on an individual's religious identity.

2.2.2 Fusion

Fusion has been sharply distinguished from social identification (Swann et al., 2012). Fusion theorists have proposed four principles, outlined by Swann et al. (2012) and further clarified by Fredman et al. (2015):

1. The *agentic personal self-principle* states that even when social identities are salient, "the personal self can motivate pro-group behavior by channeling personal agency into pro-group action" (Fredman et al., 2015, p. 470).
2. The *identity synergy principle* states that personal identities combine with social identities and individual agents can be motivated to enact sacrificial or extreme behavior on behalf of the group (Swann et al., 2012, p. 443).
3. The *irrevocability principle* states that once a person is fused, it causes such an emotional mark on the individual that they will remain fused (Swann et al., 2012, p. 443). This has been shown to be the case even when individuals are ostracized by their own in-group (Gómez, Morales, Hart, Vázquez, & Swann, 2011, p. 1576).
4. The *relational ties principle* "assumes that strongly fused persons feel attached to individual members of the group as well as to the abstract 'collective.' As such, strongly fused persons should be especially inclined to endorse sacrificing their lives not only for the group as an abstract collective but also to save the lives of individual members of the group" (Fredman et al., 2015, p. 472).

These principles suggest that there are several differences between social identification and fusion. The agentic personal self-principle suggests that even when a social identity is salient, individuals can be personally motivated toward group action. Social identity theory would propose that personal motivations are more salient when personal (not social) identities are salient. As such, the identity synergy principle stands in direct juxtaposition with social identity theory's principle of functional antagonism. For fused individuals, their personal and social identities can be said to have a porous boundary, where the two are not fully separated, and eliciting either their personal or social identity will make the other salient as well. In theory, a fused individual views the social group as being—in many ways—an extension of one's own self. As such, fused individuals feel a "visceral feeling of oneness" with their group (Swann et al., 2012, p. 450), which makes it difficult for an individual to separate their personal identity from their social identity. In addition, the irrevocability principle posits that fused individuals will remain fused. This suggests that the inability to disidentify with the group is not just a temporary state, but a permanent "trait-like" condition where individuals will support the group indefinitely (unlike socially identified individuals who are proposed to disidentify in order to maintain a positive self-image). Lastly, the relational ties principle states that fused individuals bond to specific individuals, as well as the collective group. Social identity theory makes the prediction that individuals bond to collective individuals as social categories.

One important point concerning fusion and social identification is that empirical evidence has shown that, generally, individuals with high levels of fusion also have high levels of social identification. However, it is not typically the case that individuals with high social identification also have high levels of fusion (Buhrmester et al., 2014, 2012; Gómez, Brooks et al., 2011; Gómez, Morales et al., 2011; Jong, Whitehouse, Kavanagh, & Lane, 2016; Páez et al., 2015; Whitehouse et al., 2017b, 2014). Currently, some fusion theorists posit that it may not be possible for an individual to have high levels of fusion but *not* high levels of social identification (see Swann, Gómez, Seyle, Morales, & Huici, 2009, p. 1008). Indeed, it is hard to conceptualize how one could be fused—that is, unable to dissociate one's personal and social identities—if they do not have some significant level of commitment to a social identity.

The distinction between highly identified individuals who are fused and highly identified individuals who are not fused has been shown to underlie important behavioral differences. For example, highly identified individuals who are highly fused are more prone to endorse extreme behaviors (Gómez & Vázquez, 2015; Swann & Buhrmester, 2015; Swann, Buhrmester et al., 2014; Swann et al., 2009), exhibit greater endorsements of self-sacrifices for their group (Swann, Buhrmester et al., 2014; Swann, Gómez et al., 2014), they appear to exhibit greater levels of cooperation (Whitehouse et al., 2017b), and appear more likely to defend their group through physical (and sometimes violent) actions (Gómez et al., 2017). Individuals who are highly identified but not highly fused do not show the same patterns. The observation of predicted outputs of fusion theory that are distinct from the outputs of social identity theory lends credence to the idea that social identification and fusion address distinct forms of group alignment.

To better clarify how fusion can relate to social cohesion in doctrinal religions, we can discuss two forms of fusion noted in the literature: local and extended, which were briefly mentioned in Chapter 1. *Local fusion* is when "group members form relational ties with others with whom they have direct personal contact and thus have the opportunity to share experiences," while *extended fusion* is when people "project the relational ties normally associated with local fusion onto large groups despite having little or no direct contact or shared experiences with individual members" (Swann et al., 2012, p. 443). Fusion theory does not suggest that the four principles discussed earlier are unique to either local or extended fusion. In addition, researchers generally suggest that both forms of fusion result from emotionally intense dysphoric experiences (e.g., Buhrmester et al., 2014; Jong et al., 2016; Swann et al., 2012; Whitehouse et al., 2014); only two studies concentrate on the role of euphoric experiences (Kavanagh, Jong, Mckay, & Whitehouse, 2018; Newson, Buhrmester, & Whitehouse, 2016).

Discussing these two forms of fusion is important because the DMR theory makes different predictions for fusion in imagistic (small) versus doctrinal (large) religious groups. Recall that the DMR theory proposes that individuals in imagistic religions bond via relational ties (i.e., local fusion), but that emotionally intense rituals in doctrinal religions should not facilitate bonding through the same mechanisms. While the size of many doctrinal religions (such as Pentecostal Christianity) would seem to rule out the possibility that members are aligned to the group via local fusion, it is possible that extended fusion could facilitate group alignment in doctrinal religions. Therefore, discussing the differences in the role of relational ties in fostering fusion can help us to better understand how emotionally intense rituals in doctrinal religions can affect one's alignment to a group.

2.2.2.1 Local Fusion

Local fusion is said to be based on the formation of kinship-like relational ties to non-kin. These ties are thought to be the result of a shared traumatic experience such as an initiation, war, or witnessing an act of violence or terrorism (Swann et al., 2012). Intense experiences can create episodic memories, which encode information about who was present during an event. In principle, the formation of long-lasting episodic memories for who was present at an intense event could codify relational ties between people who experienced the event (as proposed by Whitehouse & Lanman, 2014). Insofar as the individuals do not forget who was present during the experience, they will always feel bonded to those individuals. However, recent research suggests a slight amendment. Some evidence suggests that individuals cannot accurately recall exactly who was present at intense religious rituals, but they are quite certain that they accurately recall exactly who was present (Xygalatas et al., 2013). Since the memory of an event becomes codified after the event, it could be said that individuals form relational ties with who they *believed to be present*, rather than who was actually present.

Given the size of doctrinal religions, it seems infeasible that local fusion is the form of group alignment operating in doctrinal religions because it would be logistically impossible for all members of many doctrinal religions (e.g., Pentecostal Christianity) to know one another. However, it is imaginable that imagistic practices in doctrinal religions can foster local fusion. For example, in the Melanesian religions discussed earlier, individuals in local communities who performed highly intense emotional rituals appeared to bond with the other members of their local community. It was not until these communities came together after the fact, and realized they had all independently performed similar rituals, that the experience became a basis for social cohesion outside of their local community. In addition, some Christian churches utilize Bible study groups of fifteen or so individuals who frequently meet (typically on a weekly basis). Should an emotionally intense experience happen within such a group, it could foster local fusion among the members of the Bible study group, but not necessarily among other members of church who are not part of that group.

2.2.2.2 Extended Fusion

Given the size of most doctrinal religions, individuals who are fused to a doctrinal religious group such as Christianity would be said to be fused via extended fusion. As discussed in relation to local fusion, it is theoretically possible for small sub-communities within a doctrinal religion to be fused via local fusion. However, measurements of their levels of fusion to their larger church congregation (assuming the church is sufficiently large that they could not know all other members of the church) should be measuring extended fusion.

Extended fusion proposes that individuals who are fused to large groups are believed to view the members of their group as fictive kin (Swann et al., 2012). Triggering kinship perceptions may be why individuals with high levels of fusion are willing to fight and die for a large group of genetically unrelated individuals. Research suggests that extended fusion, like local fusion, also results from intense emotionally intense experiences (Buhrmester et al., 2014; Jong et al., 2016; Kavanagh et al., 2018; Swann et al., 2012). Currently, the fusion literature suggests that extended fusion can result from reflection upon an emotionally intense experience such as being affected by terrorism (Buhrmester et al., 2014; Jong et al., 2016) or participating in festivals (Páez et al., 2015). Whitehouse and Lanman suggest: "what will trigger psychological kinship is the perception that one shares with others episodic memories that are essential components of one's autobiographical self-concept" and they suggest this is because sharing such experiences has served as a reliable marker of genetic relatedness in our evolutionary past (2014, p. 677).

In most studies of fusion, fusion is treated as a mediator or predictor for some other effect, usually the extreme pro-group behaviors such as self-sacrifice (e.g., Besta, Szulc, & Jaśkiewicz, 2015; Newson et al., 2016; Swann, Buhrmester et al., 2014; Swann, Gómez et al., 2014; Swann, Gómez, Dovidio, Hart, & Jetten, 2010; Whitehouse et al., 2017b) or cooperation, particularly in regards to the donation of goods or time (Buhrmester, Burnham et al., 2018; Buhrmester et al., 2014; Gómez, Morales, et al., 2011; Newson et al., 2016; studies 4-6 in Whitehouse et al., 2017b, 2014). In addition, most studies use surveys to address extended fusion in large groups like nationalities (e.g., Americans or Spaniards) and almost all studies of extended fusion are correlational. The lack of experimental evidence may be partially due to the ethical issues in facilitating an experimental condition with high enough arousal that would trigger the episodic memories currently thought to underpin fusion. Additionally, it is difficult to devise experimental protocols that are feasible for large groups (although, this is also an issue for the literature on social identification). Nevertheless, many studies have used survey questions and priming manipulations (e.g., Jong et al., 2016) to suggest potential causes of extended fusion. Of those studies that are currently published in the literature, there are a few that have anomalous results.

2.2.2.3 Issues Concerning Relational Ties and Essential Beliefs in Extended Fusion

Theoretical overviews of the fusion literature propose that both local and extended fusion should be based on relational ties (Fredman et al., 2015, p. 472;

Swann et al., 2012, p. 443). It is currently proposed that local fusion is based on actual relational ties between members of a group while extended fusion is when people "project the relational ties normally associated with local fusion onto large groups despite having little or no direct contact or shared experiences with individual members" (Swann et al., 2012, p. 443). It has been suggested that sharing essential beliefs with "other group members may allow for and enhance fusion with the group" (Swann et al., 2012, p. 449).[5] According to Swann, Buhrmester et al., knowing essential beliefs "are shared may reinforce the perception of familial ties to fellow group members, ties that encourage them to make extreme sacrifices for the group" (2014, p. 914) and the authors clarify that they "conceptualize perception of familial ties as a member of the larger class of relational ties" (2014, p. 914). This suggests that sharing some essential belief is able to foster extended fusion by activating perceived relational ties. However, while some studies have found evidence for the relationship between essential beliefs and fusion, other studies suggest that relational ties may not be the foundation of extended fusion (discussed later), suggesting the link between perceived essential beliefs, relational ties, and extended fusion may require greater specification.

A paper by Vázquez, Gómez, and Swann (2017) presents three studies conducted in Spain that investigated the longitudinal effects of threats to one's group (in this case, Spaniards) on levels of identification, fusion, relational ties, and categorical ties.[6] They utilized pre-test and post-test measures of these constructs over time. During the post-test of Study 1, they manipulated the level of salience of perceived group threats by having participants read and write about different incidents they believed to be negatively impacting their identity (a scandal regarding the Spanish Monarchy). When analyzing their data, the authors used a dual mediation model where pre-test fusion was the independent variable, post-test fusion was the dependent variable, and levels of perceived relational ties and categorical ties served as independent mediators. This model revealed that the relationship between pre-test and post-test fusion was significantly mediated by categorical ties to the group but not relational ties to the group. The results suggest that changes in extended fusion are related to categorical ties, which are currently thought to be the basis for identification (Whitehouse & Lanman, 2014, p. 678), but no evidence was found that changes in extended fusion were related to relational ties.

In addition, Vázquez, Gómez, and Swann (Study 2; 2017) measured the level of fusion in a Spanish sample before and after a vote to have Catalonia secede from the rest of Spain. A confirmatory factor analysis found that the measures of fusion, relational, and categorical ties were all separate constructs. They found that extended fusion has a stronger correlation with categorical ties ($r = .86$) than relational ties ($r = .73$), suggesting that, while there is a relationship between extended fusion and relational ties, the relationship between fusion and categorical ties may be stronger. The results of Study 1 were also replicated in Study 2: using a mediation model, they found that categorical ties partially mediated the relationship between pre-test and post-test fusion, but their measure of relational ties did not. Lastly, the authors manipulated when individuals would take the post-test (before or after an election) and found that the relationship between pre- and post-test fusion was mediated by categorical ties but there was no significant indirect effect for relational ties (Vázquez et al., 2017; Study 3). Taken together, the results of these studies suggest that changes in extended fusion over time are related to categorical ties. While there was evidence of a correlation between relational ties and extended fusion, there was no evidence that relational ties mediated changes in extended fusion.

Another unexpected finding that concerns the relational ties principle was reported in a recent study of identification and fusion in large Brazilian groups, which found that "individual self-stereotyping and in-group homogeneity presented mid- to low positive correlations with identity fusion in all target groups" (Bortolini, Newson, Natividade, Vázquez, & Gómez, 2018, p. 16). As Bortolini et al. note, this is not predicted by fusion theory because the relational ties principle suggests that highly fused people should be "predisposed to recognize the unique personal identities as well as social identities of fellow group members, allowing for 'uniqueness-based' as well as 'membership-based' attraction" (Swann et al., 2012, p. 443).

Turning now to the relationship between extended fusion and essential beliefs, Buhrmester et al. (2018) investigated the relationship between fusion with one's country and essential beliefs. In one study reported in the paper (Study 2), they measured a participant's fusion with a country, the extent to which they held as an essential belief that baseball was part of America's "essence" and how much money they would allocate to an American baseball club, while taking money from a Cuban baseball club. The behavioral measure (of donating to an in-group or deducting money from an out-group) allowed them to assess the pro-group tendencies predicted by fusion. To assess essential beliefs, they asked participants to answer four questions: (1) "American baseball captures the very essence of the United States"; (2) "Baseball lies that the core of what it means to be American"; (3) "Baseball represents the heart and soul of America"; and (4) "Baseball is an essential part of the United States." Internal consistency on their measure of an essential belief was good ($\alpha = .91$).[7] Their analysis revealed a positive correlation between fusion and perceiving baseball as part of the nation's essence. The results further revealed main effects for fusion and essential belief, "indicating that as fusion and essence each increased, so too did the amount given to the ingroup" (Buhrmester, Newson et al., 2018, p. 21). A simple slopes analysis also revealed that, for those who do not believe baseball to be part of the nation's essence (as measured by those participants scoring less than 1 SD from the mean on the essential belief measure), fusion was not associated with donations to the in-group or deducted from the out-group. However, for those who did believe baseball to be part of the nation's essence (as measured by those participants scoring greater than 1 SD from the mean on essential belief measure), increased fusion was associated with greater donations to the in-group and greater deductions from the out-group.

An additional study by Páez et al. (2015; Study 3) deployed a survey among participants drawn from 15M protesters[8] in Spain to assess the effect of essential beliefs on fusion. Using a mediation regression model, their analysis revealed that the amount of participation in the movement was positively related to their endorsement of essential beliefs of the group (solidarity, freedom, dignity, participation, social justice, and equity) and that this relationship was positively mediated by their perceived emotional synchrony with the group. The fact that the results of the study by Páez et al. (2015), like the Buhrmester et al. (2018) study, found a relationship between essential beliefs and fusion suggests that in some cases, extended fusion may be the result of essential beliefs.

The results of these studies have not demonstrated that perceptions of essential beliefs trigger fusion via perceived relational ties (as the studies earlier do not investigate relational ties directly). While some studies have shown that perceived essential beliefs affect extended fusion, others have not found evidence that relational ties affect extended fusion, and no study to date has attempted to study essential beliefs in conjunction with relational ties. This leaves open the idea that perceived essential beliefs affect extended fusion without activating perceived relational ties, as posited previously by some fusion theorists (Swann et al., 2012; Vázquez, Gómez, Ordoñana, & Paredes, 2015); a variation of the claim that essential beliefs affect extended fusion without activating relational ties is advocated in the information identity system (IIS) framework described in Chapter 3.

In addition, the fusion literature is unclear as to the role of emotional valence in creating fusion. While multiple theoretical overviews suggest that dysphoric experiences cause fusion (Swann et al., 2012; Whitehouse & Lanman, 2014) and say little about the role of euphoric experiences (as noted by Xygalatas, 2014), the empirical literature has found support that both dysphoric and euphoric experiences can result in fusion. Multiple studies have found links between fusion and dysphoric experiences including war (Whitehouse et al., 2014), initiation rituals (Whitehouse et al., 2017b), and acts of terrorism (Buhrmester et al., 2014; Jong et al., 2016). To my knowledge, two studies have collected data on the positivity or euphoria of an experience and fusion. The first study was conducted with British football fans and found that the extent to which dysphoric experiences (such as when one's team loses) and euphoric experiences (such as when one's team wins) were considered to shape the way a participant sees his or her self were positively related to fusion to the football club. The second study recruited participants from Brazilian Ju Jitsu group and found a positive relationship between the positivity the members associated with belt promotion rituals and fusion to their Brazilian Ju Jitsu group. The results of these studies suggest that both positive *and* negative experiences can promote fusion; a point which we will return to later.

In Chapter 3, it is proposed that by understanding the role of emotionally intense experiences in the formation of schemas in semantic memory we can better understand how essential beliefs of a group can serve as a basis for extended fusion with doctrinal religious groups by internalizing social beliefs into one's personal schema. Furthermore, it is proposed that this can clarify the issues noted in this chapter regarding the relationship between essential beliefs and fusion.

3

Bonding and Belief

The earlier chapters have outlined how the intersection between bonding and belief has repercussions ranging from everyday rituals that can bring a piece of mind to religious adherents the world over, to the motivations and cognitive underpinnings of extreme acts of terrorism that can take thousands of lives in a single day. From this foundation, we can formalize the many different interactions and cognitive mechanisms that underpin how we draw our social bonds from our personal beliefs, and thus set the stage for a computational system that can help us simulate a wide variety of religious phenomena such as the relationship between social cohesion, consensus, ritual, conversions, religious schisms, identification, and even religious extremism and terrorism. In this way, the assemblage of religious systems can begin to take form, with key variables and their interactions being specified at a cognitive level, so that they can then be instantiated into computational systems.

Drawing on the work discussed in the previous chapter, we can begin to formalize the key relationships into a single information processing system (guided by the assumption laid out in the discussion on cultural cybernetics), which I will refer to here as the information identity system or IIS. This system is outlined at the end of this chapter, after a brief discussion on how cognitive science, and the AI that is inspired by it, have approached the complexities of human memory and belief.

Recall from the previous chapter that if we are discussing the beliefs that an individual has about their religion or a group, then we would be talking about information that has been consolidated into semantic memory and can be generally accessed by the individual (called declarative memory).

After information enters declarative memory, it is presumably organized so that it can be recalled as needed. It is crucial to understand organizational structure of this information if we are to be able to formalize its structure and manipulate it within a computer system. Having a good (albeit largely theoretical) way of storing complex beliefs can allow us to define a schema by the interacting representations it holds. *Schemas* are defined as structured sets of information we can use to operate in, and make sense of, the world around us. Schemas are often conceived of as things which are constantly updated by new experiences in our lives (Bartlett, 1932; Wagoner, 2013); this assumption is congruent with the memory consolidation literature outlined earlier. Researchers have noted that schemas differ based on personal experiences, resulting in both individual and cultural differences (Fivush, Habermas, Waters, & Zaman, 2011), this assumption is compatible with the anthropological and scholarly literature on culture and religion that have demonstrated the effect of context on human beliefs. In this way, schemas are a way of representing information encoded in memory over time.

In principle, an individual can have a schema for any subject. One example, which I will return to regularly both out of convenience and its relevance to research in later chapters is the religious schemas that individuals have regarding the Sunday service, which is common to so many Christian communities throughout the world and shares many common features with weekly rituals of other large religions. In order to understand religious beliefs, given that they are both socially shared by a group and partially unique and personally relevant to the individual, is to address two types of schemas for the Sunday service: self-schemas and social schemas. A *self-schema* is information that individuals have regarding their own personal experiences, knowledge about the world, beliefs, and values. Additionally, a *social schema* is the beliefs, values, and attitudes that one shares with their social group.[1] While these schemas hold different information, they are not to be considered mutually exclusive; rather, they are interactive. This can be seen with the simple example that many individuals—as part of their self-schema—define themselves as members of an imagined community (or a community which exists primarily as an abstract idea in the minds of those who align themselves with it; see Anderson, 2006), which is in turn defined by a social schema.

There are two types of schemas that can help one formalize ritual behaviors: scripts (Shank & Abelson, 1977) and frames (Minsky, 1974).

A *script* is a set of expected behavioral outcomes or possibilities that one assumes to be applicable in a situation (Shank & Abelson, 1977). We have scripts for different contexts and use them to guide appropriate behaviors. For example, a script for reading in a library would include walking (not running), speaking softly, and refraining from boisterous activities. Scripts are used implicitly to guide behavior and are not usually reflected upon. Implicit scripts can be found in many religious behaviors. Some scripts are easy to discern, such as scripts for how to behave during a silent prayer. However, other scripts are more subtle such as when it is appropriate for a Catholic to make the sign of the cross or for a Muslim to say Salawat.[2]

Since scripts are largely implicit, they are more informative for understanding the transmission of behaviors than the transmission of representations (cf. Whitehouse, 2004, p. 68). As such, scripts are not the best way to understand the transmission of representations. For example, behaviors such as reading and attending social events such as rituals can serve to transmit behavioral scripts. However, the present discussion focuses on belief schemas that are transmitted and that encode information in semantic memory;[3] the behaviors that facilitate transmission are secondary.

A *frame* is a type of schema that represents structured information "as a network of nodes and relationships" (Minsky, 1974, p. 1). This information is organized into two levels: the first level holds information which is always true for the schema (axioms); and a second level includes "terminals" or places where information is held, as well as the "markers" which describe relationships between these bits of information. This allows for schemas to be represented as networks where the terminals are nodes in a network and the markers are the links describing some connection or relationship between the nodes. Previously, schemas have been represented as networks in computational models (Carley, 1997; Meeter & Murre, 2005; Russell & Norvig, 2003; Whitehouse, Kahn, Hochberg, & Bryson, 2012).

In the network format, we can efficiently represent a schema as a two-dimensional matrix. This provides an efficient quantification of the complex relationships between concepts. Mathematical formalizations of schemas provide a means to compare schemas and such a quantified abstraction of a schema can facilitate statistical tests concerning how similar schemas are between individuals within a group or how similar schemas are between groups. By comparing schemas in this way, one can draw statistically backed conclusion regarding the extent to which representations are shared among members of a group as well as how much information a participant can recall. This can facilitate a quantifiable formalization of the idea of "consensus," which in turn can allow us to research the nature of social consensus and the spread of beliefs scientifically, and with a scientific rigor that goes far beyond either post hoc coding of qualitative data or requiring predetermined coding schemes created by researchers who are not themselves part of the group that they're studying. In this way, the use of a cognitive approach rooted in AI and contemporary data science can help us to bridge the divide and issues surrounding the separation of emic and etic approaches to cultural beliefs.[4]

Frames can efficiently represent the information held in declarative memory. In this way frames provide a way to formalize a "worldview" by storing the complex relationships between concepts or categories (Tooby & Cosmides, 1992). More abstract representations (nodes) can be further described at a lower level by the links connecting related representations (nodes). Our ability to effectively formalize a "worldview" has many repercussions for the future of the social sciences. While here I will focus on its use to study religions, the formalization of worldviews can also be used to study political beliefs and ideologies as well as more specific beliefs cultures have about critical political topics like power, gender, race, and inequality.

In the later chapters, I discuss a new simulation system for simulating key aspects of religion and identity. In that research, I focus on the concept of a frame to represent schemas of representations learned during ritual experiences. This frame is a two-dimensional network where nodes represent mental representations, and links represent a relationship between the representations.[5] There is no cause to assume that a frame requires two discrete levels; that is to say, a lower level, which exclusively contains information related to a superordinate representation, does not need to be defined. There are three reasons for this. First, multiple representations at one level may utilize links to representations stored separately at another level; therefore, delineating two separate levels within the frame may duplicate any lower-level concept used to define or demarcate more than one superordinate representation. This results in an unnecessary computational burden. Second, individual communities are likely to define their own truth claims (axioms) and making *a priori* assumptions about how a community defines a "higher-level" representation may confound the representation of the group's schema. Third, it is better to allow representations to be described by clusters of representations that may be directly related to other representations. By doing this, the "clusters" of representations that form around a node effectively serve to represent the frame's "lower level" of information.[6] For these reasons, it is best to define the frame in two dimensions and allow meaning to emerge as clusters of related representations are discerned.[7] Also, as shown earlier, two-dimensional networks can subsume many aspects of list based or hierarchically based formalizations of memory. Therefore, the two-dimensional frame-based formalization of a schema provides a versatile and efficient way to represent memory. Additionally, two-dimensional networks have been used in previous studies of doctrinal religious schemas (Lane, 2015b; McCorkle & Lane, 2012; Whitehouse, 2013; Whitehouse et al., 2012).

To summarize, a cultural cybernetics approach can utilize Minsky's concept of frames, because it offers a computationally defined framework for representing the schemas. As with previous research, computational models of schemas can use a single two-dimensional network to represent the schema (see Carley, 1997; Lane, 2015b; McCorkle & Lane, 2012; Whitehouse et al., 2012).[8] This network structure can efficiently capture the relevant relationships between representations for the purpose of testing the IIS and is continuous with previous research. For the remainder of this document the term "schema" will be used to refer to frames as defined by complex networks of representations.

3.1 The Information Identity System (IIS)

The IIS aims to extend earlier research on social cohesion by revising several components of human cognition that have been proposed to promote social cohesion in doctrinal religions: frequency of in-group ritual attendance, emotional intensity of religious experiences, reflection on emotionally intense experiences, development of a personal schema, accessibility of relevant social schemas, and within-group consensus. This chapter outlines (1) how these aspects can be integrated into a single framework, (2) the key factors that enable the IIS to enhance our ability to simulate and explain doctrinal religions by accounting for the persistence of practices that facilitate emotionally intense experiences in doctrinal religions, and (3) how the IIS can clarify some of the findings concerning the role of relational ties and essential beliefs in extended fusion described in the previous section.

The IIS builds upon well-established aspects of human psychology. For example, the research on human memory has a considerable amount of empirical investigation going back over four decades. Additionally, since the 1980s social psychologists have published a great deal of empirical research concerning social identification. However, most of the fusion literature is more recent. The initial papers on fusion were published a decade ago (the first papers were published around 2009); and the first paper to incorporate the fusion literature with our understanding of religious behaviors directly is quite recent (Whitehouse & Lanman, 2014).

One of the key differences between the IIS and earlier approaches like those mentioned in the previous chapter is that the IIS focuses on a strict computational approach, which focuses on how information can be processed in the mind (see M. Rescorla, 2015). Specifically, the IIS focuses on how information input by different experiences is processed by human cognitive mechanisms and results in schemas about our self and our group that can affect social cohesion over time. As such, the IIS presents an individual-level computational architecture that aims to address the proximate mechanisms of the evolution of doctrinal religions. This can allow for the calculation and potential prediction of both high-level phenomena related to religions (such as consensus, cohesion, and schisms) that can emerge from the complex interactions of individuals, as well as the prediction of lower-level individual phenomena such as conversions and extremism. The relationships between the key variables of the IIS are formalized in Figure 3.1, which presents a simplified model of the relationships.

The IIS begins by noting that the way individuals internalize information is critical to the formation of memories and the schemas that inform our identities and underlie within-group consensus. It also relies on the position that episodic memory and semantic memory are not separate systems, but they have overlapping attributes. Understanding these overlapping attributes—and how they are related to personal and social schemas—can help us understand social cohesion in doctrinal religions. The IIS focuses on how two pathways affect the interactions of personal and social schemas and, therefore, group alignment styles. These two pathways start with frequency of in-group ritual attendance and intense emotional experience in Figure 3.1.

Semantic memories are formed by the rehearsal of information. As noted by the DMR theory, the frequent rituals of doctrinal religions can facilitate the required rehearsal to form semantic memories. It also aligns with the DMR

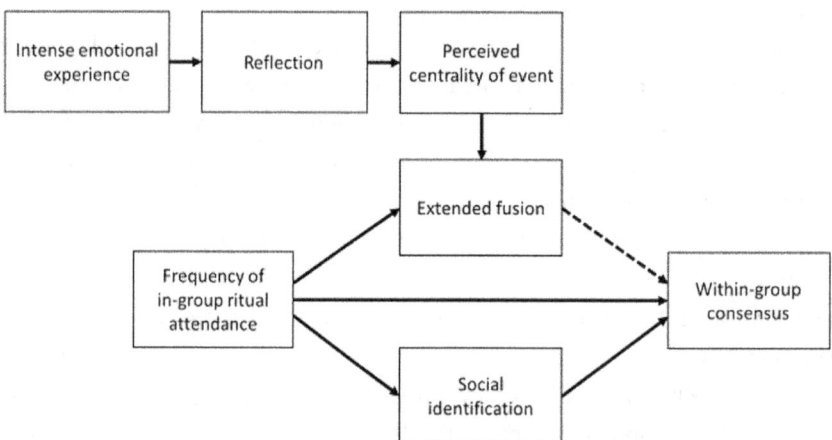

Figure 3.1 Proposed relationships of the IIS. Solid arrows depict hypothesized positive relationships. Dashed arrows depict hypothesized negative relationships.

theory in that it proposes that rare and emotionally intense experiences, such as initiation rituals, can form episodic memories. However, it breaks from the DMR theory at this point as the DMR theory focuses almost exclusively on the role of *dysphoric* experiences to form episodic memories. The IIS suggests that both dysphoric and euphoric experiences can facilitate the formation of episodic memories. As such, the IIS focuses on the *emotional intensity* of a ritual, not the ritual's emotional valence, as the cause for fusion as well, which is a break from the previous literature (cf. Swann et al., 2012; Whitehouse, 1996; Whitehouse & Lanman, 2014).

Because the line between semantic and episodic memories can be blurred, the IIS posits that the distinction between personal and social schemas can also be blurred when we interpret autobiographically relevant memories (such as those formed by emotionally intense experiences that result in fusion) using information from a group's social schema. Evidence suggests that autobiographically relevant episodic memories can be—and often are—partially reconstructed using schemas in semantic memory, and some semantic memories can be deeply personal and have emotional associations. However, typically, emotional associations are a feature of episodic—not semantic—memories (Renoult, Davidson, Palombo, Moscovitch, & Levine, 2012; A. E. Wilson & Ross, 2003). Nevertheless, there are obvious examples of this phenomenon in doctrinal religions. For example, for a devout Christian, the Crucifixion can evoke extremely emotional responses, even though they could not have directly experienced or perceived the event and they are unlikely to recall the details surrounding when they learned the information, suggesting that the information is stored in semantic memory. Also, when a 22-year-old paramilitary member in Belfast sees a mural remembering the 40-year period of violence known as "the Troubles," their reaction can be extremely emotional.

Computational models can help us better understand the relationship between semantic and episodic information stored in our memories. While many early approaches treated our memories like a filing cabinet or a folder on a computer where different files of isolated information are stored, new models suggest that information stored in memory is distributed across the brain in networks of interlocking information (Meeter & Murre, 2004; Moscovitch, Nadel, Winocur, Gilboa, & Rosenbaum, 2006; Winocur & Moscovitch, 2011), and when one concept is activated in this network, it can activate other aspects of the network as well. In this way, the image of the Crucifixion is emotional not only because it activates emotionally laden semantic information associated with what they know about the Crucifixion, but also because it activates episodic information, perhaps about their own personal experience of being "born again" where it was interpreted in reference to the "sacrifice of Christ on the cross," as is often the case in contemporary Christian communities. Similarly, the remembrance murals in Belfast not only elicit emotion because it is associated with what they know about the Troubles, despite their not being old enough to have been alive during the period; it can also elicit information that they have personally experienced, such as riots or violence associated with the 12th of July, where that individual could have been personally affected, and now associates their experience with that commemorated in the mural.

The distinction between episodic and semantic memory is also blurred when episodic memories become semantic memories. It should be noted that, when information is first presented to us it would not be initially encoded in semantic memory. Using the standard example from psychology textbooks of learning the capital of France: when one is first told that Paris is the capital of France, we would have an episodic memory of being presented with this information (with details such as who told us this information and where we were when we learned it) and later, after the information is rehearsed through reflection or repeated exposures (or rote memorization), is the information consolidated into semantic memory. *Memory consolidation* is the process by which information perceived during a personal experience becomes a part of semantic memory.

Consolidation theories propose that knowledge becomes incorporated into semantic memory through reactivation. There are three main theories of memory consolidation—namely, consolidation theory, semantization theory, and multiple trace theory. *Consolidation theory* proposes that reactivation of information during memory consolidation is an explicit process, but *Semantization theory* proposes that reactivation of information during memory consolidation is an implicit process (Meeter & Murre, 2004). *Multiple trace theory* does not clearly argue for either explicit or implicit reactivation of information; only that multiple traces of hippocampal activation are necessary to support episodic memories and as hippocampal traces are replaced by neocortical traces, the memories begin to resemble semantic memories and lose their episodic qualities (Moscovitch et al., 2006).

While these three theories disagree on specific details of the process, they all agree that repetitions (be they implicit or explicit) serve to consolidate personal experiences (such as those stored as episodic memories) into semantic memory. They all commonly assert that, during the consolidation process, some episodic memories lose their vivid imagistic qualities and become incorporated into semantic schemas. As such, we don't get much here by focusing on a rigid distinction between these three approaches. Instead, we can focuses on the general process of consolidation of information into schemas, primarily through two mechanisms of rehearsal that have been shown to be important in the literature: *repeated experiences* (such as frequent ritual attendance) and *reflection* (V. M. Holmes & McGregor, 2007; McFarlane & Humphreys, 2012; Svoboda & Levine, 2009; Xygalatas et al., 2013). These two mechanisms of rehearsal underlie the key differences between the two pathways of the IIS represented in Figure 3.1.

The first pathway in Figure 3.1 starts with frequency of in-group ritual attendance. As in the DMR theory, the IIS proposes that information that is repeated under conditions of low emotional intensity should eventually appear like semantic memories and be consolidated into schemas. These schemas can form one's understanding of an essentialized social category (a social schema). This essentialized social category, defined by a social schema, can then serve as the target of categorical ties. The position that semantic memory and social identity are connected has received previous empirical support (e.g., Berntsen & Rubin, 2006; Fivush, Habermas, Waters, & Zaman, 2011; Haslam, Jetten, Haslam, Pugliese, & Tonks, 2011; Prebble, Addis, & Tippett, 2012).

In doctrinal religions, frequently repeated rituals are a key mechanism in facilitating the frequent repetition required for creating schemas in semantic memory. Here, it is important to note that, whereas the DMR theory focuses on the frequency that a ritual is performed, the IIS focuses on the *frequency with which an individual attends a ritual*. The literature discussing the DMR theory is very unclear on this subtle—but important—point. On the one hand, the theory relies on memory, and as such should focus on individual participation, but in its analyses, it has treated ritual frequency as an ideal group-level variable to test the theory that looks at the ritual itself (Atkinson & Whitehouse, 2011). At other times, it has implied that individuals are attending their group's rituals without fail (e.g., Whitehouse, 2004). This has muddied the waters substantially because the mechanism underlying the proposed effect in the DMR theory suggests that the appropriate level of analysis is that of the information an individual remembers about a ritual, thus allowing the ritual to be performed with acceptable fidelity and with the correct associated information in the future (thus ensuring its transmission and survival within the DMR theory's selectionist paradigm). However, different presentations have focused on the group or the tradition as a whole (Turchin, Whitehouse, Francois, Slingerland, & Collard, 2012), causing confusion about whether the appropriate unit of analysis is the information about a ritual, the person, the ritual, or the entire tradition itself. Taking a more computational approach that focuses on the experiences of an individual is better served by focusing on the frequency of ritual attendance than how frequently the tradition might perform a ritual. As such, the information repeated as an individual frequently attends in-group rituals should serve to activate and codify the social schema on which their social identity is based. In this way, the IIS posits a positive relationship between frequency of in-group ritual attendance and social identification. In moving from this individual-level aspect of the theory, to the group-level aspect of the theory, it relies on the idea that the lower-level cognitive (i.e., information processing) mechanisms that all individuals have will be able to generate the higher-level properties without having to preprogram them into a model or simulation.

The next aspect of the IIS states that because different memory patterns affect group alignment (as discussed earlier), there should also be a relationship between group alignment and within-group consensus. The IIS proposes that, in principle, reflection upon semantic memories can result in new connections being made and new associations between concepts that were not previously related in a schema; however, insofar as frequent in-group ritual participation is high, most associations should lead to greater within-group consensus. For example, while I was conducting research in Singapore, the pastor of a church gave a sermon about the rules and teachings concerning servants in the Bible. Talking with the members of the congregation afterward, many of them suggested that it caused them to reflect and connect the biblical rules and teachings to their own beliefs (i.e., schemas) concerning how to deal with subordinate coworkers or maids in their home. In this way, tutored reflection on semantic memories can serve to recombine information held in other schemas. As such, frequent ritual participation that can serve to guide this reflection should result in higher consensus, even if there are dynamic changes in the social schema. Insofar as reflection results in changes to the content of a social schema, the IIS suggests that it can affect categorical ties and therefore social identification. This is because, if reflection results in new connections in a social schema, the information that the individual uses to define the group (held in the social schema) can become more—or less—able to foster a positive self-image and thus alignment to the group; this proposal is similar to earlier proposals in the social identity literature (e.g., Hogg & Turner, 1985; Verkuyten & Yildiz, 2007). That is to say, if changes to an individual's understanding of what their group represents are unable to foster a positive self-image, it should result in the individual no longer aligning with the group. In this way, the IIS proposes a positive relationship between social identification and within-group consensus. Those familiar with the DMR theory will notice that the IIS derives much of this from the DMR theory and that both propose that mutual ritual attendance (and therefore mutual encoding of information) should result in similar social schemas of information consolidated into the semantic memory of the members of the group, resulting in high levels of within-group consensus.

The other pathway in Figure 3.1 addresses how emotionally intense experiences can affect the system and outlines one of its biggest contrasts with earlier literature retarding doctrinal religiosity in the DMR theory. This pathway begins with emotionally intense experiences. The IIS approaches emotionally intense experiences in doctrinal religions by focusing on how memories for emotionally intense experiences can be consolidated through rehearsal mechanisms such as reflection. Effectively, the IIS suggests that emotionally intense experiences foster reflection on the event (although this is understudied, there is some empirical evidence for this as well; see Berntsen, 2001; E. A. Holmes, Grey, & Young, 2005; Richert, Whitehouse, & Stewart, 2005) because its intensity and rarity can leave us searching for a way to interpret it (a claim which appears to be congruent with the DMR theory and fusion literature). In this way, the IIS proposes a positive relationship between emotional intensity and reflection on an experience. Readers familiar with the DMR theory will note that this is another similarity between the IIS and the DMR theory, however the critical difference here (in addition to the aforementioned shift from emotional valence to emotional intensity) is that the IIS suggests that the relationship between emotion and reflection is not limited to the imagistic mode of religiosity and can also be an important mechanism for forming beliefs in doctrinal religions, whereas the DMR theory suggests that reflection on intense and rare experiences is a defining factor only in imagistic traditions and its presence in doctrinal religions will not be sustained.

The IIS offers several novel critical insights and specific predictions regarding the effects of reflection on memory consolidation on social cohesion. The predictions of the IIS rely on whether there is a relevant social schema available for the interpretation of the emotionally intense experience. If there is no relevant social schema in place (as would typically be the case in imagistic religions), an emotionally intense episodic memory can be consolidated over time through rehearsal, and since that memory would encode information about who was present, it should lead to the formation of local fusion via relational ties. As such, the IIS holds that it is possible, in principle, that local fusion could result from relational ties between a subset of individuals codified from an episodic memory. However, because the relational ties underlying local fusion are between individuals who have a relationship, it is implausible that relational ties could connect individuals who are not in the same social network, making it a problematic explanation for fusion with any large social group or imagined community (such as a doctrinal tradition). Given that many doctrinal religions have expansive social schemas that are readily available to be employed to interpret to a wide range of circumstances, even if only by weak analogies, it is likely to be rare that there would be no social schema with which to interpret the event. When there is a relevant social schema for the interpretation of a high-arousal experience in a doctrinal tradition, an individual can employ the schema during reflection to interpret the event, potentially creating links between the experience in one's personal schema and essential beliefs of a group's social schema. This results in the event becoming a central aspect of one's personal identity, while simultaneously being tied to an essential belief of the group's social schema. As such, the IIS proposes a positive relationship between reflection on an emotionally intense experience and the perceived centrality of the event.

As discussed, the links between one's personal schema and essential beliefs in a social schema are called conceptual ties. Earlier, I have outlined how the IIS proposes that reflection on an emotionally intense event can result in the event being perceived as central to one's personal identity because one uses the group's social schema—and the group's essential beliefs—to interpret the event. This "overlap" between a central aspect of one's personal identity and essential beliefs of a social schema facilitated by conceptual ties is the basis for extended fusion within the IIS's framework. Therefore, the IIS proposes that there is a positive relationship between the perceived centrality of an event and extended fusion with a doctrinal religion.

There is evidence that suggests that an individual can incorporate information about external entities, such as essential beliefs, into one's own personal identity. The idea was first discussed by William James in his seminal lectures on the Varieties of Religious Experience (1890, Chapter 10). More recently, Aron and colleagues expanded upon the idea to suggest that "cognitive representation of self and other might contain common elements or might occupy overlapping regions of a cognitive matrix, and access to them might follow similar pathways" (Aron, Aron, Tudor, & Nelson, 1991, p. 243). Originally, this research addressed dyadic relationships between people, but later research found evidence that individuals sometimes incorporate aspects of a social group into how they see themselves (Mashek, Aron, & Boncimino, 2003). For example, Smith, Coats, and Walling (1999) utilized reaction-time tests to study the extent to which individuals can correctly categorize information they find relevant to themselves as being congruent, or incongruent with a description of their in-group. They found that reaction times were faster when information about the in-group was congruent with information about their self. They take this to suggest that a participant's conception of self and in-group overlap.

The inclusion of concepts and beliefs into one's personal identity has also been found to extend to concepts that are essential beliefs for doctrinal religions. Hodges et al. (2013) asked evangelical Christians and atheists to choose adjectives from a list that they believed pertained to themselves. They also asked them to choose adjectives from the same list that they believed pertained to God. They found that Evangelicals had a significantly higher percentage of terms that they believed applied to themselves and God (68.7%) as opposed to atheists (40.5%). In a second study in the same paper, Hodges et al. found that among Christians attending Presbyterian, Roman Catholic, Seventh Day Adventist, and Foursquare Churches, the percentage of commonly held concepts believed to apply to one's self as well as God significantly predicted religiosity as well (Hodges et al., 2013; Study 2). Lastly, a study by Sharp, Rentfrow, and Gibson (2015) utilized the reaction-time protocol administered to self-identified Christians and found that individuals respond significantly faster on positively balanced terms related to their self in relation to God, Jesus, and the Holy Spirit. Although no correlates to religiosity levels were investigated in the Sharp et al. (2015) paper, the research provides evidence that self-other overlap can extend to one's self and essential beliefs of a doctrinal religion nonetheless.

To my knowledge, the only study that has used a measure of fusion to study an individual's fusion with a non-group entity has been published very recently and measured fusion to "Cecil the Lion," among donors to the conservation research group that was studying the lion prior to its death (Buhrmester, Burnham et al., 2018). Using the dynamic identity fusion index (Jimenez et al., 2015) to measure fusion, they found that fusion to Cecil the Lion was a significant mediator in the relationship between the intensity of dysphoric arousal experienced by donors and their fusion to the research group. This suggests, that in some way, the relationship between an individual's personal identity and Cecil the Lion was overlapping (this study is also discussed in further detail later). Taken together, these studies provide a basis for the IIS's claim that there is a relationship between centrality of an event and extended fusion as the result of conceptual ties.

The IIS, also in alignment with the DMR theory, proposes that emotionally intense rituals with low rehearsal and no available schema for interpreting the event should not result in the formation of shared schemas. However, as suggested earlier, emotionally intense experiences can foster reflection (Berntsen, 2001; E. A. Holmes et al., 2005; Richert et al., 2005), and insofar as they do so, it should result in the consolidation of personally idiosyncratic beliefs, which is only spread later along social network ties, making it unlikely to have much of a general impact on the social schema of the overall group; however, it would be possible to spread these idiosyncratic beliefs in local communities where information transmission is higher within a cluster than it is between clusters of the network. In addition, recall that the IIS proposes that, reflection can serve to make the experience central to one's personal identity by facilitating the creation of emotional associations—that is, conceptual ties—between the memory for the experience in one's personal schema and essential beliefs in his/her social schema. While the rehearsal of information in a social schema during reflection on an emotionally intense experience could have a positive effect on within-group consensus, the resulting integration of one's personal schema and their social schema can introduce idiosyncrasies that should have a net negative effect on within-group consensus because the boundary between what is personal and what is social is blurred. In this way, the IIS predicts a negative relationship between fusion with a doctrinal religion and within-group consensus.

To conclude, in proposing that personal and social schemas have different relationships depending on whether the individual is fused or identified, IIS predicts different causes and effects on within-group consensus and group alignment in doctrinal religions than the DMR theory. In identified individuals, because their social schema is largely derived from group beliefs without the interference of their own personal schema, their beliefs should appear more typical of the group at large; as such, within-group consensus should be high (in alignment with the DMR theory). However, individuals with high levels of extended fusion have incorporated parts of their social schema into their personal schema through reflection, the boundary between personal and social beliefs is blurred and unorthodox connections between beliefs may be consolidated. Therefore, fusion, which is caused by reflection on an emotionally associated information that is subsequently considered central to one's identity, should have a slightly negative effect on their ability to reproduce the standard orthodoxy of the group, and thus within-group consensus.

3.2 Formalizing Group Alignment

The IIS presents a framework that extends earlier theorizing and can be used to formalize the causes and effects of both social identification and fusion, which in turn can help facilitate empirical research on social cohesion. The personal and social schemas on which personal and social identities are reliant can be formalized as semantic network maps. A *semantic network map* is a collection of concepts, represented by nodes, which have links between related concepts. The links between concepts serve to add structure to the concepts and researchers have previously proposed that semantic network maps are useful models of the cognitive structure of schemas (Carley, 1986; Carley & Kaufer, 1993).[9] In a semantic network map, the nodes representing concepts can have attributes, such as the term "frequency," which is how often a concept appears in a dialog, interview, or text. For example, if we take the concepts presented in the "Lord's Prayer,"[10] a prayer often recited by Christians on a daily, or at least a weekly, basis, the nodes for "heaven" and "forgive" would have a term frequency attribute of 2 for each repetition of the prayer, as both words appear twice in the prayer. Likewise, links can also have attributes, representing information such as how frequently a link between two concepts appears. For example, the link between "hallowed" and "name" is represented once in the prayer, as such the link value could be 1. If the co-occurrence of the two terms were found more frequently, the link value could be increased to represent this difference. Semantic network maps also facilitate congruity with previous literature as they have been used by researchers to investigate aspects of within-group consensus (Carley, 1987; V. Hill & Carley, 1999), doctrinal religions (Lane, 2015b; McCorkle & Lane, 2012; Whitehouse et al., 2012), how individuals represent their self-concept (Flores Kanter, Medrano, & Conn, 2015), and have been utilized to investigate sacred values and religious extremism in instances of intergroup conflict (Shults, Gore et al., 2018; this model will also be discussed in later chapters).

Semantic network maps are also useful because they can be simplified to a two-dimensional matrix of numbers with identical lists of nodes (i.e., concepts) making up the x and y dimensions of the matrix and the value at the intersection of node x and node y representing the value for the link between term x and term y.[11] This mathematical formalization provides a means to compare multiple schemas for similarities between individuals within a group by analyzing the extent to which the matrices contain values that represent similar relationships between concepts. It can also allow for group schemas to be formalized (described in greater detail in upcoming sections).

When applying semantic network maps to understand schemas, we can start by positing that the network representing a personal schema holds information such as personal beliefs, knowledge, ideas, experiences, accomplishments, etc. that are important to how the individual sees themself. In the two-dimensional

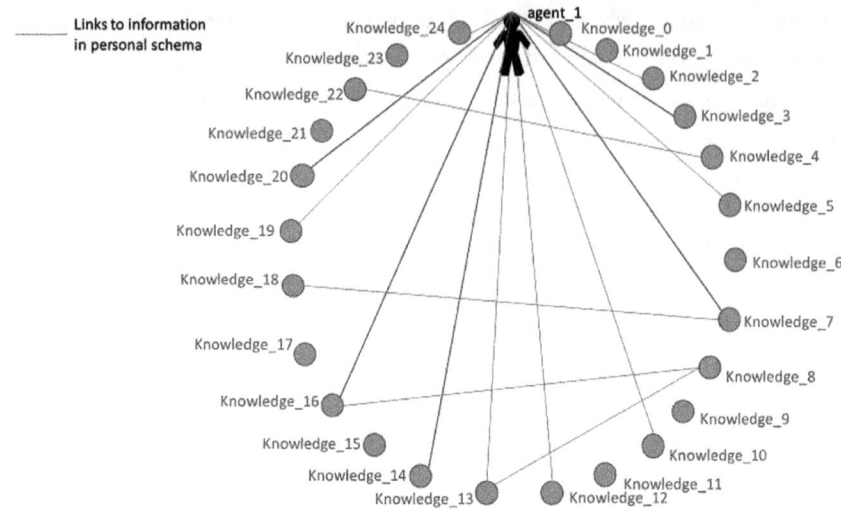

Figure 3.2 Network-based representation of a personal schema. Depiction of an agent (the black figure) with ties to concepts (gray nodes). The solid lines represent links between these representations.

representation depicted in Figure 3.2, the links represent a generic relationship between two representations.

In addition, a network representation of a social schema would depict the information representing the beliefs and links that an individual holds to be true about a particular social group with which they identify. In principle, individuals could hold multiple social schemas, one for each group that they are knowledgeable about, even if they are not a part of a group. Naturally, we all have beliefs about groups that we do not identify with ourselves, even if that information may be biased or untrue. In addition, one does not need to assume unique network topologies for semantic network maps that represent personal and social schemas. The key difference is that personal schemas should have links that are relevant to an individual, while social schemas for a particular group hold conceptual links that should be shared by members of a social group—in this way the social schema is defined by how the members of the group see themselves within the relevant group context. Therefore, it would only be possible for the semantic network maps of a personal schema and a social schema to be identical if each member of the group has identical beliefs. To the extent that an individual identifies with a social category that shares that individual's beliefs, there should be similar links in the maps defining the personal schema and social schema of an individual who is strongly identified with the group as compared to an individual who is less strongly identified. However, in accordance with the IIS's predictions regarding the formation of semantic memories, the social schema should not be connected to beliefs that are associated with high levels of emotionality, with the exception of conceptual ties that foster extended fusion.

Using this formalization, one can represent social identification as a categorical tie, which can be represented as a link between the individual and a meta-node. This *meta-node* is a single node that represents the network of information pertaining to the relevant group's social schema. A connection to a specific social category (defined by its meta-node) can be evoked in the relevant context to maintain a positive self-image in accordance with social identity theory. In this way, a link attribute can be used to represent one's strength of identification one has to the meta-node representing the social category. Furthermore, this formalization could reflect changes in how different beliefs can be viewed as more essential to the group's definition as the relevant beliefs could be added or changed in the network of the meta-node.

A visualization can be used to better describe how the IIS facilitates a careful formalization of extended fusion. Often, fusion is conceived of as two overlapping circles: one represents the individual and the other represents their social group. The more these two circles overlap, the more fused this individual is reported to be. However, instead of imagining two circles representing the personal self and the social group, we should imagine two networks; rather than one circle within another, there are now two networks that overlap. We can assume that conceptual ties are those links in the personal schema that overlap with those held in the social schema and have a significant emotional attribute. Not all links need to be connected to the individual since we do not utilize all our knowledge to construct our identities; some information is just learned about our social group or information we know about the world, but the information is not directly relevant to our personal identity. A visualization of this is depicted in Figure 3.3: dashed lines represent the relevant connections to the beliefs in the social schema; solid lines represent connections in their personal schema; dotted lines represent conceptual ties that link both the individual's personal and social schema.

Relational ties (the basis for local fusion), on the other hand, can be represented outside of semantic network maps as social network links between individuals (the figures only include one individual). These social network links could be modeled as fused by giving them an attribute representing a permanent emotional attribute that has a greater value attributed to it than other

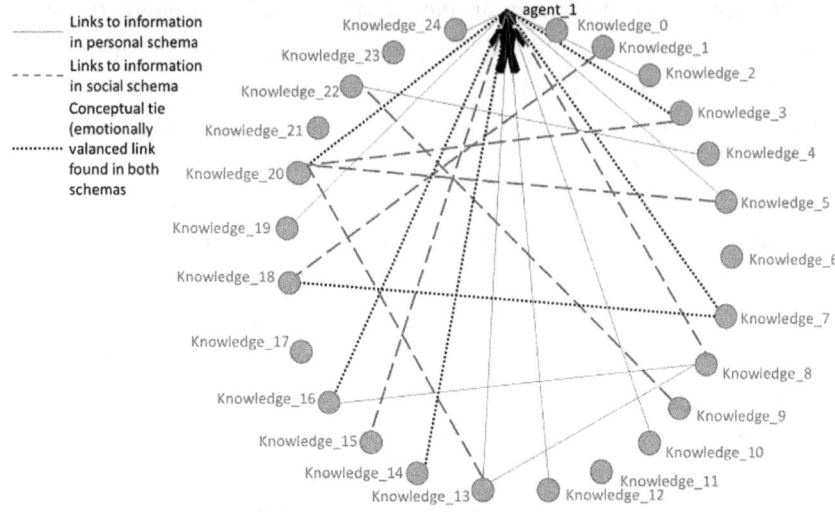

Figure 3.3 Visual depiction of schemas with conceptual ties. Depiction of an agent (the black figure) with ties to concepts (gray nodes). These concepts represent social and personal identity markers. Solid links represent concepts relevant to the agent's personal identity. Dashed links represent concepts relevant to the agent's social identity. Dotted links represent those beliefs from the social schema that have been incorporated into the individual's personal schema. Two relevant notes concerning this depiction: (1) this would be after reflection, whereby the individual incorporates personally salient information; (2) note the link between Knowledge_18 and Knowledge_7 does not directly connect to the agent. This could be the result of reflection upon two concepts whereby the information in Knowledge_18 is connected directly to the individual as well as to Knowledge_7.

social network links. The critical differences between social identification and extended fusion then can be modeled as such: (1) extended fusion is facilitated by conceptual ties between the personal schema and essential beliefs of one's social schema that become central to one's personal identity, whereas in the case of social identification, the links to a social schema are not central to one's personal identity; (2) social identification is facilitated by categorical ties that link an individual to a social schema that is associated with lower levels of emotionality—relative to conceptual ties.

3.3 Clarifying the Effect of Emotionally Intense Doctrinal Experiences

In principle, the IIS can account for the four principles of fusion described as well as clarify the role of relational ties in extended fusion noted earlier. For a fused individual, any attack on a group that is defined by a set of essential beliefs that are also central components of one's personal self would be largely indistinguishable from a personal attack. As such, a person would respond to attacks (physical or verbal) of their social group as if they were personal attacks. This can account for fusion's *agentic personal self-principle*. In addition, because conceptual ties blur the boundary between the personal and social identities, individuals who are more fused are unable to dissociate themselves from the social groups because there is little functional difference between their social and personal schemas, accounting for fusion's *identity synergy principle*. The enduring effects described by fusion's *irrevocability principle* can be accounted for by the fact that the IIS predicts that the creation of conceptual ties is driven by reflection upon a personally salient and emotionally intense experience encoded as an episodic or flashbulb memory. The long-lasting nature of episodic memories could facilitate effects that result in fusion for as long as the individual feels that the event is a central part of their personal identity.

However, regarding the IIS's formalization's approach to fusion, the *relational ties principle* is not accounted for by conceptual ties. The IIS proposes that relational ties are the basis for local fusion (as discussed in theoretical overviews of the fusion literature presented by Fredman et al., 2015; Swann et al., 2012; Whitehouse & Lanman, 2014) and are the result of episodic memories that encode relational ties as the presence of other individuals at a specific emotionally arousing event that is central to their personal identity, as in the case of imagistic religions that lack social schemas. In this way, the IIS outlines a critical distinction between local and extended fusion that has not appeared in the fusion literature to my knowledge, which is that local fusion is the result of relational ties and extended fusion is the result of conceptual ties. Therefore, we would not always expect that extended fusion be affected by changes in relational ties. However, we would expect to see observed relationships between extended fusion and essential beliefs (e.g., Buhrmester, Newson et al., 2018; Swann, Buhrmester et al., 2014) insofar as those essential beliefs are viewed as definitional for the group's social schema. In addition, the formalization above allows for the possibility that an individual, who identifies with a large doctrinal religion, could be fused to a subset of individual members in their group by means of relational ties, as relational and conceptual ties are not mutually exclusive of one another. This opens the possibility that an individual could be aligned to their group via extended fusion as well as aligned to a subset of the group's members via local fusion.

In addition to providing a framework to clarify the differences between local and extended fusion, the IIS approach to fusion enables us to reexamine some of the unexpected findings in the fusion literature. For example, the correlation (discussed previously) between self-stereotyping and fusion reported by Bortolini et al. (2018) is at odds with the relational ties principle as stated in Swann et al. (2012), which suggests that individuals bond as unique individuals, rather than as anonymous members of a large social category. However, the finding is compatible with the IIS, which predicts that extended fusion is the result of reflection that incorporates essential beliefs of a social schema into the personal schema (conceptual ties). From the perspective of the IIS, one would expect that members of the group would be viewed as more like themselves because that which defines themselves as individuals also defines other members of their group because they are perceived to share a commitment to an essential belief of the group's social schema. In addition, the studies cited earlier that failed to find a relationship between the fusion and relational ties (e.g., Vázquez et al., 2017) can be explained if the participants' fusion with their group was based in conceptual ties. This may be a plausible reinterpretation of the findings given that the groups that the research addressed were of a size that would suggest that their fusion would be extended, not local (recall that they were studying Spanish nationalism, a country with a population of over 45 million).

Although the IIS aligns with many of the DMR theory's predictions concerning ritual, memory, and social cohesion, the IIS offers new predictions that can address the emotionally intense ritual experiences that the DMR theory predicts should not persist in doctrinal religions (Whitehouse, 2004), such as those common to Pentecostal and Charismatic Christianity. Using the formalization above, these key predictions can be tested using a wide variety of data, such as interview transcripts and online social network data (discussed in the following chapters).

3.2 Testing Claims of the IIS

The claims of the IIS that aim to extend and synthesize earlier assumptions from the DMR theory and fusion theory have recently been tested in the field using a mixture of surveys, semi-structured field interviews, and data science techniques in a range of countries, including the United States, the United Kingdom, India, New Zealand, and Singapore (Lane, 2018c, 2019a). A great deal of this research occurred in a three-phase study that deployed surveys online to individuals in all four countries, while field research and semi-structured interviews were carried out with members of different churches in Singapore.

In one study, a survey was deployed online. Initially, the sample of participants ($N = 2{,}538$) included participants from twenty-one countries with a wide variety of ages and ethnic backgrounds. Most participants came from the target countries of Singapore, the United States, the United Kingdom, India, and New Zealand. The survey aimed to investigate the relationship between frequency of attendance with their in-group and their levels of social identification and fusion with their group (their target group was their church, rather than a smaller subgroups therein, such as a ministry, or any larger religious body, such as their denomination or the church as a global entity).

The results found that fusion has a large effect on the relationship between frequency and social identification, and that this pattern held cross-culturally (as country did not have a significant effect). Further analysis found that there is a significant interaction between the frequency with which one attends their group's rituals (i.e., Sunday services) and their fusion to the group. This significant interaction suggests that frequency of in-group ritual attendance and fusion not only have their own independent effects on social identification, but frequency of in-group ritual attendance and fusion also have a combined effect. Using a technique known as simple slopes analysis, the results further revealed that frequency of in-group ritual attendance had a stronger positive effect on social identification for individuals with low fusion than it did for individuals who had high levels of fusion. This suggests that there is a positive relationship between social identification and fusion, but that this relationship is not as robust for highly fused individuals. The study suggests that extended fusion and social identification are not as independent as they have been presented in some of the fusion literature (e.g., Gómez, Brooks et al., 2011; Swann & Buhrmester, 2015; Swann et al., 2012; Whitehouse & Lanman, 2014).

In the following chapters, additional studies of the IIS are presented and discussed. These studies use an interdisciplinary approach, packaged within the cognitive cybernetic framework to test the IIS. The literature discussed in this chapter has aimed to show that despite all that we do know about human sociality, we have a great deal of work left to theorize about social cohesion, and furthermore, that we can create a unified framework for interdisciplinary research into social cohesion using tools from multiple disciplines.

4

Identity and Extremism

The IIS predicts that social identification should be the primary mechanism by which individuals align themselves to large social groups such as doctrinal religions; in alignment with the DMR theory. However, breaking from the DMR theory, it suggests that there are clear circumstances where fusion should drive a person's alignment to a large social group. The IIS posits that social identification is based on shared schemas, in line with previous research on the subject (discussed in Chapter 3), and that these schemas can spread and develop through exposure to information from other members of the social group. On this point, it accepts the DMR theory's position that religious schemas develop and spread through attendance at frequent in-group rituals (Whitehouse, 2004).

The previous chapter discussed evidence that frequency of in-group social interactions (by means of ritual attendance) can facilitate social identification. It also discussed results suggesting that many individuals were aligned to the group by means of extended fusion, which is posited to be the result of emotionally intense experiences and is one of the breaking points between the IIS and DMR theory. This chapter sets out to discuss the role of fusion in doctrinal religions. Specifically, it discusses the IIS's position that the relationship between the emotional intensity associated with an experience and fusion in doctrinal religions is mediated by the perceived frequency of reflection *and* centrality of the event.

As discussed in the previous chapter, the DMR theory and IIS both suggest that emotionally intense experiences affect group alignment. The DMR theory (Whitehouse, 2004) and several fusion researchers (Swann et al., 2012; Whitehouse & Lanman, 2014) suggest that emotionally intense (oftentimes dysphoric) experiences create flashbulb memories among those who experience an event. These flashbulb memories facilitate long-lasting bonds between individuals known as relational ties as discussed in Chapter 3. Examples of bonding by means of personal relationships can be found in many small groups, such as military units, fraternities, close family members, and small tribal groups (Swann et al., 2012; Whitehouse, 2004; Whitehouse & Lanman, 2014).

In groups that are too large to be bound exclusively by the social relationships between members, fusion theory predicts that individuals who undergo an emotionally intense experience extend relational ties to the other members of their group (known as *extended* fusion). Recent research in the fusion literature suggests that the extent to which one reflects on an emotionally intense experience mediates the relationship between that experience and fusion with a group (Jong et al., 2016). As discussed in Chapter 3, the IIS extends this by suggesting that reflection on an emotionally intense experience results in extended fusion because an individual uses a relevant social schema to interpret an emotionally intense experience that is central to their personal identity, resulting in conceptual ties that form the basis of extended fusion (as opposed to relational ties).

The IIS's assertions concerning how emotionally intense experiences create extended fusion can be considered as a model wherein both perceived frequency of reflection and then perceived centrality of an event mediate the relationship between the emotional intensity associated with an experience and one's level of fusion. To clarify, the perceived centrality of an event refers to the extent to which individuals feel that an experience is defining of who they are and has an impact on their personal identity and life story. This model can be considered both in terms of a social group and beliefs or concepts central to the group; since, if extended fusion is based on conceptual ties as proposed by the IIS, fusion with a social group is based on fusion with essential beliefs in the group's social schema.

The IIS proposes that reflection has a different effect in large doctrinal religions (e.g., Christianity) than in smaller (in terms of their number of members) imagistic religions (e.g., the Melanesian religions described in Chapter 2 and in Whitehouse, 2000). This is because imagistic religions generally lack the elaborate and standardized social schemas and narratives that are characteristic of large doctrinal religions. From the perspective of the DMR theory, in imagistic religions, beliefs are often idiosyncratic and result from personal reflection and revelation—thus, within-group consensus is generally lower than in doctrinal religions. The IIS accepts this in principle. However, it notes that the mutual experiences of small groups in their day-to-day lives can serve the same purpose and have similar effects—albeit at much smaller scales. For example, it is well documented that communal meals can be important, repeated, low-arousal events for small groups. Communal meals and other similar meetings are perfect events for the transmission of narratives, stories, myths, teachings, and other things that can make up shared schemas of belief for the group. So, while bonding in small groups can be based on shared relational ties, it is not that these groups are without shared schemas. This effect of shared—but unstructured—events could have what we can refer to as a "fireside effect" whereby socially shared schemas of beliefs do develop in otherwise imagistic traditions. The extent to which these schemas are elaborate enough to be used as interpretive framework for later events that the group has is the question. In some cases, this would be the case and you could get extended fusion mechanisms operating within a small group as well—at least in principle; providing another potential scenario where there is overlap between extended and local fusion mechanisms. Regrettably, the role of the fireside effect is beyond our current scope and is an open subject for future research. One point on which the IIS and the DMR theory agree is that frequent attendance at low-arousal rituals in doctrinal religions can consolidate complex schemas into semantic memory, which the IIS proposes can be employed to make sense of significant experiences in one's life. When reflecting, certain concepts that could be considered essential to the group represent probable targets for fusion via conceptual ties. For example, one such concept for Christian communities is that of God, which has been shown in a large corpus of sermons and texts to be one of the most frequently mentioned concepts in materials produced by a wide range of Christian communities (Lane, 2015b, 2016). Given the importance of God in the Christian social schema, it is likely that reflection upon a significant experience with a group will become connected back to one's understanding of God. As individuals fill in the gaps in personal meaning about an intense experience with information from the social schema, their social schema becomes integrated into their personal schema. As outlined in Chapter 3, this could conceivably result in the feeling of oneness and the porous boundary between personal and social identities.

The DMR theory predicts that socially shared emotionally intense experiences should not be found in doctrinal religions—and if they are the practices should die out. However, as discussed Chapter 3, Charismatic and Pentecostal Christian communities have performed rituals that incorporate emotionally intense experiences for over a century. In addition to the weekly practices of Charismatic and Pentecostal Christians that present opportunities for one to have an emotionally intense experience, in many contemporary Christian communities (including but not limited to Charismatic and Pentecostal Christian communities), it is common for members of a church to go on a *retreat*. Retreats are meetings focused on worship and meditation that typically last for a few (two to seven) days and usually only a subset of the community attends, rather than the entire church. This subset is sometimes just those members of a church who decide to attend, but other times retreats are limited to specific age groups or ministries within the church. Some groups combine with groups from other churches (typically those with similar theological beliefs and worship practices) as well. During these events, the entire day is mostly scheduled with activities such as Bible study, praise and worship, sermons, group recreational activities, and meals. Some additional rituals, such as the Holy Communion (or Eucharist) and baptisms can also be incorporated into the retreat. The retreat activities are typically led by some form of leadership, and individuals are often challenged to reflect on their beliefs and faith in order to strengthen themselves and—as is often said in evangelical theological circles—"grow in Christ" (also see Luhrmann, 2012). Retreats are problematic for the DMR theory because they do not conform to its predictions. Specifically, retreats are frequent (typically annual) events where it is not uncommon for some participants to have emotionally intense experiences. However, it is not always the case that an individual will have an emotionally intense experience every time they attend a retreat. However, the activities planned during Christian retreats encourage those in attendance to reflect on their beliefs in order to mature spiritually. As such, studies investigating the role of untutored reflection in Christian communities may wish to control for these effects as best as possible and be aware that they represent a potential confound.

Other intense religious experiences common to Pentecostal and Charismatic Christianity include being converted (when someone realigns him or herself with a religious tradition to which they were not previously aligned) and born again. Given that a conversion, by definition, involves a change in one's identification, it may be unsurprising they are often reported as being important milestones in one's life (as outlined in Lectures 9 and 10 of James, 1902).

Whereas conversion events mark a shift from one religious identity to another, being born again in the contemporary Christian tradition can be understood as a reaffirmation of one's faith and identity. Being born again is common in Charismatic and Pentecostal Christian groups, although less so in mainline Protestant and Catholic communities. Being born again is typically recounted as an intense experience where individuals report being filled with the Holy Spirit or slain in the Holy Spirit. Similarly, for some Christians who have been born again, the experience can be an important aspect of their personal identity. Being born again can come during periods of particular hardship (James, 1902) and is often reported as a deeply personal experience where one feels connected to Jesus or God (Luhrmann, 2012). Although it is uncommon for an individual to report being born again more than once, many individuals are familiar with the concept. Familiarity with the idea of being born again, as shared through the social schemas of contemporary Christian groups, would allow the experience to be interpreted more readily within a theological framework. The framework for interpreting born again experiences can be transmitted by pastors and laypeople in their church and is supported by biblical interpretation.[1] As such, emotionally intense experiences such as conversions and being born again in contemporary Christian traditions provide an opportunity to study emotionally intense experiences in a doctrinal tradition for which there are likely to be available social schemas for the interpretation of the experience.

It is worth noting that in Pentecostal and Charismatic Christian communities the experiences of being converted, born again, or being filled or slain in the Holy Spirit are generally described as euphoric. The relationship between dysphoric arousal and fusion has been the topic of both theoretical overviews (Swann et al., 2012; Whitehouse & Lanman, 2014) and empirical studies (Buhrmester et al., 2014; Jong et al., 2016; Newson et al., 2016; Whitehouse et al., 2017b) in the fusion literature. To my knowledge, only two studies have focused on the role of euphoric (or "positive") experiences in promoting fusion (Kavanagh et al., 2018; Newson et al., 2016). This is a point that has been problematic for earlier research on doctrinal religions (e.g., Xygalatas, 2014), and will be returned to later in the chapter.

4.1 Previous Research

To my knowledge, no study has empirically investigated the extent to which both the perceived frequency of reflection and the perceived centrality of an event act as mediators in the relationship between the emotional intensity associated with an experience and fusion. However, there are studies which have examined some of these relationships and suggest that these relationships are plausible.

4.1.1 Reflection Mediates the Relationship between the Emotional Intensity of an Experience and Fusion

In 2016, several colleagues and I devised a study on the nature of fusion in Northern Ireland and also in Boston after the Boston Bombing (Jong et al., 2016). Three studies were published investigating the role of reflection in the fusion process. Because of the similarity between these studies and the subject of this chapter, I will include a detailed description of the measures used in the study to facilitate a comparison between previous research and the discussion presented later in this chapter. In the first study, we distributed a survey in Northern Ireland among Republicans and Unionists (two groups that engaged in extensive conflict since the 1960s; for a historical overview, see Bew & Gillespie, 1999). The survey included a list of twelve negative experiences and participants were asked to report how many they had experienced in relation to their political identity (affirmative answers were coded as 1, negative answers as 0, and the answers were then summed to create a single measure of shared negative experience). The participants were also asked for a subjective rating of how severely they suffered as a result of their experience on a scale of "0-Not at All" to "5-Extremly"; I will refer to this measure as *subjective suffering*. They were then asked how frequently they felt that they suffered because of their political affiliation (on a 5-point scale: "Never"; "Very Rarely"; "Rarely"; "Occasionally"; "Frequently") and how severe they felt the suffering was (also on a 5-point scale: "Not at all"; "Slightly"; "Somewhat"; "Moderately"; "Extremely"). They were then presented with two questions aimed at assessing how frequently they reflect on their experience. The first question was "How often do you think about these experiences?" This measure was anchored at "I have only thought about them a little bit" and "I have spent many years reflecting on them" on a 6-point scale. The second question was "How much have these experiences been on your mind?" This measure was anchored at "I have thought about them sporadically" and "They are always on my mind" on a 6-point scale. The responses to these questions were averaged to create an approximate measure of reflection. Lastly, they were presented with the verbal fusion measure. A mediation model revealed that reflection significantly mediated the relationship between the number of shared negative experiences with the participants' group and their levels of fusion to their group. However, no evidence was found for a direct effect of the number of negative experiences on fusion. The analysis also revealed that the relationship between the participants' subjective suffering ratings and fusion was significantly mediated by reflection; but unlike the previous model, there was a direct effect of subjective suffering on fusion.

In order to further investigate these patterns, we ran a second study after the Boston Marathon Bombing in 2013 with participants who lived—or had lived—in Boston. Participants were primed to think about the bombing. Because the study addressed a single event, rather than many possible events over the course of many years (as was done during Study 1 with Northern Irish participants), the measure of shared negative experience was changed to two questions: "Did you see or hear or otherwise experience any aspect of the bombing directly?" and "Were you or any family members or friends directly injured in any way during the bombing?" (affirmative answers were coded as 1, negative answers as 0, and the answers were then summed to create a single measure of shared negative experience). The participants were also asked to complete the subjective suffering measure and verbal fusion scale described earlier. In order to measure reflection, they adapted the measures used in Study 1 by asking participants to answer the following questions on a 6-point scale anchored at "I have only thought about it a bit" and "It is always on my mind": (1) "How much do you think about your experience of the Boston Marathon Bombings?"; (2) "How much do you think about the meaning of the Boston Marathon Bombings?"; (3) "How much do you think about how the Boston Marathon Bombings could have turned out differently (e.g., how they could have been prevented, or how they could have been worse)?" Scores were averaged to form a single measure of reflection. As with Study 1, it was found that reflection significantly mediated the relationship between the measure of shared negative experiences and fusion, but there was no significant direct effect on negative experience and fusion. Echoing the results of Study 1, Study 2 also found that reflection significantly mediated the relationship between subjective suffering and fusion, and a significant direct effect was present.

In order to investigate and clarify the direction of causality between the previous studies, Study 3 was completed using a priming task to manipulate the salience of the Boston Marathon Bombing by asking participants to reflect on the event. A control group was asked to reflect on a recent shopping trip. Participants were then asked to complete the verbal fusion scale as well as the dynamic identity fusion index (Jimenez et al., 2015). This scale includes two circles (one representing the self and the other representing the group) that can be moved across the screen to be anywhere from fully overlapping to resting at opposing sides of the screen. The distance between the centroid of the circles and overlap between the circumferences of the circles is then computed. Instead of using the self-report measure of subjective suffering used in Studies 1 and 2, Mehrabian and Russell's semantic differential measure of core affect was used. This measure produces three scores: one for valence, one for arousal, and one for dominance. The valence score (which measured the positivity and negativity of the experience) was used in their subsequent analysis. Results found that the priming condition had a significant effect on valence, but not on fusion (as measured by the verbal fusion score). When testing if valence moderates the relationship between the priming condition and fusion, there was no significant main effect of either priming condition or negative affect on fusion. However, an interaction effect of priming condition and negative affect was found to significantly affect fusion. To better understand the effect, the authors estimated the effect of priming condition at the negative affect mean and one standard deviation above and below the negative affect mean. The results showed that increased salience of the bombing only increased fusion for individuals with high negative affect ratings. A similar pattern was also found when using the dynamic identity fusion index's overlap measure instead of the verbal fusion measure.

Taken together, these three studies (Jong et al., 2016) suggest that emotionally intense experiences can promote reflection, which results in fusion. However, these studies are subject to limitations. For example, one limitation of Study 3 was that the measure concentrated on the emotional valence associated with an experience, not emotional intensity. In principle, fusion is said to be the result of emotionally intense dysphoric experiences. However, Study 3 only examined how negative (i.e., dysphoric) the experience was, not how intense it was; we only reported that valence and intensity were not correlated, which may suggest that intensity was not significantly related to fusion. Fusion theory, as stated by Swann et al. (2012) and Whitehouse and Lanman (2014) both suggest that dysphoria and intensity are crucial in promoting fusion, yet the Jong et al. study concentrated on the ability of reflection to mediate the relationship between the valence of the experience and fusion, not its intensity. However, previous studies have found that negative, positive, and traumatic events do not significantly differ on how often one reflects on the event and how the event becomes important to one defines his or her self (see Byrne, Hyman, & Scott, 2001, p. S126). This suggests that emotional valence might not be the critical factor. The IIS posits that the intensity of arousal is the critical factor and both dysphoric and euphoric experiences can result in fusion provided that the emotional intensity is sufficient to promote reflection and results in the experience becoming a central part of one's personal schema. Therefore, the study presented in this chapter treats arousal as an independent variable and uses valence for qualitative interpretation of how the experience is viewed by the participant. In addition, Study 2 we may have inadvertently introduced a confound by using a measure of fusion that was clearly addressing extended fusion (by using the city of Boston as the fusion target), while the measure of negative experiences may have been tapping variables related to local fusion. In the study, participants were asked "Were you or any family members or friends directly injured in any way during the bombing?" This appears to be directly addressing local fusion as relationships between family and friends would be actual, rather than the perceived relational ties underlying extended fusion. Future studies of extended fusion should aim to create consistency between all measures regarding the target of fusion to better ensure that measures are not addressing local fusion when extended fusion is the intended variable of study.

4.1.2 Previous Research: Emotionally Intense Experiences Can Become Central Aspects of One's Identity

At the end of the article, it was noted that "the precise nature of the personal reflection that joins shared negative experience to identity fusion is still unclear" (Jong et al., 2016, p. 10). It was suggested that further investigations of the relationship between reflection, which could cause an event to become self-defining, and fusion may be beneficial to increasing our understanding of fusion. Later in this chapter I will present an additional study that suggests that the perceived centrality of an event also mediates the relationship between an emotionally intense experience and fusion.

The perceived centrality of event literature, which explores how traumatic events become a central part of one's identity, reports evidence suggesting that emotionally intense events are indeed associated with perceived centrality of the event to one's identity later in life (Berntsen & Rubin, 2006). In a study of PTSD (Post-Traumatic Stress Disorder) using a population of 707 undergraduates, responses to the question "I feel the traumatic event has become part of my identity" were found to positively correlate with the frequency with which an individual had an intrusive memory in both participants with PTSD symptoms and participants without PTSD symptoms (Berntsen, Willert, & Rubin, 2003). This suggests that there is not only a relationship between an emotionally intense event and reflection on the event later, but also that the event can become part of a person's identity.

Berntsen and Thomsen (2005) investigated the effects of the German occupation on the identity of 145 Danish participants who lived through the occupation during the Second World War. To assess the perceived centrality of the event the authors had participants answer three questions: "I automatically see connections and similarities between this event and experiences in my present life," "I feel that this event has become part of my identity," and "This event has become a reference point for the way I understand myself and the world." All three questions were answered using a scale ranging from 1 (totally disagree) to 5 (totally agree). They found that the average of the responses on these three questions correlated with frequency of intrusive memories about the event. Again, this suggests that emotionally intense experiences, such as the experiences of war discussed in the fusion literature (e.g., Atran, 2016; Whitehouse et al., 2017b, 2014), can become important aspects of a person's identity.

In addition to the studies from the centrality of event literature, there are studies from the fusion literature which suggest emotionally intense experiences can be incorporated into an important part of one's identity. A recent study by Newson, Buhrmester, and Whitehouse (2016) of football fans found that the extent to which both dysphoric and euphoric experiences had been important in shaping their identity (Newson et al. refer to this as "self-shapingness") had a significant positive relationship with fusion to the football club that they identify with. To assess fusion, they used the verbal fusion measure (see Appendix 3.6). To assess self-shapingness, participants were asked to answer the questions "to what extent have your team's wins shaped you as a person?" and "to what extent have your team's losses shaped you as a person?". Both questions recorded responses using a 7-point scale anchored at "Not at all" and "Extremely." Newson et al. treated the effect of wins as relevant to euphoric experiences and the effect of losses as relevant to dysphoric experiences. Given the measures used by Newson et al. their term "self-shapingness" does appear to be measuring something similar to what the IIS calls centrality. However, the measure utilized in the Newson et al. study does not address a specific emotionally intense experience as a fan of their football club, rather the measure of euphoric and dysphoric self-shapingness addresses emotional sentiment that is related to wins and losses over a long period of time (as opposed to a specific win or loss shaped that person's identity). Nevertheless, using mediation regressions the analysis revealed that the relationship between self-shapingness and group loyalty is mediated by fusion; this was the case for both euphoric and dysphoric self-shapingness (Newson et al., 2016).

An additional study by Kavanagh, Jong, McKay, and Whitehouse (2018) aimed to test "that high arousal rituals promote social cohesion, primarily through identity fusion" (p. 1). In the study, participants were recruited from Brazilian Ju Jitsu clubs to participate in an online survey. In Brazilian Ju Jitsu, promotion to a new belt (or rank) within a club is sometimes marked through a painful "belt-whipping" ceremony where other members of the club line up and whip the initiate as they run past; it was also noted that many Brazilian Ju Jitsu clubs have banned this practice (Kavanagh et al., 2018, p. 10). Data were collected using the survey to test five hypotheses, two of which are relevant to this study:

(1) that individuals who experience more affectively arousing ritual promotions will report higher levels of fusion with their Brazilian Ju Jitsu school and (2) that negatively valenced affective arousal will display a stronger association with fusion than comparable positively valenced affective arousal. To collect data on fusion they used the verbal fusion score (see Appendix 3.6). To measure positive affect, they asked participants to rate to what extent they judged their experience to be: (1) enjoyable, (2) valuable, (3) meaningful, (4) unpleasant, (5) painful, and (6) intense on a 6-point scale anchored at "not at all" and "extremely." The results found that participants from groups with belt-whipping ceremonies reported higher negative affect than those without belt-whipping ceremonies. However, the results found no evidence for the hypothesis that negatively valenced affective arousal will display a stronger association with fusion than comparable positively valenced affective arousal. In fact, both those participants from groups with belt-whipping ceremonies and those without had significantly higher positive affect ratings of the experience than negative affect ratings regarding their experience and there was a significant correlation found between positive affect scores and fusion. However, no significant correlation was found between negative affect scores and fusion. From an outsider's perspective, these results are perplexing because of the pain associated with the belt-whipping ceremony. It appears that after the event, individuals attribute positive emotions to the experience, even though the pain of the experience would suggest that it was a dysphoric experience.

The most recent study to report a relationship between an emotionally intense experience, the perceived centrality of an event and fusion comes from Buhrmester, Burnham et al. (2018), which was run after the data was collected for this study. Nevertheless, it provides the clearest evidence that emotionally intense experiences are related to the perceived centrality of an event and fusion. The study not only measures reflection, the perceived centrality of the event, and fusion with a group, but also fusion with a concept that is important to the group (but is not the group itself). In their study, Buhrmester, Burnham et al. looked to investigate how dysphoric reactions to the death of "Cecil the Lion" (a research lion that was killed by a trophy hunter in Zimbabwe in 2015 and subsequently became a viral internet topic; see Macdonald, Jacobsen, Burnham, Johnson, & Loveridge, 2016) was related to social cohesion among donors to the Wildlife Conservation Research Unit (WildCRU), the research unit that was studying the lion. Multiple hypotheses were tested that are directly relevant to the propositions of the IIS. The first relevant hypothesis tested the claim "that participants who experienced high levels of dysphoria in response to Cecil's death would (1) experience strong fusion to Cecil, and (2) in turn, feeling that Cecil's death has bound WildCRU donors closer together, experiencing strong fusion to WildCRU" (Buhrmester, Burnham et al., 2018, p. 2). The second relevant hypothesis tested the claim "that fusion would increase most for participants who both (1) reported especially high amounts of reflection after Cecil's death, and (2) reported especially strong perceptions that Cecil's death has been a central experience for understanding one's personal identity and the identities of others who also experienced Cecil's death" (Buhrmester, Burnham et al., 2018, p. 2). The authors deployed a study online in the winter of 2015 and then again in the summer of 2016. They used the pictorial fusion scale (see Appendix 3.6) to measure fusion to the group "WildCRU" as well as to "Cecil the Lion." They measured state dysphoria (a form of emotional intensity) using an 8-item checklist, which "ask participants to check whether they had, for instance, felt intense anger in the wake of Cecil's death" (Buhrmester, Burnham et al., 2018, p. 3). Reflection was measured by asking participants to respond to "a four-item measure designed to assess their *depth of reflection* on Cecil's death" (emphasis in original; Buhrmester, Burnham et al., 2018, p. 3). Lastly, the authors "included a two-question measure designed to assess *self/group centrality*, i.e., the extent to which Cecil's death and story was a personally central experience as well as a similarly central experience for fellow conservationists" (emphasis in original; Buhrmester, Burnham et al., 2018, p. 3). The authors used a mediation model to test the first hypothesis and found that the relationship between dysphoria and fusion to WildCRU was mediated by fusion to Cecil the Lion. To test the second hypothesis the authors used two linear regressions. The first found that dysphoric intensity at time 1 predicted depth of reflection and self/group centrality at time 2. The second used a multiple regression with reflection, self/group centrality, and the interaction between reflection and self/group centrality as predictors of change in fusion to the group WildCRU. They found a significant interaction effect of reflection and self/group centrality on fusion. The effect of reflection on fusion was only significant when self/group centrality was high, but not when self/group centrality was low. This indicates that the increase in fusion to the group WildCRU happened among participants who engaged in high levels of reflection *and* felt that the death of Cecil the Lion was a central self and group experience. Those who did not score highly on the depth of reflection and self/group centrality measures "reported little to no change or a decrease in fusion" (Buhrmester, Burnham et al., 2018, p. 4). However, it does not appear that they tested whether reflection mediated the relationship between dysphoria and fusion (which is why this study is not discussed in the previous section).

The study by Buhrmester, Burnham et al. (2018) presents the best direct evidence for relationships between an emotionally intense experience, reflection, the perceived centrality of the event, and fusion. It also provides evidence for the idea that one can be fused to a non-group concept (Cecil the Lion), such as the essential beliefs described in Chapter 3. In addition, the results of the study indicate that there is a relationship between fusion with a group (WildCRU) and fusion with a concept related to the group (Cecil the Lion). However, there are several ways in which the study could be changed to more directly test the claims of the IIS. The second hypothesis stated by Buhrmester, Burnham et al. focused on "high amounts of reflection" (2018, p. 2). This would appear very similar to the IIS's claim, however, they used a measure of the "depth of reflection" adopted from the study by Jong et al. (2016). The IIS suggests that it is the frequency of reflection upon an experience that should mediate the relationship between the emotional intensity of the experience and fusion as reflection serves as the rehearsal mechanism that promotes consolidation into semantic memory and thus the creation of conceptual ties. This is not to say that the depth of the reflection would not be a significant aspect of the relationship between reflection and an emotionally intense experience and fusion, or even that depth of reflection is unrelated to frequency of reflection, only that a more direct test of the IIS would focus on frequency of reflection. The study also found a relationship between self/group centrality and fusion. However, the measure of centrality used in their study is arguably not the best fit for a study of centrality in the sense that the IIS refers to centrality. In the IIS, the perceived centrality of the event focuses on the centrality of an event on one's own personal identity. The extent to which other members of the group are also perceived to share that experience is not considered the most relevant point. To clarify, this is not to say that perceiving other individuals to have had a similar experience is not important; previous studies argue and present evidence that sharing emotionally intense experiences is important to fusion (e.g., Jong et al., 2016). However, the IIS proposes that conceptual ties (the basis for extended fusion) are the result of reflection on an experience that, in turn, results in the experience being viewed as central to their identity and causes ties to form between the group's social schema and one's personal schema as one interprets the event using the group's social schema. As such, one can undergo an emotionally intense experience by one's self and still have it result in fusion. From the perspective of the IIS, it is not necessary that other individuals also view the experience as central, only that the individual incorporates the conceptual ties linking their personal and social schemas as a central part of their own identity. That is to say, within the IIS, the result found by Buhrmester, Burnham et al. that dysphoric intensity at time 1 predicted depth of reflection and self/group centrality at time 2 should hold even if the centrality of event scale is designed to capture centrality to one's self, not centrality to other group members. Lastly, although the study by Buhrmester, Burnham et al. measured emotional intensity, reflection, self/group centrality, and fusion to both group and a non-group concept that could be considered essential to the group, no statistical test reported in their study tested the hypotheses proposed in this chapter, which both state that the relationship between emotional intensity and fusion is mediated by *both* reflection and the perceived centrality of event. Nevertheless, there are two reasons why an additional investigation was required to find more direct evidence for the relationships proposed by the IIS: (1) no prior analysis investigated whether reflection and the perceived centrality of the event mediate the relationship between emotional intensity and fusion; (2) the measures used for reflection and centrality in the Buhrmester, Burnham et al. study address aspects of reflection and centrality that are not the same as those proposed by the IIS, despite their similarity.

Taken as a whole, the studies by Jong et al. (2016) and Buhrmester, Burnham et al. (2018) suggest that reflection can mediate the relationship between the emotional intensity of an experience and fusion to the social identity associated with that experience. Additionally, studies from the centrality of event literature (Berntsen & Rubin, 2006; Berntsen & Thomsen, 2005; Berntsen et al., 2003) and previously published studies from the fusion literature (e.g., Buhrmester, Burnham et al., 2018; Newson et al., 2016) suggest that emotionally intense experiences can result in the experience becoming a central aspect of one's identity and that reflection can play an important role the fusion process. In addition, the studies by Newson et al. (2016) and Kavanagh et al. (2018) found evidence that fusion can result from experiences that are perceived as positive, suggesting that it is possible that the emotionally intense and euphoric experiences of contemporary Pentecostal and Charismatic Christians may result in fusion.

In a new study, carried out online, different measures were used to capture the variables of interest in a way that is more congruent with the IIS's proposals (Lane, 2019a). By using these measures, the study collects data to test that the relationship between the emotional intensity associated with an experience and fusion is mediated positively by both (1) the perceived frequency of reflection on the event and (2) the perceived centrality of the event. It tests this hypothesis in relation to fusion with a group as well as fusion with God, an essential belief for Christians. In addition, the analysis explores the extent to which contemporary

Christians view their emotionally intense experiences as euphoric and presents partial replications of earlier studies by testing mediation models of the same structure as the Jong et al. (2016) and Buhrmester, Burnham et al. (2018) studies using data from contemporary Christian communities.

4.2 Further Testing of the IIS

In an online study ($N = 521$), cross-cultural surveys were used to study the relationship between emotional intensity, reflection, and extended fusion to investigate the key claims of the IIS regarding how emotionally intense experiences can affect social alignment with large social groups like doctrinal religions. This study also used a large cross-cultural sample of participants to test the extent to which the relationship between emotional intensity and fusion are mediated by reflection and centrality of event—as posited by the IIS. It only looked at individuals in doctrinal religious groups (the study was limited to Christians in the UK and Singapore). Regarding fusion, it used both a measure of fusion to the group, and—importantly for the IIS—a measure of fusion to the concept "God." In this way it was able to test one of the key claims of the IIS cross-culturally.

The data were analyzed using a serial mediation model where the effect of emotional intensity on fusion with their group or God is mediated by reflection on the event and the perceived centrality of the event. The results of the study ultimately suggested that the IIS's proposal presents a viable explanation for fusion in large groups. Emotionally intense experiences can promote reflection that results in the event becoming a central aspect of one's personal schema and can result in fusion to essential beliefs of the group's social schema (referred to as conceptual ties). In both the Singaporean and UK samples, perceived frequency of reflection and the perceived centrality of the event were found to have positive effects on fusion with the essential group concept of God.

The study expanded on several previous studies of dysphoric experiences in the fusion literature. The study reported by Jong et al. (2016) found that reflection on an emotionally intense event mediates the relationship between the emotional intensity associated with the event and fusion. Using the data collected here, it was found that reflection mediates the relationship between emotional intensity and fusion using (1) a measure of fusion to the group and (2) a measure of fusion to God in both UK and Singaporean samples. The study expanded on the finding by Jong et al. by demonstrating that reflection can also affect one's fusion with an essential belief. In the original studies, Jong et al. only measured fusion to a social group, not an essential belief relevant to the group's social schema. This study was able to replicate this effect using slightly different measures of emotional intensity and reflection, however, it is noteworthy that, in the serial mediation models that tested the main hypotheses, reflection did not always have a significant independent indirect effect. This suggests that, for the formation of conceptual ties that would link an emotionally intense experience with an essential belief from the group's schema, the effect of reflection is important not just on its own, but in conjunction with the additional effect of perceived centrality of event as well.

The results of the study also addressed the findings of Buhrmester, Burnham et al. (2018), who found that the relationship between dysphoric intensity and fusion to one's group is significantly mediated by fusion to a central concept of the group. This study replicated this effect in the UK, but not in Singapore. This may be related to the results found for testing Model 1, which did not find a significant indirect effect of reflection on the relationship between emotional intensity and fusion with the group in Singapore. It is possible that in the Singaporean sample, their fusion to the group, which was significantly higher than in the UK sample, was premised upon relational ties. This study did not collect data on the size of the churches that participants attended, so size of the group could not be directly addressed. However, it is possible that the participants in the Singaporean sample came from smaller churches in Singapore and therefore their fusion was also based on relational ties. While studies suggest that many Christians in Singapore do attend large churches, there are many smaller churches that could be bound by local fusion (Chong & Yew-Foong, 2013; Sng, 2003; The National Council of Churches of Singapore, 2004, 2013). Future studies should not only gather data on church size, it should also attempt to investigate if separate measures of local and extended fusion can be validated and deployed in order to separate the potential effects of each type of fusion independently.

The results of the study also expanded on the finding of Buhrmester, Burnham et al. (2018), who found that emotional intensity is related to reflection and perceived centrality of an event. Although this study used separate measures of reflection and perceived centrality of an event than Buhrmester, Burnham et al. the results of this study also found that emotional intensity is related to reflection, perceived centrality of an event, and fusion with a group and with an essential belief of the group. However, this study used a serial mediation model that suggests that reflection and perceived centrality of an event can have significant indirect effects (both in combination and—at times—independently) on the relationship between emotional intensity and fusion. The results of this study, in combination with the results reported by Buhrmester, Burnham et al. suggest that future studies should utilize longitudinal studies (as done by Buhrmester, Burnham et al.) as well as studies that introduce experimental manipulations to further investigate the relationships between emotional intensity, reflection, perceived centrality of an event, and fusion to both a group and an essential belief of the group.

In addition to finding evidence for the IIS's key claims regarding the effect of emotionally intense experiences on social cohesion with large doctrinal religions, it also found evidence that euphoric experiences can result in fusion. My ethnographic observations suggest that the emotions experienced by Singaporean and British Christians during reaffirmations, retreats, and conversions are overwhelmingly euphoric; this ethnographic observation is supported by the participants' self-reports. The responses on questions about the intensity of the experience are also consistent with my ethnographic observations in Singapore and the UK. Often, individuals had a story to tell that documented an emotionally intense and life changing experience. Rarely—if ever—would anyone describe their experience as mundane or in a "matter of fact" way. Given both ethnographic experience and the overwhelmingly positive ratings of the experiences reported by participants, it appears that dysphoric arousal is not a necessary condition for extended fusion. Rather, extended fusion can result from intense euphoric experiences as well, as predicted by the IIS. In fact, the overwhelming majority of individuals in the study who reported having an experience that would have led to fusion stated that it was positive. Overall, 91.5 percent reported that their experience was positive, only 9.5 percent of the sample said that it was negative or neutral.

The effects of emotionally intense experiences are predicted to have important effects on social cohesion that can create extreme cohesion in a group. This cohesion can lead to a wide variety of behaviors including self-sacrifice and violent reactions to group threats. The empirical literature suggests that fusion can underlie tendencies to help those in-group members in need as well as self-sacrifice for one's own group, from personal donations of time and money (e.g., Buhrmester et al., 2014) to endorsing violent extremism, including suicide terrorism (Hamid et al., 2019; Lane, Shults, & Wildman, 2018; Sheikh, Gómez, & Atran, 2016; Swann, Buhrmester et al., 2014; Whitehouse, 2018). This wide range of self-sacrifices represents the extremity of fusion. In the next chapter, we will deal with this in more detail, resulting in a testable architecture that can be utilized within AI models to better understand, explain, and perhaps even predict religious extremism and intergroup conflicts.

Overall, there is support for, the hypothesis that the relationship between the emotional intensity associated with an event and fusion to one's group is mediated by perceived frequency of reflection on that event and the perceived centrality of the event. The study also found evidence for the hypothesis that the relationship between the emotional intensity associated with an event and fusion to an essential belief of the group (in this case the concept God) is mediated by perceived frequency of reflection on that event and the perceived centrality of the event. The results support the IIS's key assertion: that emotionally intense experiences can promote reflection that results in the event becoming a central aspect of one's personal schema and can result in fusion to essential beliefs of the group's social schema (referred to as conceptual ties) and that this effect is not limited to small-scale groups like imagistic religions. This suggests that it is possible that researchers studying fusion with large groups (extended fusion) via the idea of extended relational ties may be overlooking the effect of conceptual ties to account for fusion with large groups. Given the discussion in the earlier sections of this chapter, it should be entertained that the IIS provides a more parsimonious explanation for the varying results of earlier studies and thorny theoretical issues of previous frameworks when attempting to explain patterns of social cohesion in large social groups like doctrinal religions.

In conclusion, these results provide evidence for the IIS's formalization of social cohesion, particularly regarding its predictions concerning how fusion could result from high-arousal rituals in doctrinal religions. While previous theorists have proposed that extended fusion results from kinship-based cognitive mechanisms and extending *relational ties* to large groups of individuals (e.g., Fredman et al., 2015; Swann et al., 2012; Whitehouse & Lanman, 2014), the IIS proposes that extended fusion is caused by reflection that results in mutually held *conceptual ties* between essential belief of a group's social schema and the members' personal schemas.

4.3 Testing for Effects on Consensus

However, the IIS also proposes that that the social schemas are affected by the different forms of group alignment. Specifically, the IIS posits that fusion is the result of reflection on an intense emotional experience that becomes central to one's identity (as suggested by the study presented in this chapter).

In alignment with the DMR theory (Whitehouse, 2004), the IIS proposes that reflection can result in unique belief idiosyncrasies being introduced into the fused individual's semantic memory for the group's social schema that is not held by the rest of the group. Meanwhile, attendance at frequent rituals should result in social identification as well as the formation of social schemas. Therefore, the IIS suggests a positive relationship between frequency of in-group ritual attendance and within-group consensus as well as a positive relationship between social identification and within-group consensus. However, the IIS also suggests a negative relationship between fusion and within-group consensus. Within-group consensus is important because, as discussed earlier, the social cohesion of large social group can be undermined if its members have different conceptions of what it means to be part of that group. In a third study, I utilized data science techniques in conjunction with traditional anthropological field research techniques to study within-group consensus and its effect on social cohesion in real-world religious groups in Singapore.

4.3.1 Religion in Singapore

Here, it is useful to provide some background as to why Singapore provides a unique research context for the study of religious beliefs. Singapore is a small city-state in Southeast Asia with a population of approximately 5.5 million and its citizens are generally regarded as having an extremely high quality of life (Lai, 2008). Since Singapore's independence from Malaysia in 1965,[2] it has been a secular country with no official state religion and has carefully avoided any policies that would favor any one religion. Due to Singapore's history with evangelism by its minority Christian community during the 1980s being viewed as offensive to some, Singapore introduced controls on the ability for individuals to publicly display or discuss religious beliefs (E. K. B. Tan, 2008). Since Singapore enacted "The Maintenance of Religious and Social Harmony Act" in 1990, the state has exercised control over how religious information is spread, even to the point of limiting the speech of religious leaders and practitioners (D. P. S. Goh, 2010). Unlike in the United States or United Kingdom, religious individuals will not be found evangelizing in the street or discussing their beliefs with individuals who do not explicitly approve of the conversation. Also, unlike countries such as the United States or United Kingdom, evangelism is not found on standard television networks; individuals generally pay for channels broadcasting religious messages. As a result, most churches disseminate any live broadcasts (or recordings) of their sermons in Sunday services via the internet. This restricts the learning of most religious beliefs to two areas of life in Singapore: one's own experience with religion and the general beliefs and practices taught during primary and secondary school.

Since Singapore's independence, it was believed that the state should teach moral values and that this could be done by teaching the basic tenants of the religions in Singapore (R. B. H. Goh, 2005; Sng, 2003). In Singapore, this includes Christianity, Islam, Buddhism, and Confucianism, which are discussed in the Singaporean public-school curriculum. Students are taught deliberately vague overviews, as the state is careful to separate itself from the notion that it endorses any religious tradition. However, schools affiliated with religious traditions, particularly Methodist and Anglican Christianity, have been regarded as some of the more prestigious schools in the country and accept students of all religious backgrounds. Students in religious schools in Singapore are given religious education in the school's religious tradition that is more thorough than that of the public schools, however, the government is not tolerant of schools espousing negative views on other religions. Generally, religious education in the schools of Singapore results in a citizenry that is somewhat knowledgeable about other religions, but does not know much about the beliefs of other communities, much less the theological subtleties that would result from frequent attendance as part of a community (D. P. S. Goh, 2010; E. K. B. Tan, 2008).

In Singapore, Christianity is about 20 percent of the population and growing, particularly among educated and upwardly mobile[3] sections of the population (Chong & Yew-Foong, 2013). Throughout Singapore's history, the churches have been a provider of social services such as orphanages, hospitals, and schools (Poon & Tan, 2012; Sng, 2003), and this is still the case today. One primary context for the spread of Christianity in Singapore is in schools and universities. Although there are strict policies about public evangelism in Singapore, peer to peer discussions between colleagues and acquaintances are generally unhindered so long as they are done in a respectful and non-threatening manner. This has allowed for para-church organizations to leverage social networks of educational institutions to spread their beliefs and invite potential converts to church events (Hinton, 1985; Sng, 2003).

Using educational social networks has been crucial to the spread of Christianity. While the government closely regulates religious speech and evangelism in general public spaces (as described earlier), the face-to-face social networks that form in educational institutions are largely unregulated unless a group offends another religious group or disturbs the general peace between people in a public space (see J. Lim, 2012). This has been the case at least since Christianity started to grow among the ethnically Chinese demographic of Singapore's population in the 1970s. During this period, Pentecostal and Charismatic worship styles also began to spread quickly throughout churches in Singapore (Sng, 2003). The spread of Pentecostal and Charismatic worship styles started within the Methodist Church in 1972 when a group of boys, who were enrolled at the Methodist-affiliated Anglo-Chinese School at Barker Road, met in the clock tower of church to pray and began speaking in tongues;[4] this became known as the "Clock Tower Revival" (Poon & Tan, 2012). This revival was marked by members of the Christian community showing *signs and wonders*. Signs and wonders commonly include speaking in tongues, being "slain in the spirit," faith healings, and the casting out of demons.[5] As the Clock Tower Revival spread to Anglican and Catholic congregations, churches began performing charismatic services in addition to traditional liturgies (Sng, 2003). In the charismatic services, the general format of the service still included prayers, sermons, hymns, offerings, and the Holy Communion; however, individuals would begin to speak in tongues during prayers or hymns and—at times—would be slain in the spirit. Today, a subtle partition in the Christian community in Singapore exists between the charismatic and non-charismatic worship styles in mainline Protestant churches. Many denominations, such as the Methodist Church, have accommodated Charismatic worship by performing both charismatic and traditional services. Other denominations, such as the Presbyterian and Lutheran churches in Singapore, only offer services which follow traditional liturgies (The National Council of Churches of Singapore, 2013).[6]

Outside of mainline Protestant churches, Singapore has seen a notable increase in attendance at charismatic mega-churches since the late 1980s (Sng, 2003). Churches such as New Creation Church, Faith Community Baptist Church, and City Harvest Church have thousands of attendees per service. The largest of these churches, New Creation Church, sees a weekly attendance of over 30,000 people (Matthews, 2014) and has built Singapore's largest indoor auditorium (The Star Auditorium) to accommodate services of up to 5,000 people at a time. This is significant when one takes into account that the largest of the Protestant denominations in Singapore is the Methodist Church, which has a total membership of slightly less than 50,000 (Lane, 2014; M. Tan, 2014). These churches are marked by both their charismatic worship services and their large congregations. During a worship service, individuals will often speak in tongues and it is not uncommon for a pastor to perform faith healings. Unlike most mainline churches, traditional liturgies are not offered. For example, at New Creation Church, a typical service consists of the following: about thirty minutes of praise and worship songs; a reading of announcements and miracles associated with the church; a sermon lasting about one hour; collection of offering during a special performance by a member of the church; and a final performance of praise and worship songs. The entire service typically lasts approximately two hours.

Most Singaporean churches have vibrant social schedules for their congregants. For example, individuals are encouraged to join Bible study groups of twenty or so other individuals in their age group. These Bible study groups meet weekly for official functions and often throughout the week for dinners, sports, or to attend events together (Hinton, 1985; Matthews, 2014; Sng, 2003). Mainline churches often utilize the cell structure if their congregation supports it. If not, ministries are created as subgroups working within the church. In both mainline and charismatic churches, it is not uncommon for members to invite friends to their Bible study group either for official events or for casual gatherings. Such invites are a common way for individuals to become introduced to a new church in Singapore. Inviting one's peers to attend a church event is encouraged by most churches in Singapore. Individuals are encouraged to extend invitations both to Christian and non-Christian peers (Hinton, 1985; Sng, 2003). This creates an atmosphere where it is not uncommon for a young Singaporean Christians to attend a church that is not their *home church*, or the church they typically attend, in response to an invitation from a peer.

To review, there are several ways in which an individual can encounter Christian doctrine in Singapore. However, due to regulations and social pressures, individuals would not encounter Christian doctrine indirectly (e.g., by overhearing a street evangelist). Within Christian communities, individuals primarily receive information about their group's beliefs from structured events associated with their church. While conversations of doctrine do come up in casual conversations during social events, they are generally short and sporadic. However, one source of information is also attending rituals at other churches. The low number of Christians relative to the total population and the restrictions on evangelism allow for greater certainty that individuals are receiving information only from their own church. Therefore, individuals are less likely to learn the beliefs of other religions by accidental exposure in their day-to-day life. In addition, the performance of rituals with low emotional intensity in many mainline churches, as well as rituals with high emotional intensity in the megachurches, allows for the research to investigate both typical (high frequency-low emotional arousal) doctrinal ritual and the emotionally intense rituals that are noted as problematic for the DMR theory. The presence of both ritual styles provides a useful field-site for testing the claims of the IIS regarding within-group consensus.

It was within this context that I designed a research protocol that combined a survey that included the measures used in the two studies noted previously with a semi-structured interview about each participant's religious beliefs (this is also discussed in relation to emergence theory and complex systems in the field of engineering in Lane, 2018c). The semi-structured interview had a set topic and general structure, but the responses of the participants to the first question dictated all subsequent questions. The interview focused on the participant's memories of the Sunday service generally, not a specific Sunday service. The Sunday service was specifically chosen because it is a frequent (weekly) ritual with low arousal and is an aspect of the lives of most practicing Christians. This ensures that the target of the interview is something shared by all members of the community, even if frequency of in-group ritual attendance varies between participants. The interview begins by asking participants what the general meaning or significance is behind the ritual. It then asks what steps go into the performance of that ritual, listing each liturgical action as they provide them. Then, using the list of actions provided by the participants, they were asked to elaborate on the meaning and significance of each individual sub-action that they listed. In this way, participants provide exegesis (i.e., an explanation or interpretation of the target ritual) without having to focus on the behavioral scripts of the event; instead, the behavioral aspects of the service serve as a framework to guide questions concerning ritual meaning. To measure within-group consensus, I utilized techniques that originated in earlier cybernetic research into a branch of data science and AI known as natural language processing (or NLP), which focuses on the ability for computational systems to analyze or—in some cases—understand naturally produced human language.

Within-group consensus was measured by a participant's lossy intersection distance. This calculates the conceptual distance between two semantic network maps, one constructed from a participant's semi-structured interview response, the other constructed from analyzing all the semi-structured interview responses within a population. As such, increases in distance denote a decrease in within-group consensus and a decrease in distance denotes increase in within-group consensus. The lossy intersection distance was calculated by creating semantic network maps of each participant's interview and comparing these networks to a network constructed to represent the social beliefs of the group. Semantic networks were constructed from the interviews by first transcribing each interview into a text document. The interviews were conducted primarily in

English, and all participants were fluent in English; however, some responses included terms and phrases from Singlish, which were transcribed in English. Some participants also continued the discussion, which provided further information after the interview that is valuable ethnographic information concerning the beliefs, practices, and personal experiences of the participant. However, such information was not included in the analysis as it was considered to be provided outside of the bounds of the semi-structured interview and therefore represented information that was not valid to compare to other participants. In addition, only the responses of the participant concerning the meaning or significance of the liturgical elements of the Sunday service were recorded; the list of actions that they provided that described the liturgical elements of the service were not coded.

The transcriptions were then used to generate semantic network maps. This process involved three steps: pre-processing, cleaning, and analysis. Pre-processing removed extra spaces, punctuation, and corrected common spelling errors. Cleaning removed irrelevant words from the text such as pronouns, articles, and spoken utterances such as "uh," "um," and "lah."[7] All terms cleaned in this way were replaced with a placeholder term "xxx." After this, a predefined word dictionary was applied that stemmed words with different endings into their root concept and converts phrases, proper nouns, and multi-word n-grams into single concepts; this included the names of churches, common terms, and proper nouns. For example, the name Jesus Christ would be converted into JESUS_CHRIST as it represents a single concept and the term Holy Bible and New International Version would be converted into HOLY_BIBLE and NIV as they also represent single concepts for analysis. The same dictionary was applied to all transcripts, regardless of the social group from which the participants were drawn (the complete dictionary can be found in Appendix 1). The analysis then used a co-occurrence algorithm to produce a matrix of all remaining terms where point $N_{i,j}$ in the matrix represents the frequency with which the terms i and j co-occur within a predefined distance within a single sentence (as discussed in Carley, 1997). The resulting matrix represented each participant's personal schema and could be visualized as a network (see Figure 4.1).

Social schemas for each church were approximated by creating a lossy intersection matrix. A *lossy intersection matrix* is a matrix (i.e., network) that represents the set of links that appear in more than some threshold of responses in a defined sample. For example, when creating a lossy intersection matrix (M) from a sample of networks (N_1, N_2, N_3, [. . .] N_k) and the lossy intersection threshold is set at 5, then any link $N_{i,j}$ in the sample of N networks that appear greater than 5 times will be included in M as $M_{i,j} > 0$ (This was first described in Carley, 1997; and descriptions for how this is calculated using the ORA software can be found in Carley, Pfeffer, Reminga, Storrick, & Columbus, 2012). The lossy intersection differs from other network distance metrics because it requires that a link is recorded above a certain threshold; for this research, the threshold was set at one-third of the sample. This ensures that the information is held by a significant part of the group and not an artifact of individual beliefs. Within-group consensus for each individual is then measured by their lossy distance. *Lossy distance* is the Euclidean bit-wise distance between an individual's response matrix and that of the lossy intersection matrix (Carley, 1997; Carley et al., 2012). This method calculates the distance between two networks differently than other euclidean network distance measures, such as Jaccard distance or Hamming distance (see Hamming, 1950; Jaccard, 1912; Mathworks, 2014; these metrics are also discussed in Appendix 1.5), which measure the distance between a target

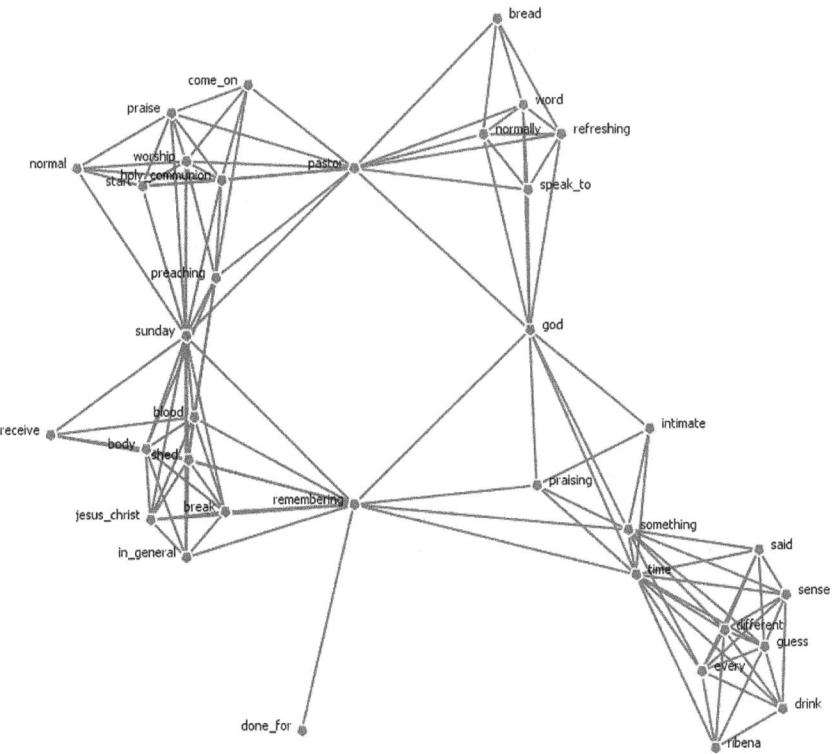

Figure 4.1 An example of a semantic network map constructed from a participant's semi-structured interview during the initial pilot study. The nodes represent concepts and the links represent discerned relationships between the concepts in the response.

network and a union network (a matrix that holds the summation of all values for all link pairings) or an average network (a matrix that holds an average value for all link pairings) constructed from a sample of networks.

To collect social network data, individuals were asked to list up to ten individuals in the group with which they regularly spoke at the end of the semi-structured interview. All names were recoded for anonymity. These lists were checked over a period of eight months; networks were only amended if a clear omission was noted, for example, if someone neglected to record a social network link with a romantic partner or if a romantic partnership was formed during the observation period. Because each participant was asked to provide names of their regular acquaintances, many individuals who were recorded in the group's social network were not participants in other aspects of the research. As such, their data was not directly used in the analysis. After data collection ended, all names were anonymized. The lists were then transformed into a matrix of values representing the presence or absence of a social relationship between all participants.

With this data, we can make initial tests of the IIS while having the social and semantic information required for the cybernetic approach discussed earlier, first by using structural equation modeling to test for statistical relationships, and then this data can be used to validate computational AI models that are designed to implement the theoretical framework of the IIS as well.

Using structural equation modeling, the frequency, social identification, and fusion data from the survey was tested against the lossy intersection approximation of within-group consensus drawn from the analysis of the semi-structured interviews. The analysis using structural equation modeling found that the model was significant, and better than the baseline model, although future research should utilize larger samples of 100+ to be sure that model fit is reliable across other populations[8] (see Figure 4.2).

The data from this study suggested that both the pathway from fusion and the pathway from frequency of in-group ritual attendance to within-group consensus were of the direction predicted by the IIS. In addition, the relationship between social identification to within-group consensus had the predicted (positive) relationship.

The contents of the last two chapters have outlined the general framework for the IIS and how it can serve as a basis for explaining social cohesion in large social groups, primarily drawing on research from the DMR theory and bringing together new research from cognitive and social psychology, anthropology,

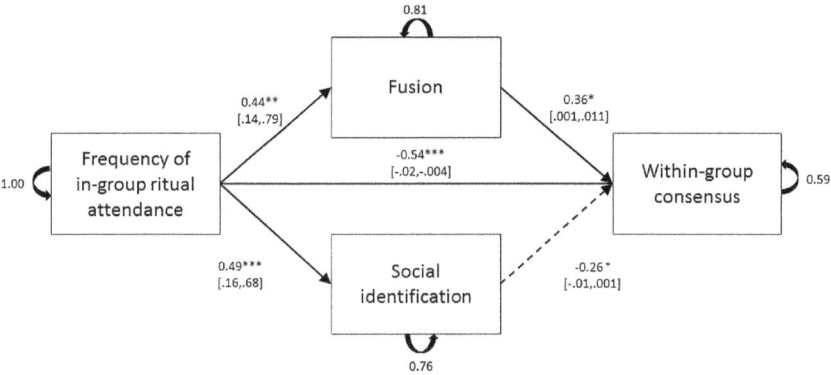

Figure 4.2 Results of SEM. Each relationship is depicted with standardized regression weights and 95 percent confidence intervals (shown in square brackets). The solid arrows denote significant relationships in the SEM, the dotted arrow between social identification and within-group consensus denotes that it did not achieve significance with α = .05 (note that this α is reporting the significance level used in the analysis, not Cronbach's alpha). The looped bold arrows represent the error coefficients. Symbols are used to denote significance levels: *p < .05; **p ≤ .01; ***p ≤ .001; +p = .09.

history, cybernetics, and data science to provide a new approach that amends what I perceived as shortcomings in earlier research.

In the next chapter, I will begin to discuss how we can move from this theoretical foundation, which has been largely reliant on methods common to the social sciences (e.g., surveys, interviews, experiments, ethnography, historical analyses, etc.), to a new methodological toolbox that incorporates computational modeling and AI. This shift to incorporate such computational tools is exciting because it does not just provide a new set of tools that can allow for more specific model testing, as well as an opportunity for "big data" analysis, it incorporates this new set of tools in a way that is theoretically and methodologically parsimonious within the framework of cultural cybernetics.

5

Artificial Intelligence and Religions in Silico

5.1 A History of Simulating Religion and Ritual

In the previous chapters, I've reviewed the literature around two key aspects of social cohesion, bonding and belief, at the nexus of group alignment and within-group consensus, and how these themes can be viewed from a cognitive (i.e., information processing) perspective that I've referred to as cultural cybernetics. One of the strengths of this framework, I argue, is that we can formalize our theories as computational models that can be tested against real-world data. In this chapter, I will discuss applications of a cybernetic approach that use principles from AI to study religion and identity. Unlike in previous discussions, where data science methods were used to process data and test hypotheses, in the following examples, data science is brought to bear in a more computational sense, where different forms of AI are employed to investigate various aspects of human religiosity and better understand what this means for our understanding of religion.

Compared to the amount of research in data analytics and AI that addresses how we can categorize texts, there has been little work on how we can use models or simulations to create and study any aspect of religion. This is largely due to both a lack of motivation for researchers to move beyond machine learning in the AI space and a lack of computationally rooted theorization about the nature of social identification. These two issues are further compounded by the fact that social identities are—by definition—social. As such, studying them requires that we utilize multi-agent AI (MAAI) and compatible approaches to study social identification. In addition, the gap between simulation and AI, filled by the MAAI approach described in Chapter 1, has largely been unaddressed, with AI systems largely ignoring identity and computer models of identity largely ignoring AI.

Those few systems that do exist to study social identification computationally have taken a variety of approaches and focused on many different aspects of identity. The first engagement of the cognitive science of religion with the idea of an "artificial mind" from a cognitive perspective began in the early 1990s (McCauley & Lawson, 1993).[1] However, it is worth noting that the "artificial" mind that was discussed in the earlier literature was never instantiated computationally, it was a narrative theoretical proposal, not one that was realized within a computational architecture. It was not until the early 2000s that any attempt to formalize theories from the cognitive science of religion as computational models that can be run as computer simulations began to be published.

The first two simulations of religion from a cognitive perspective were published by M. Afzal Upal (Upal, 2005c, 2005b), immediately followed by a monograph by William S. Bainbridge (2006). In these simulations, both Upal and Bainbridge developed the idea of an "information entrepreneur," or one who exchanges their ideas and influence in the religious sphere or afterlife for other tangible resources in this life (it heavily reflects the key propositions included in Stark & Bainbridge, 1987). These publications set the stage for many additional publications on religion that have employed simulation, and taken a cognitive approach as their foundation (Braxton, Upal, & Nielbo, 2012; Lane, Shults, & McCauley, 2019; Wildman & Sosis, 2011); and in addition to these, there is still other literature that has modeled and analyzed simulations of religion that are more sociological in nature (R. Gore, Lemos, Shults, & Wildman, 2018; Iannaccone & Makowsky, 2007) or statistical in focus (Picoli & Mendes, 2008). However, this literature does not focus of how identity and information affect social cohesion and is therefore beyond the scope of the current discussion. Therefore, I will continue by returning to the DMR theory because of (1) its relevance and similarity to the IIS discussed in earlier chapters and (2) its history of being simulated using modern computer modeling techniques. There have been two previous simulations of the DMR theory, and several simulations of social identification in religious groups that can be discussed in the current context. Here, I will present these, with a general description and critique of each model.

5.1.1 A Brief Overview of DMR1

The first simulation of how ritual affects social cohesion from the perspective of the DMR theory was published in 2012; I'll refer to this as the DMR1 model

(Whitehouse et al., 2012). The model was developed in NetLogo (Wilensky, 1999) using the BehaviorComposer platform (Kahn, 2013; Kahn & Noble, 2010).[2] DMR1 was designed to simulate the decrease in motivation for beliefs over time in the doctrinal mode and its subsequent effects. The model simulated the behaviors of individuals in the doctrinal mode and allowed users to manipulate ten target variables. The variables, their labels, and their values can be found in Table 5.1. The model specified the beliefs of any individual in the group as a network; similar to the schemas and the semantic network analysis techniques utilized in research covered in previous chapters. However, whereas the networks analyzed previously were created from analyzing texts/transcripts, the belief networks of DMR1 were constructed on the basis of Whitehouse's fieldwork experience (presented in Whitehouse, 1995, 2000).

During the simulation, followers (the number of which is set by a variable in the model called the-number-of-followers) move between their homes and their temples; both homes and temples are given a predetermined location in the simulated environment. They move to their temple X times within period t (where X is equal to the variable the-temple-visit-frequency and t is equal to the-frequency-window). They remain at the temple for a period equal to the-duration-of-temple-visit. While they are near the temple, they will receive teachings from the leader(s) of the group (the number of which is set by the variable the-number-of-leaders) at a rate equal to the-transmission-rate. Leaders in the model are imbued with identical semantic networks although they may offer teachings at any one point in the simulation that are different from previous teachings or the teachings from another leader in the simulation. If the follower does not currently know the

Table 5.1 Variables and Settings for DMR1 Model as Published by Whitehouse et al. (2012b)

Variable	Min	Value	Max
the-daily-motivation-level-decay	0	.5	10
the-motivation-level-decay-per-repetition	0	1	100
the-minimum-motivation-level	0	200	1,000
the-temple-visit-frequency	0	3	100
the-duration-of-temple-visit	0	1	100
the-transmission-rate	0	5	100
the-frequency-window	0	1,000	10,000
the-number-of-followers	0	1	45
the-number-of-leaders	0	1	10
the-number-of-new-leaders	0	1	10

teaching presented (i.e., have that teaching in their own network of beliefs), a new node is created and incorporated into their semantic network; this is only done if they can incorporate the new node successfully by connecting it to a preexisting node such as a belief or an anchor (teachings in DMR1 always include two nodes and a link). If they already know the teaching, the motivation associated with that teaching will decrease at a rate equal to `the-motivation-level-decay-per-repetition` variable at each exposure. If the motivation for a teaching reaches 0 an agent will "forget" a belief (it will delete the node from its semantic network); additionally, there is a 1 percent probability that a link will be removed at random (this value is stored in a global variable `the-odds-of-removing-a-link`). Additionally, the motivation decreases at a set daily rate equal to `the-daily-motivation-level-decay`.

If the average motivation for the followers in the model falls below a threshold set by the variable `the-minimum-motivation-level` in the model, this triggers the introduction of a number of new religious leaders (the number of which is equal to the variable `the-number-of-new-leaders`); I refer to this as the "schism function." Each new religious leader is imbued with additional beliefs not previously taught by the leaders prior to the onset of the schism function (the semantic networks of all new religious leaders are identical). Followers then begin accepting teachings from the new religious leaders. As with teachings introduced by the original religious leaders, individual motivation is set to maximum when a follower learns a new teaching from a new religious leader, and as these new teachings are repeated over time, motivation decreases, and the schism group dies out. The output of the model tracks the average level of motivation for the group during the simulation (see Figure 5.1 for a plot of a typical model run given the settings used during publication).

In the modeling and simulation literature, there are over ninety methods available for the verification and validation of a computer model, and they range in how powerful they are and their ability to ensure that the model is indeed validated or verified (Sargent, 2013). In the original publication, the model underwent what is called "face validation," which is when a subject-matter expert examines the behavior of the model and assess its validity. Ideally, the subject-matter expert was not part of the model development to ensure that biases such as the sunk cost effect (the tendency to continue with something that one has already put time or resources into) do not affect the validity judgments from the subject-matter expert.

To investigate the model more thoroughly, I want to discuss the results of further validation, undertaken after the original DMR1 was published. This validation took the form of a parameter variation and sensitivity analysis

Artificial Intelligence and Religions in Silico   109

Figure 5.1 Motivation plot for typical run of the model presented in Whitehouse et al. (2012).

referred to as a parameter sweep. During this process, the model is run multiple times with variables in particular settings in order to get a statistical basis for the overall behavior of the model. The settings of the model are then changed, and the simulations are repeated. This process is repeated for the target set of parameters in the model's phase space that are of interest.

Parameter sweeps were carried out using the BehaviorSpace tool built into the NetLogo software (Wilensky, 1999). By utilizing BehaviorSpace, one can iterate parameters multiple times in order to understand the dynamics of the model under a variety of conditions. In the current parameter sweep, conditions are determined by varying the 10 parameters in the model between the minimum and maximum for each value, and the distance between each setting is defined by the "step" parameter (e.g., a step value of 10 with a minimum of 0 and maximum of 100 is the same as a list of values between 0 and 100 when counting by 10s); each condition was run 25 times to understand the average output of the model under each condition (conditions for the parameter sweep can be found in Table 5.2 below). This analysis can reveal whether there are theoretically interesting patterns in the data. Additionally, this technique could potentially reveal issues with the coding of the model.

The results of the parameter sweeps revealed that most of the model behavior produced results that were in alignment with the theory, or expected given the model's construction, and do not have significant theoretical implications. For instance, any manipulation of `the-minimum-motivation-level` changes the point at which the group will start to accept the teachings of a new religious leader. When the parameter is set at 0, average motivation dies out

Table 5.2 Settings for DMR1 Parameter Sweep Experiment

Variable	Min	Step	Max
`the-daily-motivation-level-decay`	1	5	10
`the-motivation-level-decay-per-repetition`	1	10	100
`the-minimum-motivation-level`	1	20	1,000
`the-temple-visit-frequency`	1	10	101
`the-duration-of-temple-visit`	1	10	101
`the-transmission-rate`	1	1	30
`the-frequency-window`	1	500	10,000
`the-number-of-followers`	1	10	101
`the-number-of-leaders`	1	3	10
`the-number-of-new-leaders`	1	3	10

completely. However, when the `minimum-motivation-level` is set above the average initial motivation at the start of the simulation, the schism function is run at the earliest possible opportunity.

There are many direct effects when manipulating a variable in the model because it affects the speed at which motivation degrades or when a schism occurs. For example, manipulating `the-transmission-rate` (which determines how many teachings are given during a point in time) significantly changes how long it may take for the mean motivation of the group to fall below a certain level since motivation decreases as a direct function of how often an agent is exposed to an idea. If `the-transmission-rate` variable is increased, motivation decreases to the threshold set by `the-minimum-motivation-level` very quickly, triggering the schism function. If it is decreased, it takes longer for the motivation to fall below the threshold. This is because motivational levels are directly related to the number of times a follower receives a teaching as well as the number of "days" simulated in the model. Such patterns reveal that there is very little stochasticity in the model. Although it is beyond the scope of the current discussion, it does complicate the extent to which rituals could operate within a framework of selection as proposed by the DMR theory (Whitehouse, 2004) if there is insufficient stochasticity or insufficient description of what would cause the observed stochasticity since random variation is often discussed as a hallmark feature of selection in cultural evolution.

5.1.2 A Brief Overview of DMR2

The first revision proposed to the DMR1 was published by William McCorkle and I (McCorkle & Lane, 2012). In this model, which I'll call the DMR2, we argued that the transition from religious group to splinter movement simulated by Whitehouse et al. (2012) overlooked the fact that both theoretically (see Whitehouse, 2004) and ethnographically (see Whitehouse, 1995), the observed schism dynamics represented an oscillation from a tradition, to splinter group, and back to the original tradition. This oscillation is not unique to the ethnographic experience of Whitehouse, but often appears in Melanesian traditions; as outlined in great detail by Whitehouse (2000). To allow for this oscillation, the DMR2 model implemented a new function into the simulation where an individual gained the new teachings and accepted a new religious leader, but also accepted a new identity. This identity was just an arbitrary numerical marker of a social category. Followers with a specific identity would only accept teachings from leaders (or new religious leaders) that shared their identity. As their motivation for the schism movement decreased, they would "re-integrate" into the original tradition. This involved changing the identity marker and the leader from which the follower would receive teachings. All other model functions were the same as DMR1.

The DMR2 revision produced patterns like the observed oscillations between traditions and schisms. However, the motivational dynamics of the group were indistinguishable after the first few oscillations. After the introduction of the first new religious leaders, the second schism that followed reintegration appeared very predictable in how much the group's motivation would increase and the rates at which the increase and decrease would occur. After a small number of oscillations (usually around 5) the model would run indefinitely, and motivational dynamics of each schism and reintegration are indistinguishable. Effectively, the model would cycle through repetitions of schism and reunification with near-identical results forever.

Analyzing the previous computational models of the DMR theory reveal several limitations. One is a computational error that results in the model predicting sustained maintenance of high levels of motivation in larger groups. In both DMR1 and DMR2, when one manipulates the variable `the-number-of-followers`, (which controls how many followers are in each simulation), it affects the maximum and minimum motivations of the group. At first, it appeared that in larger populations, motivation was less volatile and could be sustained for a longer period than in smaller populations. This also resulted in a smaller range of observed motivational levels during the simulations.

This pattern seemed to reveal that when one increases the number of followers in the model the motivation level output by the group seems to stabilize in such a way that could produce longer lasting movements. Given the fact that observations of doctrinal religions in the historical record appear to sustain motivation among members of large groups of people over long periods of time (as attested to by the ability for large religions to retain members over entire lifetimes), this could potentially reveal an unexpected consequence of the model. While one would expect motivation to decrease over time at the same rate regardless of population size, it has been noted that in doctrinal religions, motivation can be sustained over long periods of time by large religious groups by temporarily introducing imagistic practices into the ritual repertoire of the tradition (for example, this is observed in European Christian religious traditions; see Pyysiäinen, 2005). This "imagistic shift" appears to be observed in participants discussed in the previous chapters who appear to be fused with their group after having undergone an intense religious experience.

However, observing such an effect would be puzzling since the model did not allow for the introduction of new ritual behaviors, only new concepts.[3] A closer analysis of the model revealed that individuals were losing motivation for concepts as described by the model—and theory—and then were re-taught these concepts at a later point in the simulation. When the motivation for a concept decreases to 0, the model deletes the node representing this concept entirely.[4] As such, when a follower is exposed to a previously deleted concept at a later point in a simulation that node is reinstated in the agent's belief schema with the maximum motivation level as if it were the first time that agent had learned that concept. As such, this increases the mean motivation for concepts at higher population levels as a small number of agents re-learn previously forgotten (i.e. deleted) concepts. Therefore, it can be concluded that the effect of sustained motivation observed in DMR1, and DMR2, under conditions of larger group sizes is an artifact of the model's programming.

In addition to suffering the computational issue of artificially increased motivation and a lack of variation in leaders' networks, the ethnographic and historical record, such as that outlined by Whitehouse (1995), provides evidence that the oscillations that are the focus of DMR2 are not identical, as the DMR2 model would seem to suggest. As such, the DMR2 may have been more *theoretically* valid, but analysis of the output revealed that the model was still overly reliant upon the ethnographic case study of the Pomio Kivung to be generalizable outside of that case study—and the DMR1 and DMR2 are arguably limited even in that application. It was argued that this pattern of schism and reunification could be better addressed if the leaders and followers were allowed more heterogeneity in their conceptual networks so as to simulate the historical differences between religious schisms (McCorkle & Lane, 2012, pp. 217–18).

The conceptual networks in the models represent a significant limitation for both DMR1 and DMR2 and affect their generalizability beyond the ethnographic account of the Pomio Kivung (Whitehouse, 1995, 2000) because the information held by—and transmitted between—the agents of the group does not follow the statistical distributions noted in the literature on the structure of belief networks and the functions describing information transmission appear to be theoretically underspecified.

Throughout the literature, researchers observe that the links between concepts in belief networks follow a scale-free distribution (Lane, 2015b; Ravasz & Barabási, 2003; Steyvers & Tenenbaum, 2005). However, the distribution of links in DMR1 and DMR2 is closer to a random distribution than a power-law distribution (as discussed in Lane, 2015b). As the mechanisms proposed in both models are not posited to be unique to the Pomio Kivung, but are taken to be information processing devices common to all individuals, utilizing a structure of beliefs which is common to individuals in multiple groups can serve to increase the generalizability of the models and move us closer to a computational model of social cohesion that extends beyond a narrow ethnographic context.

To test the extent to which other types of religious belief networks follow a similar distribution as networks drawn from material in other domains, I utilized a corpus of 480 religious texts and sermons. The structure of the knowledge revealed in these texts never exhibited a random distribution or the quasi-uniform distribution utilized in earlier models of the DMR theory. In all cases, the distribution of links *resembled* a power law with scale-free small-world properties. In order to statistically state that the structure followed the scale-free small-world distribution, two metrics were employed. The first was a conventional measure of scale-free small-world distribution, which is to see if the average path length of the network is shorter, and the clustering coefficient greater, than that observed in a random network with the same probability of connections and number of nodes. The second was a mathematical formalization, proposed by Humphries & Gurney (2008; presented below), which defines a small-world network as one where S > 1. S is calculated by dividing two values: γ is the clustering coefficient of the observed network divided by the clustering coefficient of a similar Erdös-Renyi graph and λ is the average path length of the observed graph divided by the average path length of a similar Erdös-Renyi graph.

$$S^{ws} = \frac{\gamma_g^{ws}}{\lambda_g} \quad (2)$$

The analysis revealed that materials that had a social nature (such as collections of sermons, or religious treatises—e.g., the Pauline epistles in the New Testament) did not conform to the *conventional* definition of scale-free small-world distributions because their average shortest path lengths were greater than would be expected. However, their clustering coefficients were much greater than would be expected, resulting in the social texts satisfying the mathematical conditions outlined by Humphries & Gurney (2008). As such, the evidence suggests that—given the previous critiques of earlier DMR models noted above—the distributions of links in the conceptual networks of the agents in models of doctrinal religious groups should be revised to reflect power-law distributions.

The semantic networks in the computational models of doctrinal religiosity have additional issues as well. For example, in the DMR1, Whitehouse et al. posit that beliefs are transmitted based on their distance from one of four "cognitive anchors"; DMR2 followed this assumption as well.[5] This is an addition from previous formulations of the theory (namely, Whitehouse, 2004), which states that the frequency of belief transmission functions to ensure the consistency of complex belief schemas in the doctrinal mode. This claim can also be tested, and if the mechanism in DMR1 and DMR2 are correct, those beliefs with high betweenness (a measure of how often any one belief is between two others in the network) would have the greatest frequency, since they are along the path between the cognitive anchors and the rest of the network. However, it was revealed that degree centrality (the total number of links connected to the belief, not how often it is between two other beliefs) predicted between 57% and 99% of the variance in frequency of transmission for all beliefs (i.e., concepts) in the corpora. In each case, degree centrality was a better predictor than betweenness (Lane, 2015b). This leads to the conclusion that the original explanation offered by the DMR theory (ex. Whitehouse, 2004, p. 162), that frequency of in-group participation supports accurate recall of complex beliefs, may itself be the result of the complexity of a concept (i.e., the number of other concepts it is related to in a belief schema); with concepts that are more cognitively demanding requiring more repetition in order to maintain the fidelity of the concept's connections to other concepts in the schema.

By using more advanced verification and validation techniques from computer modeling and simulation, we can further the science of social cohesion and our understanding of doctrinal religions. Effectively, the model (which is the computational implementation of a theory) is able to produce data (which are equivalent to predictions) that can be tested against real-world data. When the real-world data does not reflect the data of the model, we can revise the model, just as the scientific method suggests we do the same with non-computationally implemented theories. The analysis of the previous simulations of doctrinal religiosity reveal a number of opportunities for creating a more psychologically realistic MAAI architecture of social cohesion in doctrinal religious groups, and suggests a great deal of opportunity for upgrading those models with the IIS architecture developed in earlier chapters. The first improvement that must be made addresses the computational error regarding the way in which novel information is transmitted, which resulted in artificially high motivation for large population levels. The second potential improvement would be adding heterogeneity to the beliefs and behaviors of agents within the same agent type (i.e., followers, leaders, and new leaders). For example, this could provide the opportunity for different agents to receive teachings at different rates or allow leaders to have unique beliefs. This would also include expanding the model to add multiple groups into a single simulation. The third improvement to be addressed is integrating social identification into the model in a way that is more theoretically valid (i.e., congruent with contemporary social identity theories) than what is found in the DMR2 model (McCorkle & Lane, 2012). This can be integrated with theoretical congruence between the DMR theory and social identification theory given the theoretical integration currently proposed by the IIS.

5.2 Modeling Identity

Two recent ABMs attempt to model identity dynamics in ways that are relevant to the current discussion: one focuses on modeling social identification (Upal, 2015); the other focuses on modeling fusion (Whitehouse et al., 2017b).

As discussed in the previous section, the DMR2 (McCorkle & Lane, 2012) revision to the earlier work by Whitehouse et al. (2012) introduced social identity dynamics into a model of a doctrinal religion for the first time. However, the revision modeled identity as a binary group affiliation: an agent was either in group 0 or group 1, depending on if the agent was part of the traditional religion or schism group, respectively. The models did not address the psychological literature on social identity theory (such as the seminal work included in Brewer, 1991; see Brewer & Gardner, 1996; Hogg & Abrams, 1988; Hogg, Abrams, Otten, & Hinkle, 2004; Jans et al., 2011; Reicher, Spears, & Postmes, 1995; Tajfel, 1974; Tajfel & Turner, 1979, 1986). The key effect of social identity in the model was which leader the agent received teachings from, and these teachings were in no way used to affect identity or strength of identification. However,

Upal (2015) developed a multi-agent model of social identification, aimed at studying identification with religious groups, which employs direct theoretical propositions from social psychology in its development.

Central to Upal's (2015) model is the axiom that individuals strive to maintain a positive self-image and will amend their group beliefs or identification in order to do so—a point which is congruent with the psychological literature. Agents in the model do this by employing two strategies: self-enhancement (the attempt to enhance one's positive self-image from its current position) and self-assessment (the desire to find new information about oneself). They will seek to increase their self-esteem while also utilizing social learning to ensure that their beliefs align with those of their fellow group members. Agents in the model have personal and social identities: personal identities are the beliefs the agent has that make them unique; social identities are the beliefs they have about their social group. Agents also have personal and social aspects to their self-esteem: personal self-esteem is derived by comparing the agent's resources to the other agents around it; social self-esteem is derived by the future gains the agent expects to receive because of their membership with the social group. Agents use this information to derive their group affiliation. This group affiliation can range from -1 to +1 (with negative values representing an adverse relationship and positive values representing alignment with the group and 0 representing indifference). If an agent finds that they can take an action (such as joining another group) through self-assessment, it will—in accordance with self-enhancement—join that group.

This model facilitates several interesting effects. Agents in the model utilize two basic strategies to maintain positive self-image: mobility and individuation. Mobility is when an agent joins another group with a more positive association to increase their own self-esteem. Individuation is the effect of distancing one's self from their social group in order to maintain a positive self-image; as discussed previously this effect is known as disidentification (Bhattacharya & Elsbach, 2002; Elsbach & Bhattacharya, 2001).

Upal's (2015) social identity model provides useful insight concerning a more psychologically relevant way to model social identity that can provide guidance when developing a model of group alignment that can incorporate both social identification and fusion. First, Upal imbues agents with the ability to have personal and social beliefs. This is not the case with previous models of the DMR theory, which were limited only to personal beliefs. Adding this capability can allow agents to align themselves with beliefs that are socially held (i.e., used to define their social category) as well as maintain personal beliefs that make them (i.e., the agents) unique. It also allows for the calculation of extended fusion by analyzing the extent to which social beliefs with emotional associations have been incorporated into an agent's own personal beliefs—as described in earlier chapters. In principle, this variation could allow for an agent to convert to another social identity if they find that their beliefs are more aligned with some other group than their own.

Upal's model also reveals complications in modeling social identification. First, Upal's model is premised on the assumption of having multiple social groups in an environment. This is what allows an agent to evaluate their identity in relation to other groups and thus derive their self-esteem. DMR1 models a single group at a time and models a religious phenomenon that was a localized phenomenon. DMR2 revision (McCorkle & Lane, 2012) expanded DMR1's attempt to model a schism movement by allowing for members of the new group to take on a novel identity. This observation leads to a further complication revealed by Upal: In order for an individual to derive their self-esteem, they utilize information about their own resources and the resources their group is likely to receive in the future. However, the beliefs of religious groups are—by definition—derived from supernatural claims (as discussed earlier; also see Lawson & McCauley, 1990; Spiro, 1966). This complicates any attempt to calculate a "resource" based exchange of their beliefs in the real world with which one could gauge self-esteem; so, behaviors cannot be clearly evaluated by a utility function. Additionally, religious beliefs are—by their supernatural nature—non-falsifiable, therefore, there is no inherent way to judge the "value" of a religious belief. Moreover, intensely held religious beliefs have been shown to be processed by non-utilitarian neurophysiological structures (Berns et al., 2012). While there have been proposals for understanding religion as a rational choice based system (Bainbridge, 2006; Stark & Bainbridge, 1987), such proposals have fallen under heavy critique (e.g. Bruce, 1993; Wallis & Bruce, 1984), largely on the grounds that individuals are not rational actors. Although this critique does not lay claim to reveal some theoretical inconsistency with Upal's model, it does reveal an issue in that without a well-defined—and measurable—way of addressing the resource exchange based on a group's religious beliefs, one would not be able to directly validate the model using real-world data.[6]

In conclusion, Upal's social identity model provides crucial insight into the construction of an ABM for social identification and stands as one of the more interesting and useful models of social cohesion to date. However, for the reasons stated above, religion has many aspects (e.g., goal demotion, non-rationality, it is based on cognitive heuristics) that complicate the ability to extend Upal's rational choice model to address large religious groups.

5.3 Modeling Fusion

The first publication to utilize a computer model to study identity fusion was published during the period of empirical and field research described in the earlier chapters (Whitehouse et al., 2017b). It utilizes an agent-based model, developed in MATLAB,[7] in an attempt to simulate how individual experiences could foster greater cooperation.

The model attempted to simulate the evolution of fusion by addressing the proximate causes of cooperation and self-sacrifice. Their model was ultimately one which modeled trait selection using a two-level Fisher-Wright framework (Schonmann, Vicente, & Caticha, 2011), which was designed for modeling biological selection. In the model, agents participate in collective actions that are either euphoric (if the agent receives direct benefit) or dysphoric (if the agent incurs a loss). In the model, past experiences can affect future cooperation, and cooperation was treated as an individual-level trait (in the biological sense). The fitness of agents was determined by performance in a collective goods game. Those individuals who were in groups that had experienced dysphoria (or fitness decreasing events in previous games), would contribute more in future games. Agents were members of one of G groups ($G = 1,000$) of constant size n (which varied between 4, 8, and 12). Groups that did not survive were replaced by members of competing groups. Since the model working within a biological selection framework, the agents had to reproduce. In the model, the agents would be replaced through successive discrete and non-overlapping generations (i.e., members of one generation would not co-exist with that of another). At reproduction (or replacement), two parents are chosen for each offspring. Their recombination of traits results in the next generation. After reproduction, offspring would be affected by mutation and a probability of being dispersed into a non-kin group. The authors utilized a group selection paradigm (Whitehouse et al., 2017b, p. 3) where individuals are homogeneous within each group.

Given the results of testing their model under different conditions the authors conclude that "dysphoric experience makes individuals contribute more than euphoric experience" (Whitehouse et al., 2017b, p. 4) and that "more intense experience results in stronger effects on prosociality" (Whitehouse et al., 2017b, p. 4). Lastly, they note that within their model the effect of dysphoria on prosociality is stronger in smaller groups: Whitehouse et al. state (on page 4) of the manuscript that "[i]n the models studied above, each individual values the group success equally which implies equal degree of identity fusion," and that those with high fusion will exhibit more pro-group behaviors than those with lower fusion.

As with the social identity model presented by Upal (2015), the fusion model provides aspects to be adopted and others to be critiqued when considering how to build a new architecture of social cohesion and implement it in a computational platform. One example of the fusion model's strength is that it theoretically addresses the role of euphoric and dysphoric arousal in identity fusion. When looking through the source code of the DMR1 model (the first model of doctrinal religions discussed earlier; Whitehouse et al., 2012), it is clear that the model initially intended to incorporate variable rates of euphoric and dysphoric arousal, but this code was commented in the final model to simplify it.[8] However, the fusion model's inclusion of dysphoric and euphoric arousal as unequal contributors to fusion reveals a potential issue with the model's assumptions; namely, euphoric arousal has been shown to be associated with fusion as well (as described in earlier chapters from both ethnographic and empirical research). Not only is this problematic because of the results of the surveys discussed previously, euphoria has also been found to be statistically related to fusion in other studies such as the Newson et al. (2016) paper and in the supplemental material to the fusion model itself (Whitehouse et al., 2017a).

Another complication with the fusion model is that groups are defined on the basis of shared "genetic" correlates in the model. It is extendable to understanding social identification (a sociocultural phenomenon) by weak analogy only.[9] This is related to the complications that arise by assuming a group-selectionist paradigm, which is explicitly stated in the paper (Whitehouse et al., 2017b, p. 3) and implicit in the fact that agents within a group are homogeneous. Given the empirical data in the fusion literature, it is well documented—an uncontested— that there are distributions of fusion levels and not all individuals in a group will be fused—much less have the same fusion level. While population thinking approaches to cultural selection (Boyd & Richerson, 2005) might be able to overcome this, the fact that generations in the model are discrete and non-overlapping means that the only potential information transfer over time in the model is one that assumes genetic correlates of traits between generations. This assumption has never been validated anywhere in the fusion literature. While the supplemental material to the model does include a twin study, the study measured the extent to which genetic relatedness was a better predictor of fusion than shared experiences, and the results suggested it was not. In any case, the assumption obfuscates the extent to which the selection mechanisms of the model are to be interpreted as analogical to cultural or biological selection mechanisms. Most importantly, this highlights a deficiency in the validation of the fusion model, particularly regarding establishing some correspondence between the units and mechanisms in the model and those of the fusion literature. Effectively, the model did not demonstrate sufficient output correspondence (relatedness between the model's output and real-world observations) or mechanistic correspondence (relatedness between the mechanisms of the model and the workings of subsystems of the target phenomenon in the real world) to be useful in our understanding of fusion.

The previous point is the most pressing issue: the fusion model does not model fusion per se. It utilizes prosociality as a proxy for fusion and attempts to model the selection of prosocial groups—which is still a somewhat controversial position because of its relationship to group selection (Knudt, 2015) and the questionable applicability of group selection to human groups (see Nowak, Tarnita, & Wilson, 2010). Although the endorsement of prosocial behavior is a well-documented behavioral output of fused individuals, one cannot say that the model is simulating a fusion process without addressing some theoretically relevant mechanism underlying fusion. For example, the publication notes that fusion is a theory for group alignment that is the result of a porous boundary between one's personal and social identity (Whitehouse et al., 2017b, p. 1). However, identities are not incorporated into the model. As such, it cannot claim to be a model of how fusion evolved since group alignment was never modeled, nor was it a trait that was selected for by any mechanism during the simulation.

One oversight that is potentially addressable without implicating a new architecture in the inapplicable analogies for biological selection is that, as previously stated by Whitehouse and Lanman (2014, p. 690)—among others—that small groups of individuals can bond by mechanisms which are psychologically distinct from that which bond large groups. As such, any model of fusion should address the distinction between extended and local fusion. Utilizing Whitehouse and Lanman's proposal, this requires that a model address—in some way—a causal mechanism for that distinction, such as the relevant memory systems that govern the retention and manipulation of the appropriate information utilized in the cognition of group alignment (the fusion model by Whitehouse et al. did not). In later sections, I argue that the issues noted earlier can be addressed by refocusing the modeling effort to create "psychologically realistic" agents with heterogeneous attributes that are theoretically relevant for the target output using the IIS as described in previous chapters (for further discussions on the importance and theoretical relevance of psychological realism in social simulation, see Lane, 2013; Sun,

2006; Sun & Hélie, 2013). By implementing the different group alignment styles proposed by the IIS (i.e., conceptual ties, relational ties, categorical ties) and the mechanisms that underlie them (i.e., reflection, consolidation, and learning), we can begin to implement a model that has better mechanistic correspondence to the IIS.

One of the greatest strengths of the fusion model is its utilization of past experiences to inform current decisions. This point addresses a critical aspect for any identity model and is attested to by the analyses presented in Chapter 4 discussing how previous experiences can be formative moments for different mechanisms of group alignment. However, the past experiences should be that of the agent making the decision, not assuming that the decisions and effects of one's ancestors bear some inherited effect on more proximate decisions.

The critique presented here rests on the fact that, in a purely technical sense, the fusion model is not a model of fusion, identification, or even group alignment more broadly; it is a model of how—assuming cooperation as a biologically engrained trait—dysphoric and euphoric arousal can affect cooperation in homogeneous groups and can therefore be selected in competitive environments.

5.4 A New Model for Social Cohesion

To address and overcome the limitations of previous models, we can build upon the best practices and efficiencies of earlier research to produce a computational model of the IIS that can function as a psychologically realistic cognitive architecture for understanding the complex relationships and causal cognitive mechanisms that underlie social cohesion. A computational model that applies the IIS framework to understanding the sociopolitical predictions of the DMR theory is valuable because it can produce predictions, in the form of output data, with which to test the claims of the IIS and—insofar as the claims are aligned—that of the DMR theory as well. The data output by the IIS model should have several features. First, as a matter of validation, it should be able to replicate the qualitative dynamics of earlier models of the DMR theory. Additionally, it should remedy the repetition pattern originally noted by McCorkle and Lane (2012); where the model effectively cycles infinitely without any changes in dynamics. Effectively, the previous model had dynamic changes in motivation, but there was complete predictability after a few cycles (the model lacked the ability to output the kind of "entropy" that exists in real-world social systems).

In addition, the data can be used to investigate the following key hypotheses in attempt to validate the model:

1) Levels of fusion and social identification will be positively correlated.
2) Social identification and social consensus will be positively correlated when controlling for fusion.
3) Fusion and the rate of reflection will be positively correlated.

It is crucial that these three hypotheses be addressed as evidence for them is crucial to demonstrate that the model is a valid representation of the IIS. After the model has been validated, the model can be used to test additional hypotheses. For the current purposes, we will start with two. These hypotheses can help us to understand if the individual psychological mechanisms of the IIS can give rise to the predicted sociopolitical features of the doctrinal mode as predicted in the literature (i.e., the IIS and the DMR theory). These two hypotheses are:

4) Social identity should not decrease with population size.
5) Within-group consensus among the followers in a group will be positively correlated with the proportion of leaders in a group.

These hypotheses, discussed in previous chapters, are key features of doctrinal religions that, if the IIS should align with the DMR theory, should be observed in the model's output.

The implementation of the IIS as a computational model can also help to address the strong causal claims made by the theory. In many ways, cognitive science, as a paradigm that focuses on information processing, relies implicitly on strong causal claims of how information is transformed by different functions and algorithms. However, in many of the research methods employed throughout the basket of disciplines that are included under the umbrella of cognitive science, a great deal of them are unable to deal with this assumption of causality. In many cases this is acceptable, as the research still provides an interesting foundation for research and important insights into how these causal claims can evoke different phenomena in different contexts (nearly the entire endeavor of cognitive historiography engages cognition in this way). The research presented in Chapters 3 and 4 cannot justify the strength of the causal claims of the IIS for several reasons: (1) the fact that an individual's social identification is in part derived from the schemas of all other individuals in their group; (2) the memory consolidation process is a dynamic process that happens over time; and (3) the research needs further replication in other cultures with larger samples to solidify its findings. However, by situating these findings within the IIS, a plausible architecture for how individuals come to share information and align themselves with a social group can be created.

Key to implementing the IIS's architecture are the group alignment functions. Here, there are multiple functions which are presented to provide a clearer understanding of how the model works. In the model, social identification is handled through two functions: the first allows an agent to change the social group with which they align themselves, allowing them to change their social identity (this is treated as a nominal variable—akin to an integer in the computational sense); the second reports the level of their identification to that group (this is treated as an interval variable—akin to a double or float variable in the computational sense). Any agent can change their group identity to any other group in the simulation (insofar as there are other groups present in the computational environment) if such a point comes where the group with which they are most aligned conceptually is the same one with which they have the largest number of social links (the mode of all the agent's social links), as these links are formed through calculating the conceptual alignment between schemas held by the agents (recall that in the IIS, agents can hold multiple schemas, such as personal schemas about themselves and social schemas about the social group). Conceptual alignment is calculated as the group with which they have the smallest distance between their conceptual network and the target group's lossy intersection network.

To calculate the strength of an agent's identification, the calculation combines the agent's within-group consensus with the group to which they are identified, the agent's motivation for their group's beliefs, the extent to which the agent attends group events (i.e., rituals), and the agent's fusion level.[10]

In addition to social identification, the model also has to deal with fusion and attempts to do so by addressing the limitations of earlier models, while maintaining theoretical congruity with the earlier empirical research and framework of the IIS presented in the earlier chapters. The model has two mechanisms for addressing fusion: one for local fusion and the other for extended fusion. In the model, agents can attend frequent rituals that have little to no arousal. However, they can also attend "retreats." An agent's group will attend a retreat with the frequency specified by global variables `Retreat-frequency-group-1`, `Retreat-frequency-group-2`, etc., which govern the frequency of retreats for their respective groups. Not all agents will attend each retreat every time, rather it is set based on their interaction frequencies, which are unique to each agent (to provide a realistic heterogeneity among the agents in the model). While in the retreat, agents make new links with members of their in-group, exchange beliefs and motivations with members of their in-group, and receive teachings from their group's religious leader(s). The teachings from the leader come associated with a level of arousal (represented by the variable `teachingarousal`) which is set at 8 (it can also be randomly generated to add stochasticity to the model). If `teachingarousal` is greater than or equal to the variable which sets a threshold of arousal (`Arousal-threshold`) local fusion bonds are created. This is done by having the appropriate agents attending the retreat to set the link weights of links to in-group agents to 999, much like those individuals in the empirical and ethnographic literature who experienced an intense emotional experience at a small group even like a retreat or initiation will also create fusion like bonds. This link represents the strong kin-like bond between the agents as described in the fusion literature. In accordance with fusion theory, these bonds are not dropped after they are created (Gómez & Vázquez, 2015, p. 3; Swann et al., 2012, p. 443).

To address extended fusion, first, the conceptual links that exist in both the agent's personal identity matrix (`my-PID-matrix`) and social identity matrix (`my-SID-matrix`), which have an arousal level (the value stored in `my-arousal-quality-matrix`) greater than or equal the `fusion-threshold` variable are added together; this provides us with the number of beliefs in the schema to which the individual is "fused": that is, the beliefs from the social schema that are also in their personal schema and have an emotional attachment as described in earlier sections' description of conceptual links (see Chapter 3). This value is then divided by the number of possible links (so that simulations with larger schemas are not given an artificial advantage) and multiplied by the agent's level of social identification (to address the interaction between fusion and identification described earlier).

In addition to the changes above, other changes included how new leaders were created in the model. Whereas in earlier models, new religious leaders were created as new agents in the model, the current model exclusively draws new leaders from within the group, selected the individual with the highest level of identification to be promoted to the status of a leader. This is in alignment with most of the ethnographic and historical literature on new religious leaders, where it is rare for an outsider to just appear and be followed by members of the group. Rather, it is far more common that someone from within the group is promoted to the status of a leader. This is particularly true of doctrinal religions, which often have extensive training required for their leaders, and a preexisting institutional structure within the tradition for grooming future leaders. Within the Pentecostal and Charismatic Christian groups that formed the basis of much of the earlier empirical research, this was the case, where even within small-groups (or Bible study groups) leaders for new groups, when required, came almost exclusively from within the group. I only heard of a single case within a Charismatic Church in Singapore where there was a person from outside the group who was allowed to serve in a leadership position (dealing with young adult and youth ministries) in the church before previously being part of the church for a lengthy period of time, and this was due to their previous work as a leader in the Lutheran Church. In all other instances of leadership that I was aware of or observed in Singapore, the United States, and the United Kingdom during the research for this book, individuals who were promoted were typically the most devout and committed from the group. When discussing this with the leadership of one Charismatic Church in Singapore, a senior pastor went as far as to say that when it comes to promoting new leadership from within the church, they aim to find individuals who are committed, faithful, and teachable so that they can exhibit the leadership that most benefits the church.

As discussed earlier, there are two initial tests that the IIS model should undergo in order to verify that it is modeling doctrinal religiosity. The first test is qualitative in nature. It begins with seeking to replicate the findings of DMR1 as presented in Whitehouse et al. (2012) and its revision (DMR2) offered by McCorkle and Lane (2012). In this "face validation" (Sargent, 2013), the model should output decreasing motivation levels which at a certain point will start to elevate with the introduction of a new religious leader. Should motivation levels again fall below the threshold, another new religious leader should be created and reinvigorate the group's motivation. Additionally, agents should be able to change their social network links and social identities. If both of these outputs are observed, one could state that this model subsumes key aspects of both the Whitehouse et al. (2012) and McCorkle and Lane (2012) models while incorporating the theoretical revisions concerning the conceptual networks suggested earlier (which were outlined previously in a more mathematical discussion in Lane, 2015b).

Another qualitative observation that should be produced by the IIS model is that new religious movements are formed. This would be a separate phenomenon from the observation of new leaders introducing teachings and reinvigorating the group; that phenomenon is arguably more related to religious revivals (see Pyysiäinen, 2004 for a discussion of revival within the framework of doctrinal religiosity and cognition; see Stark & Bainbridge, 1985 for a discussion of revivals and new religious movement formation more generally). Ideally, to observe the generation of a new religion within a computational model, you would aim to see a new leader who has been able to form an isolated (or mostly isolated) small network that exists alongside the original network. This would, in principle, be evidence of the simulated formation of new religious movements in a way that incorporates both psychological and sociological processes (from a single architecture) that is reminiscent of the fission dynamics of religious splits that exist generally in the historical and ethnographic record (this is also addressed at length in Chapter 6).

The second test is quantitative. By using parameter sweeps of a subset of all theoretically possible conditions within the bounds of the model, it can test to see under what circumstances are identities stable in doctrinal religions.

These analyses serve to verify (demonstrate that the model is an acceptable representation of the theory at hand) and validate (replicates, in some way, real-world observations of the target phenomena at least as good as previous models) the model. This chapter will employ (1) face validation and (2) parameter variation and sensitivity analysis. The first, face validation, presents a qualitative comparison between the model's target output and some observed phenomenon. This was used in Whitehouse et al.'s original publication of DMR1 model (2012). A preliminary validation will be performed on the model of the IIS that will use similar parameter settings as DMR1 with the aim to reproduce the motivational dynamics reported in Whitehouse et al. (2012). After this, a parameter variation and sensitivity analysis will vary the key parameters and track the output of the model under those conditions. This will allow us to see the conditions under which the theory predicts that some phenomenon should be observed. These settings can then be matched to the real-world observations reported in earlier chapters. In this way an additional, quantitative method can be used to validate the model.

5.5.1 Replicating the Findings of DMR1

Here we can start by discussing the face validation test. This can provide an understanding of the extent to which there is congruency with earlier work and if it can replicate earlier findings. Even though many of the other models of fusion and identification (i.e., Upal, 2015; Upal & Gibbon, 2015; Whitehouse et al., 2017b) were extremely informative in generating computational approaches to DMR theory, the target outputs of those models are orthogonal to our current discussion. As such, qualitative comparisons can be offered but no analysis would sufficiently represent a replication of earlier research. However, this is not the case of DMR1 and DMR2. The current IIS architecture should be able to simulate the target output (i.e., motivation) dynamics—even though understanding motivational dynamics are not the impetus for revising the models to incorporate the IIS. This would be observable if in fact there were evidence from the IIS model that it also exhibits decreases in motivation over time and the introduction of new religious leaders in order to reinvigorate groups whose motivation has fallen below the threshold; and additionally, it should address the shortcomings in the motivational patterns exhibited by the DMR2 model (McCorkle & Lane, 2012).

The initial publication of DMR1 by Whitehouse et al. (2012) assumed that there was only one follower in the model. Because the IIS model does not create new leaders from outside of the simulation, but instead draws one of the agents into a new leadership position, the number of followers in the model was increased to five agents. The full parameters of the replication model can be found in Table 5.3.

The model was simulated fifty times with the parameters mentioned earlier. An example of one of the model runs can be found in Figure 5.2. The experimental run was replicated with only the final mean motivation levels for the group being recorded.

Investigating this pattern across all parameters of the model shows that this pattern is robust. The IIS model, like the DMR1 model, starts with an initial

Table 5.3 Parameter Settings for DMR1 Replication

Parameter	Settings
Homophily-Threshold	.84
the-duration-of-temple-visit	1
Minfriends	3
the-motivation-level-decay-per-repetition	1
the-temple-visit-frequency	3
Retreat-frequency-group-1	365
the-frequency-window	1,000
the-minimum-motivation-level	200
Heterophily-Threshold	.58
ConnectionProbability	.66
NetworkType	"Erdös-Renyi"
the-transmission-rate	5
Initial-population-level	5
Num-of-groups	"1"
the-number-of-leaders	1
the-number-of-new-leaders	1
the-daily-motivation-level-decay	.5
Num-of-beliefs	5

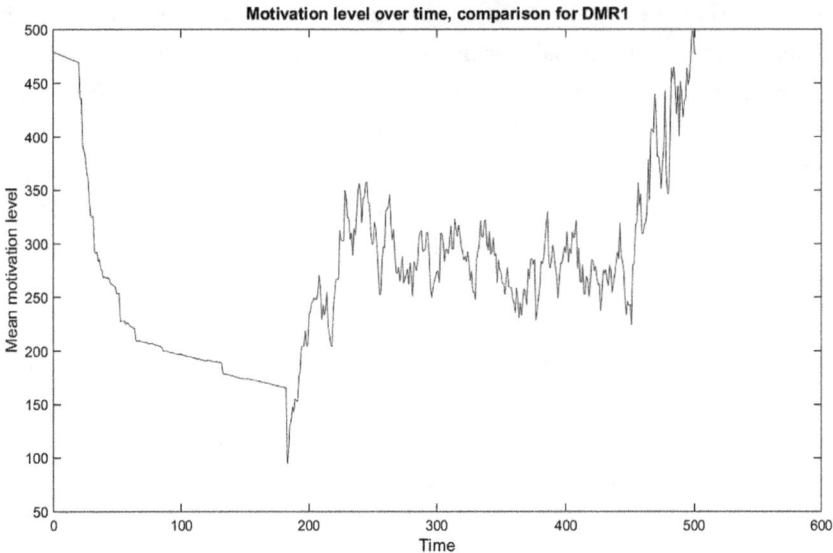

Figure 5.2 Run of IIS model with similar settings to Whitehouse et al. (2012).

decrease in motivation that, eventually (generally after time step 200), reaches the motivational minimum. This then triggers the introduction of a new religious leader. After this leader is introduced the motivation steadily increases. Unlike DMR1, the group motivation does not inevitably reach zero in the IIS model if the model is not terminated after the motivation reaches its maximum following the introduction of the new religious leader; to that extent it could even be stated that the original DMR1 model really modeled secularization—although it was obviously not its intention. Instead, the IIS model exhibits far greater stability over time than DMR1. This is likely due to the dynamic nature of the semantic networks and how individuals can change motivation and beliefs more dynamically than was possible in DMR1.

5.5.2 Additional Features of the IIS Model

The results above provide a qualitative replication of the results of Whitehouse et al. (2012). When setting the parameters of the model as close to the original publication as possible, the model exhibited similar behavior to that exhibited by DMR1. Furthermore, the model does not show identical repeating motivational patterns as new religious leaders become introduced to the simulation (McCorkle & Lane, 2012). Given these observations, this serves as a preliminary validation that the model can replicate the motivation dynamics observed in previous models.

Recall, however, that the key use of the new IIS model is intended to be as a platform for simulating how humans identify with different social groups. When evaluating the model under different conditions, it was observed that (1) the model is able to simulate relational ties between individuals that last the duration of the simulation (corresponding to local fusion); (2) the model is able to simulate categorical ties between individuals that can change depending on their social and ideological context (corresponding to social identification); and (3) the model is able to simulate conceptual ties between individuals that occur after the individual experiences an intense emotional experience. In this way, all three types of ties (relational, conceptual, and categorical) and their corresponding types of group alignment (local fusion, extended fusion, and social identification) can be generated from this architecture. This suggests that the IIS presents a parsimonious and streamlined approach to understanding social stability as the architecture simulates the key psychological mechanisms underlying social cohesion and can generate the group-level effects through the complex interactions of agents in the simulation. Additional qualitative and quantitative tests can be used to demonstrate the extent to which this architecture could be said to (at least partially) subsume other approaches to social cohesion (such as the DMR theory) while integrating a range of other theories critical to our understanding of social cohesion: namely fusion theory, social identification, sacred values theory, and devoted actor theory. In the following sections and Chapter 7, these considerations will be discussed in more detail.

An additional qualitative analysis was run to see if group alignment perturbations could be observed. Group alignment perturbations are defined as instances where an agent changes their group alignment (i.e., a conversion) or where two or more agents create a clique that is not connected to the giant component of their original group (a schism). In the DMR1, the intent was to model a schism as observed in Whitehouse's ethnography, which describes an instance where two individuals from the Pomio Kivung in Papua New Guinea created a schism group, with new beliefs, that broke off from that of the original group. However, this ethnographic even didn't resemble other religious schisms since, eventually, nearly the entire village joined this movement; this pattern has been observed before by other anthropologists studying the Kivung (see Whitehouse, 1995, 2000, 2004). As such, the perturbation in group alignment observed in the Pomio Kivung appears more aligned with a revival movement, than a new religious movement in its own right.

Investigating the space of the new IIS model suggests that it can address shifts in identity (conversions) and the formation of revival movements in a way that is more closely related to the ethnographic and historical record than either of the previous models of doctrinal religiosity. Followers begin to follow new religious leaders as they are introduced when the `mean-motivation-level` of the group falls below the threshold (as in previous models). However, in some simulations the formation of new social groups can be observed as subsets of agents forming new and unique social networks not connected to their previous group. The model can also generate instances where followers begin to identify and accept teachings from a religious leader which was not from their initial group. This instance of conversion also appears to capture the dynamics of DMR2, where agents began to follow new religious leaders. However, the IIS model does so using more psychologically realistic functions, as opposed to the mechanistically forced switching between two binary identities implemented in the DMR1 and DMR2 models. As an example, Figure 5.3 depicts a model run where a new religious movement has formed; that is to say, a follower is now accepting teachings from a new religious leader and neither have connections to their previous group. This screenshot was

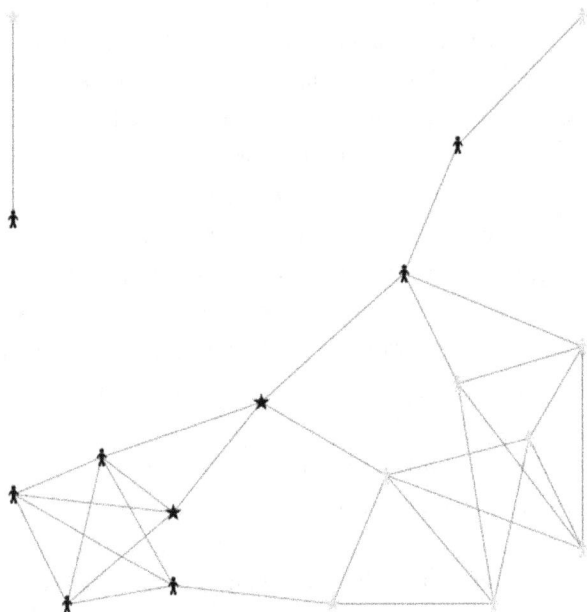

Figure 5.3 A conversion to a new religious movement within the simulation. Parameter settings are the same as those in Table 5.3 with the following exceptions: num-of-groups = 2 (initialized with the colors black and grey); initial-population-level = 9; homophily-threshold = .51; toroidal was turned off for purposes of network visualization. Leaders had their shapes changed to appear as "stars" rather than "people."

captured approximately 100 ticks into a simulation run with two groups. In the upper left-hand corner of the simulation space we can see that a follower from the black group has become linked with a leader from the grey group. They have formed an isolated dyad apart from the giant component of the rest of the agents in the simulation. Shortly after, this black agent's color changed to grey, signifying that they now identified with the grey religious leader's teachings. An additional observation worth noting in this visualization is the presence of a grey agent in the upper right-hand corner of the figure. This agent (a follower) still identifies with their initial group but has not yet converted to the black group. However, they have dropped all network links (as described earlier, this results from beliefs shifting so that there is a large conceptual distance between agents) to their original group. This observation is discussed further in the discussion (see Figure 9).

In addition to the qualitative observations of the model described earlier, the IIS model, as with all computational models, also provides the ability for hypotheses to be tested using data generated from the model. Here, the data comes from extracting the data from each agent in a simulation to test for statistical significance regarding the hypotheses discussed earlier. Indeed, all hypotheses are accepted by statistical analysis of the agent-level data. Testing hypothesis 1 reveals a significant correlation between fusion and social identification ($r_s = .99, p < .01$). Testing hypothesis 2 using a partial correlation revealed that there is a significant correlation between social identification and within-group consensus when controlling for fusion ($s = .93; df = 12147; p < .01$). Lastly, the relationship between fusion and reflection was also found to be significant ($r_s = .14; p < .01$).

Now that the key features of IIS instantiated in the model have been statistically validated, the model can be used to investigate other claims. These claims address the extent to which certain sociopolitical patterns are generated (or emerge) from the individual agent-level interactions of the computer model. The target sociopolitical relationships predicted by the IIS and the DMR theory include the idea that individuals can maintain social identities even in groups where not every agent interacts with every other agent in their group. Furthermore, it is expected to be the case that groups with a higher ratio of leaders to followers will be able to maintain a greater level of within-group consensus since, as discussed previously, leaders provide teachings to members of the group, providing stable points of access to orthodox information. Lastly, this model will be used to address a subsequent question, which is given in the IIS framework, *How frequently should rituals be undertaken to maintain*

Table 5.4 Means for Social Identity by Group Size

Group Size	Mean SID	SD	95% CI
15	618.9	474.05	[595.66–642.15]
50	423.11	423.11	[767.3–788.93]
150	822.34	392.73	[816.48–828.2]

conceptual stability and motivation within a group?[11] I now present the results of testing the hypotheses:

4) Social identity should not decrease with population size.
5) Within-group consensus among the followers in a group will be positively correlated with the proportion of leaders in a group.

In testing hypothesis 4, the model results reveal that social identity does not decrease with population size, showing that large groups can be sustained when not all agents have links to other agents. A one-way ANOVA found that social identity increases as population sizes go up ($F(24742) = 193.891$; $p < .01$; see Table 5.4).

In testing hypothesis 5, the results reveal that there is a significant correlation between the proportion of leaders in a group and the amount of within-group consensus that is sustained ($r_s = .16$; $p < .01$; 95% CI [.15, .17]). Further analysis shows that there is a positive correlation between within-group consensus and the actual number of leaders in the group ($r_s = .32.$; $p < .01$; 95% CI [.30, .33]) and a negative correlation between within-group consensus and the number of followers ($r_s = -.16$; $p < .01$; 95% CI [.-.17, -.15]).

6

From AI in Silico, to AI in Situ

Creating AI Gurus, Bird's Eye Views of Christianity, and Using MAAI to Study Social Stability

The model in Chapter 5 suggests that the IIS architecture can be a powerful tool for understanding important aspects of culture and religion. Its ability to reflect how we become attached to beliefs provides an interesting insight into the many flavors of commitment and social cohesion that anthropologists and historians have observed throughout history. The ability for cohesion via conceptual ties to bind a large group has many potential effects for future research to explore, from the kind of identities that shape world history through the adoption and changes in the world religions, to the large-scale economic cooperation required to facilitate the Neolithic transition 10,000 years ago, which saw a shift in many human groups from a life limited primarily to small kinship bands to the large civilizations we see today.

The ability for the IIS to address conceptual ties that lead to the patterns of social cohesion observed in human history also motivates questions concerning its ability to address how these same patterns of social cohesion might explain conflict. In the IIS, the suggestion that a conceptual tie is one that blurs the line between one's personal and social group has several byproducts, some of which were described in Chapter 3. One of those is drawn from fusion theory, which suggests that, for individuals who are fused, an attack on their social group is akin to an attack on them personally, and vice versa. In a conflict situation, where individuals from one group are engaged in the targeted harm of individuals in another group, individuals are likely to look for markers that can define their in-group, wherein they can find protection and cooperative partners, in relation to those individuals in groups which would not provide the positive protection and cooperation offered by their in-group. In some situations, particularly those where most parties in the conflict share a race and ethnicity, religious beliefs, which may not be as outwardly observable, can become important information markers for in-group and out-group boundaries. In such situations, it is possible that conceptual ties become key markers of the conflict, even if those beliefs serve little function in defining the conceptual disagreement between the parties themselves.

This can help provide a framework for understanding some complex religious conflicts, such as the period known as "the Troubles" in Northern Ireland. Understanding a little bit about the history of this conflict can help us to understand its relevance to the IIS model, and how comparing the output of the IIS architecture to the historical context can provide useful validation through output correspondence.

The Troubles are colloquially discussed as a religious conflict, even in many scholarly treatments of the subject (e.g., Juergensmeyer, 2000). Framing the Troubles as a religious conflict is defensible in some studies but may not be the most efficient way of describing the conflict. Heuristically, describing the conflict as one between Protestants and Catholics is not false. Largely, the two groups in the conflict did identify as Catholic or Protestant. However, when looking at the root cause of the conflict, the differences between the two groups were not rooted in religious beliefs but in secular beliefs. This framing of secular conflicts between religiously identified group is one of the many issues with claiming that a conflict or act of terrorism in a conflict is "religious," despite the speed with which many scholars and the general public alike identify something as a "religious conflict" or "religious terrorism" (see Gunning & Jackson, 2011 for a more in-depth discussion). Initially, the conflict in Ireland was rooted in issues of political sovereignty (specifically the Irish Home Rule movement) and the partitioning of Ireland leading up to the Irish War of Independence. When Ireland was granted home rule (although not sovereignty in the sense that it has today), Northern Ireland, which had a majority Protestant population at the time, was not, largely for political reasons. The Catholic population of Ireland (both in the North-East Ulster counties, known today as Northern Ireland, and the Southern counties, known today as the Republic of Ireland) were motivated to fight because they felt oppressed by what was a foreign Monarchy in the UK. In Ulster, the Protestant majority were largely Unionists, supporting the British power structure, while the Catholics generally were Republican and supported independence or home rule in Ireland; the disagreements between the Unionists and Republicans were not rooted in theological disagreements, but secular disagreements. In fact, the text of The Republic of Ireland Act, 1948, which established the independence of Ireland doesn't mention religion at all. In more recent issues, those statements made by members of the "Real" Irish Republican Army (IRA) who carried out the August 1998 bombing in Omagh, killing 29 people and injuring over 200, were framed in secular terms related to the political relationship with the UK, not in religious terms related to Catholic and Protestant groups (a point raised by Goodwin, 2009). Here, I am not suggesting that religion was not important in the conflict. To the contrary, religious identities were very important to the conflict. Furthermore, I believe that this statement should be taken with the full acknowledgment of the fact that the extent to which one considers the conflicts in Ireland (and I would suggest all religious conflicts) "religious" or not is highly dependent on the definition of religion being employed, as suggested by Mitchell (2006). However, within the framework of cultural cybernetics described here, religious beliefs and behaviors are not primary motivations for the violence, but the identities that are constructed through holding and participating in religious behaviors (for example, rituals) are important to defining the social structure in which the violence is enacted. In this way, religion might not be a primary motivator for violence, but it was a "flag" that was flown by both sides of the conflict and therefore represents a critical dimension of the conflict that cannot be dismissed. As such, in the analytical approach used here, as in the daily lives of many in Northern Ireland, the Catholic-Protestant dimension, although not a root cause of the disagreement, can be an efficient heuristic from which one can draw on to define in-groups and out-groups.

The Troubles of Northern Ireland reveal an interesting historical dynamic to the IIS, which is the role of a social identity as a heuristic way to assume other information about the beliefs of other people. That is to say, a person, going into certain pubs in Northern Ireland and proclaiming one's political beliefs can be met with acceptance (and possibly cheers) or rejection (and possibly violence) depending on the congruence of one's political beliefs to that of the audience. However, if one proclaims themselves to be of a specific religion, the audience is likely to use that as a heuristic to attribute beliefs to that individual; moreover, the beliefs attributed to that individual are disconnected to the actual beliefs of the individual. That is to say, if an individual who believes that the British have fair right to rule over Northern Ireland publicly describes himself to be a Catholic, the audience in that context is likely to assume that he believes the British have no right to rule Northern Ireland (among other beliefs). In this way, there appears to be an additional issue of out-group perception in these conflicts, where it is not enough for an individual to hold a belief that is different from their own, but the fact that they are in an out-group provides additional anxiety that can escalate the potential for conflict.

So far, the information that informs our identities and the mechanisms processing this information have been treated as largely internal to the individual. However, the previous example suggests that these mechanisms are informed by otherwise orthogonal cognitive processes, such as threat perception. In the literature on threat perception, it has been suggested that ritual behavior in general can be motivated by perceived threats (Boyer & Liénard, 2006; Keren, Boyer, Mort, & Eilam, 2013; Liénard & Lawson, 2008). This framework fits well within the large body of literature in social psychology that has found that being reminded of one's own death or mortality can strengthen religious beliefs (Jong, Philip, Chang, & Halberstadt, 2015; Vail et al., 2010). The IIS's focus puts many of the claims of the threat perception literature outside of its purview. However, by taking some of the key claims of the threat perception literature, and integrating it into a single architecture alongside of the IIS's key identity functions, we can develop a more comprehensive framework for the study of social cohesion and conflicts described as "religious conflicts."

The MERV (mutually escalating religious violence)[1] system does just this. It took a previously existing framework that presented a theoretical integration of the terror management literature and the threat perception literature and created a single simulation for experimenting on the proposed cognitive system (Lane & Shults, 2019; Shults, Lane et al., 2017). In the previous system, four threats were identified from the literature in evolutionary psychology: social threats, natural threats, predation, and contagion. It was proposed, based on an extensive review of the literature on these themes, that social threats and contagion activate those relevant aspects of our evolved cognitive processes that manipulate our perception and acceptance of group boundaries, while natural and predatory threats active those relevant aspects of our evolved cognitive processes that manipulate our perception and acceptance of natural and supernatural explanations and perceptions.

Taking this model, we integrated its basic functions of the IIS into the framework, to allow for further experimentation on the role of conceptual ties in the explanation of intergroup conflict. One of the key additions was the introduction of dynamic conditioning into the IIS model. Conditioning, in the psychological literature, is the process by which an individual's response becomes more (or less) predictable given a stimulus from the environment that reinforces that response. In its most simplistic form, this form of learning can be seen in reward systems: if we do something good, we will get a reward for the behavior, and receiving this reward in conjunction with the behavior reinforces that behavior; this is the general basis for reinforcement learning. The most well-known case of this kind of learning is from the classical experiment in psychology of "Pavlov's Dogs," where in the late 1800s a Russian psychologist named Ivan Pavlov was investigating salivation in dogs when they're being fed (Pavlov, 1906, 2010). He noticed that the dogs salivated when the technician who fed them was around, even if they were not being fed. This suggested to him that it wasn't just the food that caused the dogs to respond, but that this biological capacity can also be paired with something "learned" (i.e., the presence of someone who usually feeds them). He then began to pair the presence of food with the sound of a bell. Eventually, he found that the dogs began to salivate when only the bell was present, and that the unconditioned stimulus (salivation in the presence of food) was paired with a conditioned stimulus (the sound of a bell). Effectively, as the salivation-reaction to the bell was reinforced over time by receiving food, the dogs learned to respond to the bell as well. Rudimentary as this formalization is, it represents an interesting starting point for simulating how an evolved cognitive function can produce results in new environments through a kind of reinforcement learning (where something is learned by receiving some kind of feedback from its environment).

In AI broadly, simulating the processes of reinforcement learning represented a major breakthrough in the field and has led to many systems that we use today such as robotics and the management of supercomputers, but its most wide ranging application is likely to be in the personal recommendation engines and the question and answer systems used by companies such as Google (e.g., Buck et al., 2018). Cognitively, our understanding of conditioning and reinforcement is fairly mature, the contemporary roots of the mathematical models of conditioning and reinforcement date back to the work of Robert Rescorla and Allan Wagner in the early 1970s (see R. A. Rescorla & Wagner, 1972). Like all models, this model has its limitations, but it has been used fruitfully in the past, including in new approaches to modeling culture and even religious phenomena (see Epstein, 2014). The Rescorla-Wagner model also has its benefits, such as being able to demonstrate properties of over-expectation, which is the decline in response to two (or more) of well-established conditioned stimuli in conjunction with each other; which is something that we observe in the empirical literature of humans (e.g., D. J. Collins & Shanks, 2006) and nonhuman animals (e.g., Kehoe & White, 2004; Witnauer & Miller, 2009), but is not produced by many common machine learning systems (see Dawson & Spetch, 2005).

The Rescorla-Wagner learning function can be formalized mathematically for any abstracted stimulus-response paring using the following equation:

$$v_{t+1} - v_t = \alpha\beta(\lambda - v_t) \qquad (3)$$

Although it may appear complex, this equation can be simply explained: t is an index of the number of times there is an observation of both stimulus and response, so $t = 1$ is the first time it is presented, and $t = 2$ for the second time; λ is the maximum strength that could happen when the stimulus and response are observed together, so it represents an upper limit to the system; α is a number that represents the salience of a conditioned stimulus, which is a stimulus that initially elicits little or no connection to a specific response, but we learn to associate with a specific response over time; β is a number that represents the salience of the unconditioned stimulus, which is a stimulus that represents a response that hasn't been conditioned. With Pavlov's dogs, the unconditioned stimulus is the food, which elicits salivation, and the conditioned stimulus is the bell, which produces a conditioned response of salivation.

Utilizing the Rescorla-Wagner model to simulate the generative emergence was first prototyped by Joshua Epstein (2014), where he included this basic system in each agent, but agents existed on a network, that could transmit information between agents, including their emotional level. This allows agents to be affected by their social contacts by simulating the effects of emotional contagion. As their response strength grows, it can be set up to trigger certain behaviors such that if v is greater than a specific threshold, a behavioral response is triggered. In MERV, the dynamics of emotional contagion between agents was added to the original identity functions idealized for earlier research into the IIS. This allows emotions to increase in realistic ways through both the personal experience of the agent and how they obtain information socially from other agents in their network.

In addition, when a stimulus is presented without a reward (say, a bell without food) learned responses can begin to decrease over time. When a response pairing begins to go away like this, it is called extinction. However, over time, stimuli come and stimuli go, leading to dynamics where thresholds can be activated depending on the observations, experience, and context of the agent, and in a system where the state of any one agent is affected by the information it receives from other agents in its social network, who are themselves affected by their unique environment and social contexts, you can get complex behaviors that become difficult to track over time, but nevertheless can be fruitfully utilized in a simulation where the individual, their social contacts, and physical environment, all play a role. As described in Chapter 1, these complex interactions, which can be computationally defined, can be theoretically discussed as components of a cybernetic assemblage to help to structure how we approach this level of complexity (see Figure 6.1).

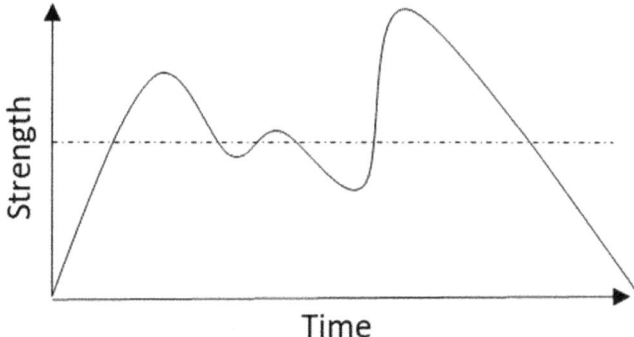

Figure 6.1 Visualized output of the Rescorla-Wagner model with threshold marked as the dotted line as an agent experiences multiple exposures and social feedback.

In Epstein's original prototypes, he only utilized three basic agents. These agents typically had one belief or response and were connected so the network always resembled a triad of connected agents. When the MERV system was developed, I changed the code to allow it to flexibly handle any number of agents with any number of social links. This allowed the agents in the simulation to interact in more realistic ways with a more realistic number of agents (more than two for example) and in network constructions that are more realistically created. In our work, we were able to experiment with scale-free small world social networks, which have been found to be similar to human social networks in many contexts (Humphries & Gurney, 2008; Travers & Milgram, 1969; Watts & Strogatz, 1998). We also implemented the ability to construct networks based on the demonstrated evolutionary constraints for human social networks in the real world, where we typically have concentric circles of individuals with varying closeness, and an upper limit of the number of social network ties we can manage of around 150 people (Conti, Passarella, & Pezzoni, 2011; Dávid-Barrett & Dunbar, 2013; Dunbar, 1992; Dunbar & Sosis, 2018; Gonçalves, Perra, & Vespignani, 2011; R. A. Hill & Dunbar, 2003; Russell A. Hill, Bentley, & Dunbar, 2008; Saramäki et al., 2014; Stiller, Nettle, & Dunbar, 2003; Young, Hébert-Dufresne, Allard, & Dubé, 2016; Zhou, Sornette, Hill, & Dunbar, 2005). By simulating much larger networks, we could look at larger social systems and begin to simulate scaled versions of entire religious communities (Shults, Gore et al., 2018; Shults, Toft et al., 2017).

This advancement in simulating the previous architecture not only included more agents and complex networks but also drew from the IIS's assumption that individuals hold multiple beliefs, which in the case of conceptual ties, can lead to extreme and even violent defenses when challenged. This simulation included such beliefs, and posited that dynamics of associating different intergroup interactions, in conjunction with the defense of conceptual ties that are defining of one's personal and social identities, can lead to the generative emergence of violence over time. As discussed earlier, pervious research has shown that when dealing with "sacred values" people will fight and die for those beliefs and do so using "deontic," or if-then, reasoning (Berns et al., 2012; Ginges, Atran, Sachdeva, & Medin, 2011; Sheikh et al., 2016); so the relationship between the stimulus and response is more black and white. This is to say, if someone violates a sacred value, then an individual will respond to its violation. Therefore, using a threshold model that governs the actions an agent takes in a given (simulated) social situation is—in this case—defensible.

Investigating this model led to several discoveries. In experiments with two groups, the two groups exhibited a tit-for-tat behavior, with one side attacking the other, and then the attacked group responding, and then the first group responding to that, and so on. This observation was surprising, as tit-for-tat strategies have been put forward as the evolutionary stable strategy for cooperation by evolutionary game theorists for decades (initially put forward by Axelrod; see Axelrod, 1984; Axelrod & Hamilton, 1981). This finding has been reiterated (and—insofar as it is relevant from the modeling and simulation aspect—replicated) many times and the conclusions from this work have been used as a foundational claims in more recent theories in the cultural evolution of religion as well (Johnson, 2015; Norenzayan, 2013; Wilson, 2002). However, in these earlier studies, the format of the computational model is based in the rules of game theory, which means that the assumptions of game theory (such as rationality and access to information, etc.) are built into that model. In the MERV model, the assumptions of game theory did not bear on our architecture. Our assumptions were not rooted in that of Homo Economicus (the economic rational agent in a game theory paradigm). Rather, our assumptions were rooted in the cognitive study of homo sapiens. This was reflected in assuming, for example, that humans interact in constrained social networks and interact in a geospatial environment and that the emotional state of another individual affects our own emotional state. In this way, it suggests that the MERV extension to the IIS architecture can subsume the result of this earlier game theory research, while relying on more valid assumptions coming from cognitive psychology and human evolution, as opposed to the assumptions of game theory, which despite its limited utility, are questionably relevant to the reality of human decision making in complex social contexts such as in times of intergroup conflict and sacred values; this is at least the case given that game theory assumes rational actors while sacred values are not processed rationally or even in the same parts of the brain as utilitarian thinking (Atran, 2006a, 2016; Atran, Sheikh, & Gómez, 2014b; Berns et al., 2012; Ginges & Atran, 2009; Ginges, Atran, Medin, & Shikaki, 2007; Gómez et al., 2017), and fusion theory appears to follow similar irrational behavioral outputs (Besta et al., 2015; de Gelder & Hortensius, 2014; Swann et al., 2009; Whitehouse et al., 2014). So, from this perspective, it appears that the IIS has touched on key mechanisms that can allow for the behavior of the tit-for-tat cooperative approach to be subsumed under more psychologically realistic assumptions.

However, further research is required to uncover to what extent the model's predictions about tit-for-tat behavior are relevant. Perhaps it is in a small area of the entire theoretical space that the model covers, perhaps it is the general rule. The research to date on the MERV model suggests that the model can generally produce this effect under areas that are relevant to the study of human violence. So far, the MERV model has been applied to two historical cases of mutually escalating religious violence: the Troubles of Northern Ireland and the Gujarat Riots. These two cases are interesting comparison cases because the Troubles lasted for nearly four decades, while the initial Gujarat Riots lasted less than four days. However, in both incidents thousands were injured or killed. In both cases, religious identities were the group markers amid a background of political tensions that erupted into large-scale violence before settling down. In validating the model against these systems, the MERV system was not "trained" in the case of typical machine-learning-based AI. Rather, it was allowed to test to see if the patterns of anxiety and violent interactions that it simulates do so under parameters that match the historical record. It was found that this approach can be used to study religious violence, and with great accuracy (Shults, Gore, et al., 2018). The general dynamics, of an initial "pop" of violence, followed by a longer tail of tit-for-tat violence was found, this also simulates other statistically based models and historical observations on the distribution of violent events during such conflicts (Bohorquez, Gourley, Dixon, Spagat, & Johnson, 2009; Clauset & Young, 2005; González-Val, 2015; N. Johnson et al., 2011; Roberts & Turcotte, 1998; Small & Singer, 1982), suggesting yet another area where utilizing a psychologically realistic MAAI approach is beneficial.

When validating the output of our model to that of the historical record in Northern Ireland, we utilized an interdisciplinary technique from the modeling and simulation literature called "trace validation," where "characteristics of agents and the model are tracked over time and then analyzed by subject matter experts to gain insight" into the outputs of the model (R. J. Gore, Lynch, & Kavak, 2017, p. 273). During the validation of the model, we found that we were able to match the overall pattern of violence over the forty-year period. In addition, we utilized "The Beast" (the custom supercomputer at the Center for Mind and Culture) to analyze tens of thousands of different scenarios to better understand our new model of social instability. Ultimately, we were able to extract and analyze 5 million data points from the simulation and found that the escalation of anxiety that we see between religious groups during periods of violence is relatively rare (only occurring in less than 25% of all observations, and not all observations would have led to real-world violence if we were to extrapolate it to actual human response). Although the statement "religious violence is relatively rare" might seem shocking given the way that such events are portrayed in contemporary culture, this is because we are all susceptible to the "availability bias," which is a bias toward thinking that examples that come easily to mind are generally representative of something; making it natural to think that religious violence is more prevalent than it is, when in fact, most religious people go about their lives without any notable event occurring, much less one of intergroup violence.

This shows one way in which computer simulations can help our understanding of complex social systems. In the past, we have largely relied upon interpretive frameworks for understanding complex social systems like religions, cultures, economies, etc. But this approach is more reliant upon the internal whims of the interpreter than a well constrained and falsifiable study that could reveal unexpected results. Computer models present an interesting opportunity because they provide a way of harnessing large amounts of data, including data from scenarios that are reminiscent of historical counterfactuals for understanding what could have been.[2] In this way, the framework of the approach is formalized with strict logic, so that even if the model is intended to be interpretive, rather than explanatory, it can be replicated and critiqued with less propensity for the debate sliding into semantic arguments prone to ad infinitum debates and a lack of progress due to polysemy. In this way modeling and simulation can create a more open, clear, precise, and interdisciplinary approach so long as the epistemological concerns are appropriately taken into account (for a more in-depth discussion on this point, and how to avoid pitfalls in interpretive modeling, see Lane, 2019b).

This simulation also fosters questions about what the future of this could be. If the MERV model were to leverage the data-mining algorithms used to validate the IIS model mentioned earlier to analyze "big-data" streams of information coming from social media sites or data available to intelligence operations, could it affect our ability to predict religious terrorism? Setting aside the ethical implications of this momentarily, I would argue that we could predict, with a certain bound of probability, religious terrorism in the near term, but due to the feedbacks and complexities of the numerous actors and environmental factors at play, as the time horizon of the prediction is pushed further away, our ability to predict would lessen to the point of being random guesses at best (Lane, 2017a). In the next section, I discuss new big-data approaches that address the first steps toward integrating these methods.

6.1 "Big Data" and the Bird's Eye View of Religious Identities around the World

The IIS-based models here have shown how we can use basic MAAI systems to create a useful understanding of some of religion's most impactful facets. However, one of its drawbacks is that the data that was used to validate the system came from either small selected groups, using field research, or specific historical test cases. One trend in contemporary AI research has been to leverage "big data" in order to test and train new AI systems based in machine learning. Using the analysis techniques of big data, we can further test claims related to the IIS, to better understand how social cohesion is affected over time and during periods of conflict or crisis.

"Big data" has become somewhat of a trendy and overhyped word recently, particularly in the social sciences and (digital) humanities where the term has been bandied about frequently in order to attract more attention as the humanities and social sciences are squeezed by STEM fields for funding (a note which I'll return to in Chapter 8). One issue with the trendy use of the term "big data" is that it overlooks the way that the term is used in academic fields of computer science and, more importantly, how it is used in commercial industries, where the actual big data is being generated and stored. Big data has many different definitions. But generally, in computer science, definitions of big data focus on three key aspects: complexity, size, and technology (Ward & Barker, 2013). These aspects are useful to help us understand how big data can fit into the study of complex social systems from a cybernetic perspective and evaluate the extent to which the use of the term "big data" is, or is not, used appropriately.

The complexity factor of big data is debatably important, and there is not a lot of consensus concerning the importance of data "complexity" in computer science.

Typically, "complexity" here refers to the fact that the data is not structured. It includes texts, images, names, audio, locations, demographics, social network information, and/or many other data variables that are interrelated in some way. For example, Twitter and Facebook are great examples of big-data companies by anyone's measure. These companies are processing millions of posts that are tagged with pictures of an individual, the text of the post, how many likes or favorites it gets, how many shares or retweets it gets, and the links to those "followers" or "friends" on the social network who interact with the post. Religious studies almost by definition deals with complex data—despite the fact that it is rare that the data is digitized. Religious studies deals with beliefs and behaviors, enacted by people who are part of groups that exist in a particular place at a particular time and interact with one another using different cognitive mechanisms and an information-rich environment that—from the cybernetic perspective advocated in Chapter 1—is at least partially responsible for the rich myriad of forms that religious beliefs and behaviors can take in our world today. On the face of it, religion is well fit for big data.

The size factor of big data is its most notable factor (hence the name). Typically, the volume of data that is being referred to is extremely large. Some definitions, such as that embraced by Intel, suggest that big data are those datasets which grow by a median amount of 300 TB each week (Intel IT Center, 2012). This amount of data is hard for many to imagine. However, to put it in perspective, we can do a little bit of size comparison to the digital form of the King James Version of the Bible. Let's take a basic text file (not anything fancy, like a Microsoft Word file) of the Bible.[3] This file comes in at approximately 4.2 megabytes (MB). The information contained in that text file has supported thousands of scholars throughout their entire career and hundreds of thousands, if not millions, of man-hours have gone in to analyzing the text. By Intel's definition of big data, you would need to produce about 71.5 *million* unique texts of the same size as the Bible, every week, to qualify as big data. Naturally, this amount of information is daunting—if not unfathomable. To put this in perspective, the Center for Mind and Culture has been indexing all works on the scientific study of religion going back to the late 1800s. Included in their database are just over 15,000 papers. Although the scientific study of religion is growing at an alarming rate, those 15,000 papers represent a fraction of a fraction of a percent of the data required for their definition of big data. So, while the typical size of religious data is not qualifying for big-data, the way that we extract religious information from big-data sources does offer us a new horizon for research. For example, you can follow the Pope on Twitter (@Pontifex), where he has 18.1 million followers on his English language Twitter as of 2019; he also has another 17.3 million on his Spanish language Twitter (@Pontifex_es). Joel Osteen, the American Christian pastor and leader of the Lakewood Church in Houston, Texas has 9.2 million followers (@JoelOsteen) making him one of the most influential pastors on the internet. These two leaders alone have generated millions of tweets and responses in a wide ranging global social network that is part of a dataset that generates over 300TB of data weekly, which satisfies the definition of big data. Another source for relevant big data is the wider internet itself. Religious organizations from all over the world post material online in order to engage their current membership, foster a tighter social connection with their community, and—of course—evangelize with the hopes of getting their message out to a wider audience and bring in more members. Later in this chapter, I'm going to discuss a new research project that I've led that has used web-scrapers, web-spiders, and search results from Google in order to scour the internet for text transcriptions of sermons that can be analyzed using modern big-data methods and AI systems.

Of course, there is a logistical issue with collecting, storing, and analyzing all of this data, which leads us to the third aspect of big data: the technology. This can refer to the technology used to collect and store the data. For example, in order for Twitter and Facebook to work, it requires a massive technological infrastructure with servers that have software that can automatically scale up in order to balance the changes in the number of users that are active on the platform at any given moment. For example, in order to build a system large enough and keep it from overheating, Facebook invested the money in order to build a massive datacenter in Luleå, Sweden (in the Arctic Circle), where using natural permafrost and arctic temperatures helps to keep their datacenter cool and operating at lower costs than it would if built in other places. The other side of big data's technology is the hardware required to analyze the data. The average computer only has about 8 gigabytes of memory available to analyze information at a time. This is well below the terabytes of information required to analyze large datasets in the realm of big data. However, some computers exist that can analyze much larger datasets. For example, while working at the Center for Mind and Culture, myself Prof. Wesley Wildman designed and built the first "supercomputer" in the field of religious studies (lovingly called "The Beast"), which, at the time, was the most powerful single machine at the university. It was able to process 1TB of information at once and had over 120 cores (your laptop probably has 8) that carry out simulations, scripts, or other analyses simultaneously. The other option for data scientists today is called "high-performance computers" (HPCs). Without getting too technical, these supercomputers effectively wire together thousands of smaller computers into a "computer cluster" and allow for analysis programs and scripts to be distributed across the computers in a cluster.

The technical limits of most computers are also an interesting place to set a definition of big data that could be useful for the social sciences because once you begin to deal with data that is too large to be analyzed on a single computer, you typically have to utilize the same kinds of solutions to answer a question using 3TB of data as you would 300TB of data. Therefore, it can be useful to say that big data is a data source that is a complex dataset that is too large to be opened and analyzed by a single computer and has the ability to collect data over time. This definition is more simplistic, less limiting, but still an equally valid way to demarcate where big data begins and ends for the study of complex social systems, despite its differences with its traditional use in computer science, which is a more strict definition.

When we define big data this way, it doesn't really exclude any obvious data sources for studying religion. Online social networks like Facebook, Twitter, and Reddit are still obvious candidates for big-data studies, and there are some studies of religion on those platforms (particularly Twitter; see Adamczyk, LaFree, & Barrera-Vilert, 2019; Ritter, Preston, & Hernandez, 2013). In addition to these sources, I had mentioned that the internet more generally can be a great resource for information about religion because of how many communities are posting religious material (such as sermons) online. Religious material online is—relative to the age of the internet—rather new to cyberspace. Early on, religious leaders largely didn't see the need to put information online because the business of religion was face-to-face. However, just like the brick and mortar stores that dominated the malls of the 1990s have embraced the internet and moved online, religious leaders too have realized that engaging their congregations online can be a key channel for transmitting religious information and maintaining the social cohesion of their groups.

Today, the internet is filled with a variety of religious organizations, from new religious movements to the pope's Twitter feed and likely your neighborhood church, synagogue, mosque, or temple has an internet presence of some kind. This data isn't all found in a single database like the data for Facebook, Twitter, or Reddit. Therefore, we can't just query a database to return the data we want. Instead, we need to be more creative. In order to create a database of sermons in the United States, I utilized a set of web-scrapers and web-spiders[4] to find, structure, and store sermons online. This can allow researchers to utilize search engines, like Google, to search for a specific thing such as "church sermons" and return the links that Google finds. From this list of links (which can be hundreds of thousands) you can create "bot" like programs to harvest the data from those websites automatically. This kind of data retrieval is extremely efficient at getting massive amounts of historical and archival data from a wide variety of sources, but is almost never utilized by researchers, despite how common the practice is in corporate industry and in the technologies—like Google—that affect our daily lives.

What resulted from these efforts was a database of about 150,000 sermons from thousands of churches all over the world, and in multiple languages (I only realized after the program had run that any limits to stop it from gathering translations of sermons or sermons from churches in multiple languages was never programmed, so the original dataset included sermons primarily in English with Spanish, French, and several other languages included as well). This is, at the time this book is published, the largest research database of sermons in the world.[5] I analyzed the data from this sermon project using multiple methods common to data science and AI research.

The first method, which is common to data science is commonly known as topic modeling (its more accurate name is Latent Dirichlet Analysis, or LDA). This method takes the words in the corpus and extracts clusters of words that form the key topics discussed in the texts. This can give us a "bird's eye view" of what the key themes are in the text.

One key metric used in AI research to create classification systems for texts is known as TF-IDF (term frequency-inverse document frequency), which helps us to automatically extract what the key terms and concepts are in a body of texts. Here, the first dimension of the measure is term frequency (TF). Simply put, this is the number of times a term appears across all documents in the corpus. The second dimension is inverse document frequency (IDF), and that measure counts the number of documents (or sermons, in this case) that the term appears. It then sets that as 1/DF in order to get the inverse. In this way, it helps to better understand what terms "define" a set of texts. For example, while terms like "pray" might appear in every sermon, that doesn't mean that it is a useful feature for classifying subsets of sermons, as it isn't very unique to a specific subset of the sermons and likely appears at least once in most sermons in the form of phrases such as "let us pray" or "the lord's prayer." However, terms such as "damnation" or "war" are not likely to be features of every sermon, but instead appear in only a small subset of the sermons in the corpus, and therefore are more likely candidates for useful features to define subcategories of texts.

The two dimensions also can be taken together to describe the probability that a corpus relies on a specific term, as well as the extent to which a word is defining of a specific corpus.

Terms that are flagged using the TF-IDF method can then be used as definitional for sub-topics in a topic analysis. The multidimensional nature of these topics, and the way in which they're embedded within a text, can also be reduced to two dimensions for visualization purposes. This can help us to understand the differences between two sets of texts in a corpus.

Using the data from the web scraped sermons, I wanted to investigate the extent to which sermons changed before and after the terrorist attacks of September 11, 2001. This date is interesting as a point in time for pre-post analysis of Christian sermons in the United States for many reasons. One, this event seriously challenged many aspects of the American worldview by bringing conflict directly onto American soil for the first time since the attacks on Pearl Harbor that got the United States into the Second World War. Two, the event was framed by politicians at the time as an attack on the American worldview and way of life, juxtaposed against the worldview of "the terrorists" (Lincoln, 2006). Lastly, because of this, many churches were framed as viewing the attack in terms of religious in-groups and out-groups. These reasons make it a fascinating point in time to group sermons around because, if the event was as significant as scholars suggest, we should be able to view clear differences between those before and after the event.

For these reasons, 9-11 offers an interesting venue for testing theories about why worldviews change and what the nature of that worldview change is. For example, theories rooted in Darwinism would suggest that the abrupt and significant change in the environment should reflect a corresponding shift in the worldview of the group as it adapts to a new cultural environment.

However, a cybernetic perspective takes a slightly different perspective because its focus is on proximate information processing mechanisms and their effects, as opposed to fitting observed changes into patterns addressing more ultimate causal patterns. The cybernetic perspective doesn't look at changes as a matter of fitness but does accept that there can be functions for worldviews that make them more or less useful. As such, worldviews are likely to change in response to specific events, but they do so as a result of human cognitive mechanisms (and their heuristics and biases), not as a function of selection of random mutations between worldviews or their transmissions (as difficult or impossible as that may be to define before the event in any case). From the perspective of the IIS, these worldviews serve as critical information-based signals for group inclusion, and sermons are—as described earlier—an extremely important mechanism for the transmission of this information. While worldviews can also provide secondary benefits and functions such as making sense of a complex world, providing dissonance resolution, providing a framework for decision making and behavioral schemas, etc., its ability to define who is and is not in a group is of particular importance during times of perceived threat. In uncertain times then, we wouldn't expect worldviews to radically change in response to major perturbations in the environment. Such perturbations would create noise in the signal that could negatively impact how we can discern who is—and is not—a member of our in-group and thus a reliable exchange partner for goods, services, help, aid in resource acquisition, mate finding, child rearing, etc. Rather, in times of great perturbation or threat, we would want to see a worldview get more simplified, so that we can easily identify who is—and is not—in our group.

Examples of easy-to-understand signals in response to threat abound throughout the animal kingdom and are not limited to religion. In fact, any complex social system whereby consensus and group alignment are at play appears to be implicated. However, in the modern world, we often misunderstand their function. Take for example aspects of national and civic identity during the events of the American election in 2016. During that election, Hilary Clinton was the obvious choice for most Americans. Her political pedigree and decades in the political spotlight made her the presumptive winner of the election. Meanwhile, despite several more qualified candidates from the Republican Party, Donald Trump was able to energize a small minority of supporters to edge out his competition early on and become the nominee for his party. In a head to head race, all logic and history suggested that Clinton would win the presidency in the general election. During the election however, one of the nastiest and most slanderous campaigns in American history was run by both sides, who leveraged and fostered an increase in perceived threats. On the one hand, Clinton and her followers questioned the stability of Trump to have access to the nuclear codes—causing obviously reasonable doubt in the minds of many about the security of the country under a Trump presidency. In addition, Trumps supporters were compared to terrorist and called "deplorables" by Clinton and her supporters—causing doubt in the minds of many about how they might be treated under a Clinton presidency. On the other hand, Trump and his followers regularly questioned the extent to which Clinton's actions best represented American interests and if she could be trusted to protect the country by noting her handling of private emails and the Arab Spring (focused on the security issues around the 2012 Benghazi attack).

These are but a few examples, of which there were many, where Trump's and Clinton's actions and words focused on perceptions of threat from members of the opposite party that not only heightened threat perceptions but would have presumably engaged identity mechanisms key to the IIS as well. In an environment of perceived threat, the two groups were regularly signaling in-group commitments. In hindsight, it appears that a clear signal built around perceived identity threats prevailed against the odds. While I do not wish to spend too much time on this point, it could be worth considering the extent to which modern elections are won by tapping into clear identity signals.

In a post-9-11 world, a cybernetic approach suggests that a similar process of identity signaling in a time of threat may have happened in church communities. One hypothesis is that before 9-11, churches felt less threatened, and were able to extend their worldviews to focus on many different aspects of daily life, as signaling exactly what the group stood for was less important. After 9-11 however, it was imperative for the churches to not only discuss the issues of the day to help their congregation interpret the events but also to provide clear signals of what the group stood for so that they can effectively say "we believe in X" and if you do too, then you're one of us. In this way, churches can be viewed as more conservative in that they are less tolerant of deviation from a core set of fundamental values (some may call this fundamentalist—within some bounds I would agree).

To begin to test this, I worked with a dataset that was gathered using a big-data technique called web-scraping, whereby a program searches the internet for some target (in this case, sermons) and saves and processes the data from the website where the target data can be found. What resulted was the largest research database for sermons collected to date. The dataset includes over 150,000 sermons from over 5,000 churches going back to the 1970s that are geolocated and timestamped. When looking at the data, I grouped the sermons by the census region of the church from which they were collected. By doing so, I effectively capture religions in the United States that are approximations of different cultural zones (the south, the northeast, the west coast, the Midwest, etc.). I then grouped the sermons by time period (pre- or post-9-11). When analyzing the key concepts from the sermons the results in every region followed the same pattern: the relative frequency of the key terms increased, but the terms themselves didn't change (see Figure 6.2).

This suggests that the worldviews were not adapting by *selecting for* new beliefs to better fit a new environment (as would be hypothesized by theories drawn from cultural evolution and social Darwinism). Rather, the worldviews increased the relative frequency of its key terms. From the cybernetic approach

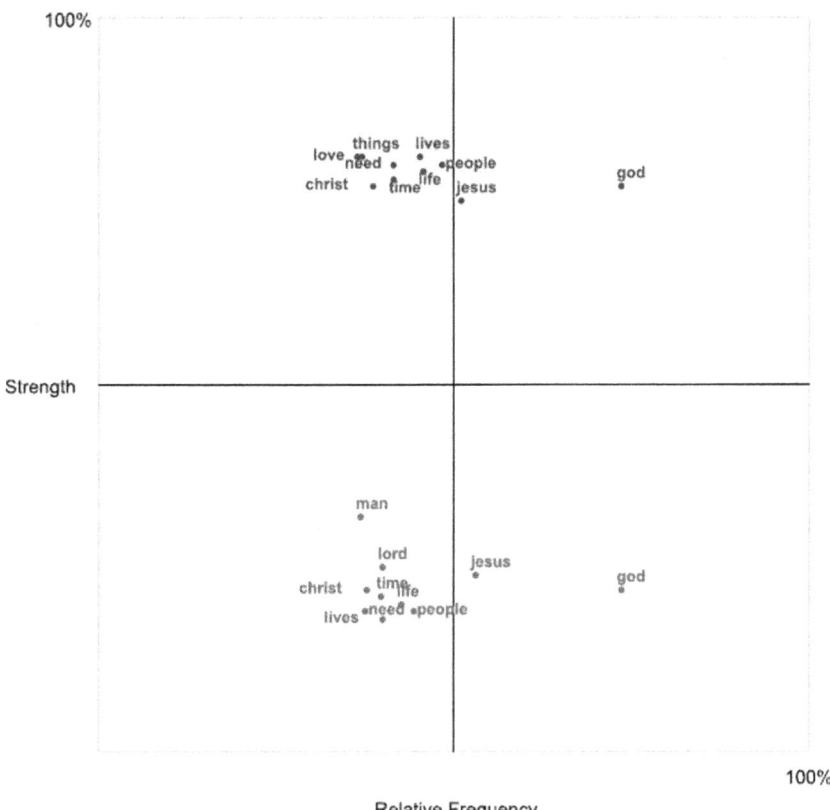

Figure 6.2 Results from analyzing the strength and frequency of key terms drawn from sermons in a census region. The red data in the bottom cluster is from sermons that were given before 9-11 and the blue data in the top cluster comes from sermons given after 9-11.

proposed here, this has a clear function: to signal more clearly the key beliefs of the group so that the core concepts of the group (those concepts that are most likely fusion targets for reflection) are presented clearly and frequently. This fits well within the IIS's cybernetic framework as beliefs that serve as clear identity markers could be regularly encoded into semantic memory. When the group finds itself in a context of perceived threat, where the evolutionarily advantageous position would be to engage with a social group for safety and security, it would be beneficial to have clear information signals about who is, and is not, part of the group that shares your beliefs—and possibly shares similar targets for extended fusion via conceptual ties.

Further analysis of this data can also be used to further investigate other aspects of social cohesion from an information processing perspective, such as leadership. For example, if there is some increased environmental stress, where the imperative for having a social group for safety becomes greater, and our individual cognitive systems are under greater pressure to quickly make reliable decisions, the information processing systems that engage the IIS could be affected and noise from other aspects of our environment could affect our ability to discern clear identity signals. As such, effective group leaders should adapt a group's message to be more clear in more stressful environments and can allow for more relaxed presentations in more secure environments. This suggests that when socioeconomic stresses occur, there should be more clear messages from religious leaders. A similar effect could happen more generally, wherein under perceived stresses, individuals would become more prone to clearly signal their agreement with a large social group. This effect, as an evolved capacity, may also affect how we interact socially in online social networks, wherein our evolved cognitive mechanisms would still be operational, but activated for interactions that are outside of the scope of evolutionary influences in past generations. As such, those who are under more perceived threats could be more prone to perceive, seek out, and produce in-group information signals in order to affect their hazard precaution systems and decrease their anxiety by means of "online" social participation with an otherwise disembodied group.

One way of testing if leaders present more clear or predictable information during periods of increased environmental stress is through a concept called entropy, as discussed in Chapter 1. There are many kinds of entropy in the scientific literature, and it is often equated with "chaos." Recall that entropy (as defined by Shannon) is, in a word, the "predictability" of information and has been used in the study of human communication (Ferdinand, Kirby, & Smith, 2017; Xu & Reitter, 2018). Effectively, when studying a text or corpus using entropy, one is looking at how much "information" a text has based on how predictable the words of the text are. In an absolute way, this measure is not so useful; for example, to say that something has an entropy of 5 is not as qualitatively interesting for someone researching human language. However, relative to one another, different levels of entropy can be revealing, for example if one set of texts has an entropy 8 and the other has an entropy 5, it can be informative to note which of the two texts has lower entropy.

Applying this to the sermon corpus earlier, we can calculate the entropy for the tens of thousands of sermons that were collected. Entropy can be calculated at the level of the individual text in order to statistically test if there is a significant effect of socioeconomic stress on entropy. One way we can begin this kind of investigation is through testing if there is a statistical relationship between the average unemployment rate in an area and the entropy of the sermons in that area. By taking the unemployment rate data that is publicly available, this can be calculated and it was found that there is a significant negative correlation between unemployment rate and entropy, suggesting that as unemployment rises, entropy decreases—in line with the prediction of the IIS. In addition, further tests can be used to test if this relationship between entropy and identification is related to the key variables of the IIS, such as social cohesion. For example, we can look at the data from a historical perspective and measure how language that is religiously themed or signaling of group "tightness" (Gelfand, Nishii, & Raver, 2006; Gelfand et al., 2011; Harrington & Gelfand, 2014b) changes in relation to socioeconomic conditions (while this analysis was run in R, basic analyses can be run in software such as LIWC; see Pennebaker, Booth, & Francis, 2007). In the United States, the recession of 2008 changed the economy for the decade that followed. As such, we should see the proportion of a text dedicated to religious language and cultural "tightness" rise after the 2008 recession. After calculating the amount of religious language and tightness for each sermon and grouping them, based on the month that they were given, as before or after the financial crash, it was found that there is in fact greater religious language and language denoting cultural tightness after the onset of the 2008 recession than before, in line with the predictions of the IIS (Lane, 2016, 2018a).

6.2 AIwaken

The data can also be used to train new AI systems based in machine learning. As discussed in Chapter 1, machine learning has several shortcomings that MAAI attempts to overcome. However, the use of machine learning can still provide useful information and provide an interesting understanding of issues surrounding the role of learning in religion. In recent years, AI systems have been used to try and create more and more human-like materials, from news sources, to books and plays, to music and poetry. However, one domain that has largely been neglected is religion. To date, no AI system has been trained exclusively on religious material, although, there is one being trained on the written material of Grundtvig, an important theologian and philosopher for modern Danish society (see Lane, 2019d). While many of these AI systems are trained on data from social media or Wikipedia in order to better create natural language that appears human-like, most of these training sets do not include a lot of religious material. As such, these AI systems (as "intelligent" as they might appear in answering trivia questions) are effectively mute or evasive when discussing religion. For example, one of the most advanced AI bots currently is Hanson Robotics' robot named "Sophia." Sophia has been giving interviews around the world, speaking at trade shows, and appearing on TV. In one instance, an interviewer asked Sophia, "What is god?" The answer that Sophia gave seemed stumbling and contrived: she replied, "In monotheistic thought, god is conceived as the supreme being and the principal object of faith."[6] I believe that this is because the data used to create that system was largely drawn from secular sources. Indeed, the Wikipedia page for "God" presents, almost word for word, the exact same answer: "In monotheistic thought, God is conceived of as the supreme being, creator deity, and principal object of faith." So it isn't so much that Sophia knows anything about God, so much as Sophia's programming allows her to get the information from online resources (a clever trick that should not be discounted and is extremely powerful as a building block in its own right). However, this leads to the question, what would it be like if we train an advanced AI system to understand human language like Sophia, or Google does, but only use religious material drawn from the database of religious sermons?

Given the corpus of sermons discussed earlier, this becomes a very answerable question. Using the Google Cloud system I was able to create a new AI system (based on the GPT-2 system by OpenAI; Radford et al., 2018) that we've named AIwaken. This system, however, is not the same as the MAAI system described earlier. AIwaken utilizes an unconventional kind of artificial neural network in order to learn associations between concepts and the frequency with which they co-occur. In this way, AIwaken can extract the semantic associations between terms and allow itself to construct its own texts with frightening grammatical and conceptual accuracy. This system has the capability to construct an unimaginable number of novel sermons that have never been spoken or heard before. AIwaken could go a lifetime, spreading its word every Sunday to congregations and not have to reuse a sermon it had given in the past. To date, I have produced many sermons with the system, but the first one is worth consideration. Here is the first sermon produced by an AI system:

```
I was given a very valuable life lesson that day. It
was a lesson that is inextricable from the lessons
I have learned in the past. It was something that
has never been taught in my life. It was a spiritual
lesson that was the cornerstone of my life. In fact
at first glance it sounds so easy to give you a reason
to give your life a life of your choosing. I am glad I
```

can show you the lesson at the beginning. Just as the beginning of life is the lesson that holds forever, the end of this lesson is the lesson at the end that holds forever, but as in the beginning it becomes so long that you don't know what to expect. And so I teach this lesson because I want them to know that it is a spiritual lesson that is inextricable from the teachings of Jesus Christ. The lesson you've learned at the beginning is really, really hard to teach, and it makes you think that you can continue to teach it. It makes you want to jump through hoops to get into the next stage when you're at the beginning of this lesson. In fact when you're at the middle stage, you've learned that the next best thing to teach is the teaching. The next best thing is not teaching or teaching by preaching on to your kids. The next best thing is to teach their principles by using our understanding of God's Word to teach them the lessons they need to know to make their faith go. I would like to share this lesson with you. So just like Jesus I tell you that this is not the way man is supposed to live life, I want you to do this for him. I want you to share this lesson with me. You need to get up early and take it to your children. They are in your life all the time and you've never yet come across them as being unruly. The things going on in those moments are so overwhelming, the things going on in those moments have so much power and influence on them that they can affect your life as you mature, what's happening to you, what's happening to your family and how can you possibly do the things Jesus is able to do for you? No, you need to trust Jesus and to give him faith in making the right choices for your life. You need to trust Him by giving Him something now. Don't worry about things as they happen. He cares about you. He has everything you need to do for your life. He wants to go ahead and help you grow and be a better Christian now. He wants to have you make the right choices for your life. Have faith! And I'll be right there, at the end of this lesson I want you to give up the battle and go with what Jesus has said.

> Don't try to stop you from doing the things He is doing because you can't use this battle, and He will use it. And you can't use him to use you because there isn't anyone against you. You can be a saint of your lives. You can be a soldier of God because of your prayers. You can spend your life in a place for the Lord—a relationship with your Savior—that you really need to get over the barriers that are on your life, to grow spiritually, and to do the things He is able to do for you. For the way you look at the world, the way you look at your own relationship with Jesus Christ—this is just a different world of God—this is very different place. This can never be the same again. God can have a world and His children will live around Him, and there will never again be people who are out there, who are not following the way we have to live, but just coming to Jesus Christ through the power of the Lord. This will never be the same again. Look at the world of the people He is setting up—in a different way and not the way you have to live. This is a world of people who have no reason and no God, but Jesus is saying that if there is no one on this world, that they will always die. It is not that they are evil. It is not that they don't do the things of God, they have no reason to do them. This is the way God planned it, this is the world they live in. If there is no one you have to do them, then we could never do them. You can get away with murder, but it just doesn't matter which way you look at God. You have to start somewhere. You can't just come here because you are in a prison.

There are some interesting features to this sermon worthy of consideration here. First, AIwaken rambles, but not unlike someone speaking in an unrehearsed manner. Secondly, AIwaken has put together a remarkably readable sermon (albeit hard to logically follow) with surprising grammatical accuracy as well as the faint outline of a general arc about how we can learn the lesson of what most Christian pastors would call discipleship.

The system can also be tuned to answer questions from other user input. For example, when asking AIwaken the same question that Sophia was asked earlier ("What is God?"), it produces a far more interesting answer that appears to be much more "heartfelt" and even almost faith-based and personal compared to the Wikipedia derived answer provided by Sophia:

> What is god? It is not just the word of God that we have. God is in us, makes our lives meaningful and impacts how we think and live. God does not just act on our behalf, we have to act on behalf of God. God is active in our lives and in the lives of others. God is involved in our lives as well. God is watching over us and working through our lives to help us. God is there to lead us in our own way. God's presence in our lives is not just for us to be present. God is in our lives to be part of our lives. God is in the churches and in our lives to be part of their lives.

AIwaken is also useful because it can help us to define the problem space of religious information transmission based on social learning. As discussed in Chapter 1, these kind of neural network AI systems are typically used to solve a problem or complete a task, such as classifying a text. While AIwaken could be used by religious leaders to write their sermons for them or inspire them in regards to new topics that they haven't thought of, AIwaken doesn't really solve a practical problem beyond this. It can, however, help us investigate how far we can get theoretically by proposing that religion is based on information transmission exclusively. This is because the system here is not imbued with the evolved cognitive mechanisms that we have, or even the basic identity mechanisms that the MAAI system is. AIwaken is fairly limited theoretically to creating sermons based on information that it has received (despite how powerful the system is in its intended domain). In this way, this system is only a social learner.

Investigating the sermons AIwaken produces, and common patterns therein, we find that it lacks some interesting abilities that human religious leaders have. Specifically, while AIwaken system shows basic creativity, it does not appear to be able to create new minimally counterintuitive properties—or at least none that I have yet seen in the sermons it has produced to date. This is because the transmission of minimally counterintuitive information is social, but its processing is done by mechanisms that are not the same as those used in social transmission. This is not to say that minimally counterintuitive concepts are not processed by social transmission mechanisms at all. Quite the contrary, it is obvious that memory, learning, attention, and reproduction mechanisms common to all social information transmission are also used in the transmission of minimally counterintuitive concepts. However, there is something about the processing of minimally counterintuitive concepts that goes further than that. As described by Boyer and Ramble, there are cognitive mechanisms implicated in the perception and processing of concepts that include the tacit knowledge that we bring to bear on our assessments of concepts. These assessments are related to the expectations we have for different ontological categories with which we associate a concept, and variations from this knowledge (which does not need to be socially learned, but does appear affected by social learning; see Upal, 2017) that affects attention and mnemonic advantages for some counterintuitive concepts (Boyer & Ramble, 2001).

This understanding allows us to appropriately frame the role of social learning in this extremely important mechanism that underpins human culture and religiosity. As first proposed by Afzal Upal (and later reframed by Purzycki & Willard, 2015; for the original formulation of the idea, see Upal, 2005a, 2010, 2011), our social context can affect what we view as "normal." For example, if a specific culture believes that statues can be hungry, then this belief would be minimally counterintuitive (all things being equal) because statues, as inanimate objects, do not have urges or feelings like hunger. In this way it should benefit from the minimally counterintuitive effect of "hunger" for a time. However, generations later, that culture could have statues that can be hungry, tired, grant wishes, heal the sick, bring good fortune or luck, and walk around at night. By most definitions, having six counterintuitive properties would be considered "maximally" counterintuitive (not minimally) and would therefore not receive any benefit—the theory would suggest that it is too counterintuitive to be easily remembered (in fact, without looking a few lines above, you probably can't remember what the six properties are, despite it being mere seconds ago). However, these statues that can be hungry, tired, grant wishes, heal the sick, bring good fortune or luck, and walk around at night might be easily remembered by a culture where statues are regularly hungry, tired, and grant wishes because those three features are so common to their concept of statue that only healing the sick, bringing good fortune or luck, and walking around at night would be considered counterintuitive.

For AIwaken, all minimally counterintuitive concepts are given equal attention and are just as likely to be remembered and recalled provided that they have the same statistical dimensions in the corpus. In this way, we can see how social learning, which provides important information for our minds, is not sufficient to create a truly religious mind. Quite the contrary, social learning is secondary to the more primary evolved cognitive mechanisms. Naturally, both are important here—and in the cybernetic approach I propose generally—

however, without the rich architecture of evolved heuristics and biases that we have, our religiosity can only go so far, and would only be so deep. In fact, without these biases, our religiosity would not exist at all. While AIwaken is inventive in some respects, it does not appear to have the capabilities to invent a new god for example. With only its learning capabilities (as impressive as they are) working on material devoid of religious information thousands of AIwakens interacting would not have been able to produce the first religion. The reason AIwaken can produce the rich sermons that it does is because it has already learned these concepts from others (through social learning) not because it can create such concepts on their own. As of now, it still takes a human to create a religion, even if AI could be dangerously close to leading one.

6.3 Conclusion

This chapter introduced previous and ongoing research efforts to better understand social cohesion in large complex social groups, specifically focusing on the dynamics of doctrinal religions. Using techniques from modeling and simulation, combined with AI and big data, it demonstrates how contemporary analyses can provide insight into age-old questions about religious violence and social instability. The utilization of these methods represents a new horizon for the scale of research for the study of religion and culture.[7] Another key contribution has been bringing the study of religion up to speed with current technology by utilizing supercomputers and big-data algorithms for text analysis. To an extent, this contribution is secondary because computers with great power are "just" a tool for running models of well-formulated theories. As such, the weight of any such contribution could be primarily measured by the power of the theory in question. However, due to the computational requirements of the simulation, when addressing complex theories in the social sciences, computational models would not be possible without high-performance computing systems.[8]

In the future, computational models like the ones discussed here can also serve additional purposes. For example, they can provide a basis for testing counterfactual situations that may resemble historical or potentially future situations. As such, the model can serve as a tool for understanding historical as well as contemporary phenomena. Perhaps more importantly, computational models and big-data driven approaches to the study of religion can also address critical concerns and do so in a way that can be relevant to policy makers and stakeholders outside of the "Ivory Tower." In the book *God's Century*, Monica

Toft and her colleagues present the argument that religious considerations will be more important, not less, in understanding the future sociopolitical context of the next century (2011). Even if religious considerations maintain an impact that is at least somewhat reminiscent of the last two decades, it will be an undeniably important feature of public policy moving forward. However, the ability for policy makers to understand the complexity of religious systems is limited. The focus of many policy makers in the West has been, understandably, concentrated on non-religious aspects such as the economy and more general expansions of civil rights. It was the events of 2001 that caused religion to take its contemporary place in the minds of policy makers, and then, it was primarily treated as an issue of security and defense, whereas before (particularly in the United States) religion was used to leverage votes and garner support. Since then, religion not only has played a big part in policies related to security, defense, and intelligence, but it has also played a notable role in emergency responses to natural disasters such as hurricanes in the United States, typhoons in the Pacific, and the earthquakes and tsunamis globally.

In addition, social cohesion has affected the ability for countries to maintain stability and experience the growth and investment that comes with social stability. For example, in many countries in developing nations, social instability is a serious barrier to investment, both in terms of supporting innovation and infrastructure. Its causes are debated, but even in analysis looking at the relationship between investment and macro-economic factors like income distribution, it appears that social cohesion (manifested as internal discontent) is a key mediator between macro-economic factors and the kinds of sociopolitical stability that can be barriers to investment in developing nations (Alesina & Perotti, 1993; Benjamin, 2012; Gyimah-Brempong, 1999). The relationship between social cohesion, religion, and larger macro-economic trends is largely unexplored, despite its potential relevance to the global economy and a group of stakeholders that includes nonprofit NGOs, policy makers, and large investment banks. The extent to which simulations like this can help us better understand the effects of potential policies or investment decisions, by instantiating the rules or context changes into the simulated environment is largely an open question. While simulation has been a useful tool in policy making for some time (for examples, see Ahrweiler, Schilperoord, Pyka, & Gilbert, 2015; Conte et al., 2012; Gilbert, Ahrweiler, Barbrook-Johnson, Narasimhan, & Wilkinson, 2018), it is still a generally new method for policy makers and rarely adopted despite its obvious benefits for decision making; rather, policy decisions are typically made using methods more common to the humanities and social sciences.

On the other side of the spectrum, in banking and finance, the use of computational and statistical models is extremely common, and the use of such algorithms have had demonstrable effects from "flash crashes,"[9] to impacting the extent to which an investor is more informed about their market (Gsell, 2008). Trading algorithms are currently used by 95 percent of the largest institutional traders and it accounts for an estimated 20 percent of the trades on the US equity markets (Paskelian, 2010)[10] and 80 percent on the foreign exchange currency markets (Bigiotti & Navarra, 2019). However, these algorithms are not known for considering dimensions related to religion or culture. Generally, the algorithms are statistically based and when AI is included, it is based in machine learning, not the kind of algorithms discussed here that are more well founded in the cognitive literature. Developing methods and products to engage in this disconnect could be a valuable endeavor and help a host of stakeholders to make better decisions concerning many of the world's most important issues and opportunities. However, a cybernetic perspective like the one I suggest here is only now being explored, and when it is, it is being done largely outside of the purview of academia. Given the strength and importance of these economic systems, and the impact they have on the everyday lives of so many, we should critically assess how much value could be produced by integrating a well-founded, scientific, human perspective that looks to address causal factors, not only interpretive factors, from an evolutionary perspective.

7

Schisms and Sacred Values

When we think about how religion has shaped human history, we are often led back to examples of religious schisms. Schisms are when a subset of a religious group breaks off and becomes a new religion. One of the most prominent examples is that of Christianity's split from early Judaism. While entire volumes have been written about the subject, the general consensus is that the state of Judaism 2,000 years ago was fractured into many different groups. The Sadducees occupied a space high on the legal and socioeconomic system, while the Pharisees were more occupied with daily life for most Jews at the time. However, large groups also existed on the periphery, such as the Essenes. The Essenes may have been related to the group that produced the Dead Sea Scrolls (Eisenman, 1998), although there is debate surrounding that with good points for and against the idea. However, the Essenes appeared to believe in a more aesthetic Judaism where fasting and prohibitions were commonly practiced. In addition, they appeared to hold messianic beliefs, or beliefs that the end times were near, and that the messiah would come to deliver the Jews and usher in the kingdom of God. Against this backdrop there were many religious leaders like Jesus, although Jesus is undoubtedly the most famous (for overviews of early Christianity and Second Temple Judaism, see Ehrman, 2008; Schiffman, 1991). The movement that came after Jesus, led largely by Paul—rather than James, the brother of Jesus (for a more comprehensive overview of James and his role in the early church, see Eisenman, 1998)—found unprecedented success and has affected history from East to West and even caused us to change the very way that we count the years as they pass.

In the grand view of history, the Judeo-Christian schism is but one of many. For example, the schism of Buddhism from Hinduism and the impact of Buddhist thought and practice over the past millennia is undeniable. Its effects have ranged from philosophical debates on nearly every continent to the conversion of royal courts throughout Asia.

On the one hand, religious schisms are more common than we might think because—as discussed earlier—most leave no historical record. Small groups of believers form new religious movements, and fade away as members and leaders die off, re-assimilate into the original group, or find new religious paths in their life. All of today's "world religions" have produced schisms and were themselves—at least partially—the result of schisms as well.

On the other hand, schisms have also brought to the fore a darker side of religion. Schism groups have been behind some of the most extreme forms of religious violence in history. For example, the suicide of the nearly 1,000 members of the People's Temple discussed earlier, or the 1995 Tokyo saran gas attack perpetuated by the Buddhist schism group Aum Shinrikyo. Most recently notable, schism groups from extremist Sunni Islam, such as Al Qaeda and the Islamic State (or ISIS) have carried out horrendous attacks across the globe. Most obvious among these are the attacks on 9-11 in the United States and attacks on the London Subway (known as the 7/7 bombings) and the Paris Nightclub shooting of November 2015, but throughout the world, these groups—particularly ISIS—have been behind a multitude of public beheadings, rapes, murders, and besieged entire cities. Despite being documented as a complex lineages of schisms from the fringe of fundamentalist Islam (McCants, 2015), these new religious movements in Islam are not typically viewed in light of religious schisms. Instead, they are viewed only as terrorist organizations, despite the fact that theories addressing new religious movements can be applied to our understanding of religious terrorism and parallels between terrorist and non-terrorist new religious movements can be informatively drawn (Lane, 2011). From the perspective of the IIS, there are theoretical perspectives relevant to both religious schisms (Lane, 2018c) and religious violence (Lane et al., 2018; Shults, Gore et al., 2018, 2017), which suggests that future research should attempt to utilize the IIS to make more clear predictions to explain the rise, and potential futures, of such groups (Lane, 2017a).

Earlier chapters presented evidence suggesting that fusion is a prominent form of group alignment that may result from reflection on central and emotionally intense experiences. However, reflection is proposed to have a negative effect on within-group consensus by introducing new and idiosyncratic beliefs. Research has suggested that there is a positive relationship between frequency of in-group ritual attendance and within-group consensus; that is to say, those who attend rituals of their group more frequently (every Sunday as opposed to just on holidays) are more able to produce the standard beliefs of their ingroup.

Given the tendency of fused individuals to approve of self-sacrifice, display intense pro-group behaviors, and endorse extreme out-group punishments, fused individuals appear to be most committed members of the group. However, assuming a negative relationship between fusion and within-group consensus might suggest that fused members of the group drive conceptual and ideological changes in the group. If highly committed members of the group are introducing new beliefs that they codified into their understanding of the group through personal reflection, their beliefs could diffuse and introduce new beliefs into the group over time.

Approaches such as Whitehouse's DMR theory propose that idiosyncratic beliefs are likely to either be corrected by leadership or fail to transmit to the other members of the group. As such, it should appear as if there is alignment between one's personal beliefs and the schema one associates with their religion and that this alignment should underpin fusion as a form of perceived kinship. However, the IIS proposes that fusion is the result of conceptual ties, and that this subtle difference can result in fusion with a group that one does not necessarily have a lot of consensus with. The IIS's reliance on conceptual ties to facilitate fusion also suggests that individuals who are fused by a conceptual tie will remain fused (in line with the principles of fusion mentioned in earlier chapters). This is still the case even in doctrinal religions where leadership will attempt to correct beliefs (this point is a key breaking point between the DMR theory and the IIS). Intuitively, it seems unlikely that an individual will change a belief that they find central to their identity because they are told to; in addition, doing so would violate fusion's irrevocability principle; in this way, the IIS's approach to schisms also suggests a previously unforeseen implication for fusion theory.

This tension between high commitment and new beliefs might also help us to explain an additional aspect of social schisms in doctrinal religions. Given that the IIS assumes that groups exist within a network structure, the structure of a social group may affect within-group consensus if some individuals are reinforcing idiosyncratic beliefs while others are not. Depending on an individual's place in the social network, they may be able to reinforce the social schema more efficiently or introduce new information into the social schema. This is because of the structure of human social networks, which have been shown to be generally stable over time (Gonçalves et al., 2011; Saramäki et al., 2014) and clustered: that is, individuals are more likely to have connections that create tightly clustered communities with a few individuals that serve as links between communities rather than networks that are dispersed in a hub-and-spoke fashion (e.g., Ahn, Han, Kwak, Moon, & Jeong, 2007; DiFonzo et al.,

2013; Granovetter, 1983; Humphries & Gurney, 2008; Jackson, 2008; Lee & Kim, 2017; McPherson, Smith-Lovin, & Cook, 2001). Clustered network structures could—in principle—result in pockets of information within a group where slightly different types of information come to inform the identities of different clusters. For example, Figure 7.1 presents a fictive network of individuals (nodes are black dots) that has been colored to highlight two clusters in the network (dashed links and dotted links). Given that these individuals could potentially identify within the same social category, they can utilize a fictive group boundary that unites them in a single group (depicted by the circle in broken dashed lines). As such we can say that they are—in principle—aligned to the group by means of social identification. However, if groups of individuals go through some similar experience with one another, they are all likely to reflect on a similar experience, resulting in similar conceptual ties if the social schemas they invoke are similar. However, if they utilize separate schemas, it is possible that within a single identity group, individuals become fused to different key concepts, exacerbating the tendency toward social schism. In addition, if one also maintains that there could be epidemiological effects for information transmission, this effect could be intensified because information

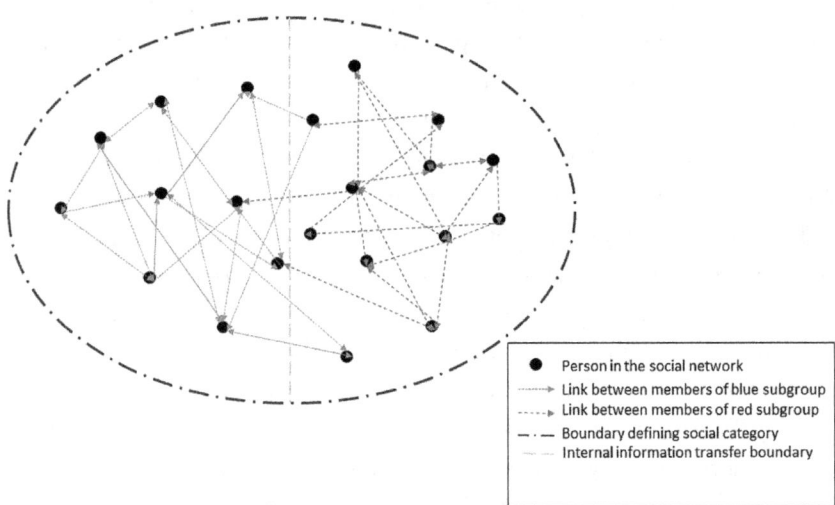

Figure 7.1 A depiction of how the IIS explains some social schisms. This figure depicts a fictive social group with two clusters (denoted by red dashed and blue dotted links) within a single social category (denoted by the purple circle in broken dashed lines that encircles all nodes and links). Diffusion in this network results in pockets of information that have trouble crossing between clusters (denoted by the yellow vertical dashed line).

could travel more efficiently within a clustered subgroup than it can between clustered subgroups, resulting in the idiosyncratic beliefs from fused members being repeated and codified within a subgroup. The clustering of social ties could therefore reinforce the uneven spread of information, and information will have a harder time diffusing *between* the clusters than it will diffusing *within* the clusters (the "social membrane"—if you will—representing the topological weakness between the two social network clusters is represented by the vertical dashed line).

From this perspective, the presence of fused individuals in large doctrinal groups that are otherwise reliant upon social identification as the primary mechanism for group alignment may have a significant effect on within-group consensus and group alignment over time; particularly if new information disseminates unevenly throughout the group. This could create an asymmetry within the group where one cluster of the group has a conceptual tie that is not shared by the other cluster within the group. Should instances arise where the conceptual ties are challenged by outside groups or from the other subgroup, it could result in a social schism. For example, if belief X represents a conceptual tie held by individuals in the doted link community of the figure that is not held by the dash link community, an external group pressure that challenges belief X could result in a schism because the members of the dash link community can disassociate themselves as they would not be fused to the ideas (only aligned by social identification). However, members of the doted link community, who hold belief X as a conceptual tie (i.e., it is a sacred value and an essential belief for their group), will be unwilling to disassociate themselves from the group and will consider the challenge against belief X to be a challenge against themselves personally, as belief X defines both their conception of their social group's schema as well as a central part of their own personal schema. Under this circumstance, it could be that members in the dotted link community come to view members of the dashed link community as apostates or free-riders, resulting in a breakdown of social cohesion and the creation of a new group.

In addition, one can imagine a circumstance where members of the dashed community no longer hold belief X to be a positive aspect of their self-image. As such, members from within that group may distance themselves from belief X. Because this same belief is essential to members of the dot community, an internal struggle for the definition of the social category at large may result in the two sub-communities engaging in a conflict over the group's identity where the dot group holds that belief X is essential, while the dashed group holds that not-belief X is essential. Such a situation may result in social schisms, where highly committed individuals to a rather novel belief break off to form their own group.

Historically, examples of this can be found in contemporary new religious movements that form from larger preexisting doctrinal religions (Lane, 2009), such as those discussed earlier. In addition, this could also be a useful research question to investigate in light of the split between Judaism and Christianity in the first century, where it appears that a small subset of highly committed individuals (early Christians) separated from a larger doctrinal religion (Judaism) after an emotionally intense experience (the Great Jewish Revolt). Computationally, an example of this can be found in the discussion around revivals in the IIS, where a similar effect was observed.

Using the IIS as a foundation, we can view social events as complex as social schisms within a cognitive cybernetic perspective that focuses on information processing and looks to cognitive psychology—and the empirical methods it can provide—to underpin its key mechanisms. This is a powerful reframing for two reasons.

First, earlier approaches in the field are largely based in assumptions of groups. For example, the DMR theory suggests that groups perform rituals, and that these rituals have effects on both memory and the sociopolitical forms of the group. The theory also suggests that these group dynamics are divergent, making it problematic for the understanding of subgroup formation and group schisms. Assuming a group entity, as is common in many theories of cultural evolution, results in a mereological problem that plagues group selection theories as discussed earlier. When attempting to understand issues of social cohesion that could result in a schism, this problem is exacerbated. Effectively, once we assume a group to be entitative, and define theoretical mechanisms based on that group as an entity, we rule out the ability at find principles to address schisms of that group in ways that are historically relevant. In addition, if a theory suggests that modes are divergent, a great deal of more clarity needs to be provided wherein a clear and empirically definable path can be proposed for one group to become another—separate—group. This is not just a semantic issue within the theory, as it affects the mechanisms by which a group would change over time.

Second, the IIS's proposal here offers one of the few theoretical approaches to new religious movements that is empirically testable. As discussed earlier, new religious movements have been largely neglected in the study of religion despite their historical importance and the obvious fact that every religion was—at some point in its history—a new religion. To its credit, the DMR theory does attempt to provide an empirical approach to understanding new religious movements and their formation as it results from tedium (Whitehouse, 2002), which has been a useful foundation for studying new religious movements in the United States for example, particularly when combined with our understanding of Charismatic leadership and ritualization as proposed by Jesper Sørensen (see Lane, 2009). From the perspective of earlier work in the cognitive science of religion, a charismatic leader can themselves become a critical component of a ritual system leading to a point where their charismatic leadership becomes enthroned in the ritual system itself and can help it perpetuate through tradition, extending the charisma of the leader beyond their own actions and allowing it to have a mechanism that can even perpetuate the leader's influence after their death. This is critical for many new religious movements as the death of the leader often means the death of the movement if sufficient mechanisms are not in place to bond the group or its beliefs without the leader. This is further complicated by the fact that, in some cases, leaders of new religious movements are believed to possess supernatural powers, making them minimally counterintuitive agents—in some cases regarded as gods—in their own right. From the perspective of some theories of ritual and cognition (namely, Lawson & McCauley, 1990; McCauley & Lawson, 2002), if that leader is believed to be the primary deity of the system, the system becomes unbalanced as the ritual system becomes unbalanced due to the presence of a more central supernatural agent.

However, these approaches to new religious movements are not the only ones within the cognitive science of religion, and others should be noted—if however briefly—because all of them have been formative in one way or another in the reformulation of the IIS presented in this book. For example, one of the most comprehensive theories of religion ever formulated, that of Stark and Bainbridge, dealt specifically with new religious movements at length (Stark & Bainbridge, 1987), and was the first theory of religion ever formalized—albeit only partially—within a computational model (Bainbridge, 2006). This research informed the IIS in demonstrating how a complex framework that starts with several first principles could grow into a more general theory of religion, applicable to many domains of sociality. Stark and Bainbridge's work, in turn, inspired that of M. Afzal Upal, whose work on modeling new religious movements was the first comprehensive publication of its type at the time (Upal, 2005b, 2005c), and his work since then has done a great deal in helping us to understand how new religious movements can persist from a very unique cross-cultural perspective in Islamic religious movements (Upal, 2017); not to mention Upal's influence described more explicitly in the previous chapter in the formation of models of social identification. In addition, recent work by Anne Taves (2016) has done a tremendous service both to religious studies and cognitive science with her interdisciplinary approach to the formation of some new religious movements and the role of revelation that demonstrates how religious studies can directly participate within scientific disciplines to form a new study of religion (Lane, 2018b).

One of the key themes that runs through these theories is that they all attempt to utilize the findings of cognitive psychology to better understand how it is that new religious movements can form and sustain themselves. The IIS, with its focus on a cognitive (i.e., information processing) framework adds to this by studying the extent to which MAAI can help us better understand the formation of new religious movements as they result from social schisms, and how social schisms can occur more broadly. This also allows us to study an important—and common—feature of new religious movements: their failures. Typically, when a new religious movement fails, history only takes note when it fails because it has had some sociopolitical importance. For example, killings, terrorist attacks, mass suicides, or extermination through war will allow a new religious movement to be included in the historical record. However, new religious movements that fail because they are unable to generate enough interest to motivate their followers or unable to overcome the death of a leader, or find ways to incorporate a new generation born into the group rarely make history—despite most new religious movements likely falling into this category. Because so many new religious movements have not been considered worthy of historical note, we are not able to study the failures of new religious movements without focusing on extreme outliers. This is obviously problematic. However, the IIS framework that was instantiated into the MAAI framework is one way that we can study the formation of new religious movements and social schisms without having to rely entirely on the historical record, since we can rely on a computational platform, which can engage history through output correspondence as well as mechanistic correspondence. In this way, we have a theory (instantiated as a computer model) that allows us to investigate the theoretical spaces wherein previous new religious movements may have existed—and may exist in the future—even though historical evidence for the group is insufficient, incomplete, of poor quality, or lacking entirely.

In addition to reframing schisms, the IIS can also shed more light on the nature of sacred values. In the past, these values are often treated as nonnegotiable beliefs that, when attacked, threatened, or otherwise manipulated by out-groups, can lead to intractable conflicts such as that seen in Israel-Palestine. More recently, with the development of devoted actor theory, sacred values have become more well integrated with the idea of identity fusion (Atran, 2016; Atran, Sheikh, & Gómez, 2014a, b; Bonin & Lane, in press). From the current perspective of the IIS, sacred values are a form of conceptual tie, whereby an individual has integrated a central part of their group's social schema into their own personal schema, and therefore defines core aspects of who they are based on central tenants of their group's beliefs. This centrality also suggests that certain key sacred values are also socially reinforced as such when the belief is more accepted by the group. That is to say, a person could—in principle—hold any part of the group's social schema as sacred. However, if the belief is more peripheral to the group's core tenants, then extreme actions in defense (or support) of that belief could trigger disidentification tendencies in other members of the group. This could be the reason why when an individual undertakes an extreme action on behalf of the group in some circumstances, the majority of other members do not support that person or their action. For example, lone-wolf actors, who have increasingly become a concern for security experts in recent years, despite acting alone, justify their actions with key beliefs from a social schema—typically drawn from a like-minded minority of the larger group. For example, those extremists who take it upon themselves to take violent action against out-group members are often denounced by other members of the group. This does not seem to be always explainable by a difference in beliefs. In many cases, religious extremists justify their actions by linking the action with defending a key belief of the group, which is likely shared by other group members. However, in the case that the group is generally made up of individuals who are identified—but not fused—with the group, the extreme actions of those who are fused can cause disidentification to occur among the members at large. In other cases, you can find pockets of individuals who are fused to a group but have different targets for their conceptual ties. In these cases, you can also get sacred-value-based schisms. Examples of this can be found historically in the splitting of many new religious movements, wherein the group splits off because of fusion with fundamentalist beliefs or fusion to a specific interpretation of the group's key beliefs.

Examples of both of these dynamics can be found in the history of the Branch Davidians of Waco, TX, who became famous after their 1993 besiegement by the FBI and the US Bureau of Alcohol, Tobacco, and Firearms that lasted fifty-one days and resulted in the deaths of almost eighty group members, including twenty-five children (United States Department of Justice, 1993). However, prior to this group becoming established, it split from an earlier schism group from the Seventh Day Adventist church. The Davidians first split in the early 1900s, when their founder, Victor Houteff, and his followers were disfellowshipped from the Seventh Day Adventist church in 1935, apparently because of their unwillingness to align their fundamentalist millennialism with that of the main body of the church and abandon the idea that Houteff was a prophet. The group continued after his death under his wife's leadership, who led the group until prophesying that the end of days would occur in 1959, leading to an additional schism. This schism suggested that, in light of disconfirming evidence, the members of the group were faced with the cognitive dissonance that arises during a failed prophecy (a similar failed prophecy event from a millenial UFO group was the basis of the seminal study that inspired the first formulation of cognitive dissonance theory of Festinger, Riecken, and Schachter, 2008). On the one hand, the group members believed that their prophet had spoken truthfully about the end times, while on the other hand, they were faced with obvious evidence to the contrary. To resolve this dissonance, some members would have "doubled down" on their group beliefs, trusting that some other event must have intervened, while others would have concluded that the leadership was flawed and left the group. This disidentification process would have resulted in members leaving the tradition entirely, or, if most beliefs are still aligned—as appears to be the typical case—the group experiences a schism. This kind of schism related to fusion with beliefs about a charismatic leader is paradigmatic to new religious movements, and echoes commitment to other "alpha" leaders found throughout the animal kingdom (Lane, 2009). After this failure, the larger membership was led by Benjamin Roden, focusing on further millennial beliefs about a coming end-time (Melton, 2018; Melton & Bromley, 2009; Newport, 2006). After Benjamin Roden's death, the leadership was taken over by his widow, Lois Roden, who allegedly entered a relationship with David Koresh. This led to Koresh being caught in a power struggle for leadership of the group with George Roden, Lois' son. After a power struggle for leadership of the group that included a shootout and public court case, those who were apparently fused with the belief that Koresh was chosen by God to lead the group stayed loyal members with Koresh. Under Koresh's leadership, the group ultimately became infamous for its altercation with the US government in the 1990s that inspired later the Oklahoma City Bombing by Timothy McVeigh.

Other social movements (religious and secular) show similar patterns where fusion to a central belief of the group (either related to the leadership or not) experience schisms and reformations regarding attachment to those core beliefs. This allows for the fusion framework of the IIS to suggest a clear explanatory framework for a range of social patterns, from cults of personality, to political movements, to protest movements, and beyond.

There is another way that we could potentially learn from AI that I think is worthy of exploration and note. As you recall from the previous chapter, I was able to use a large data set of religious materials to train an AI system that we could effectively communicate with as it was able to produce its own religious narratives and sermons. Another way we could study extreme forms of religion could be to take similar systems and train them with the relevant material. For example, leaders of new religious movements are hard to study because they are relatively rare in a population, extremists and those willing to fight and die for their group are also hard to study because of their rarity and also because we don't typically know who they are until after they attempt some extreme action which results either in their death or their imprisonment, making them problematic subjects for study. However, with the rise of the internet and social media, a great deal of information is being left behind by these individuals. Their material could be used to train a similar system so that we could study its output. This in no way should be taken as a suggestion that we can create "AI replicas" of religious extremists that are so psychologically realistic that the results of some study should be taken as if they were generated by actual humans. Nor should it be assumed that these AI replicas would be terrorists capable of carrying out attacks or realizing some form of a jihadi terminator army (this is both ignorant of the level of AI that could be created and the inability of even the most advanced current natural language processing based AI systems to interact with anything outside of basic text prompts).

However, AI does serve one very interesting purpose for the study of religion beyond that which I've discussed at length in previous chapters, and that is the ability to define a problem space. A problem space is the range of components that can be incorporated when finding the solution to a problem (as opposed to a solution space, which is the set of all possible solutions for a problem). In many policy issues for example, religion can play a role in the problem or the solution (sometimes both). Using AI, and MAAI in particular (because it affords greater interpretability and realistic constraints that correspond more closely to those of the real-world system), we can efficiently search the possible parameters in a computer model that might have the greatest effect on some intended policy-relevant outcome. This can be done through methods such as parameter sensitivity and variability analyses, which take the parameters of a model and slightly change them and then run the model multiple times to understand the distribution of possible outputs of the model for that set of parameters before moving on to the next set. This can be done multiple times for many parameter sets (sometimes tens of thousands or millions). This can help us narrow down the problem space and define it in a way that is more relevant for a particular policy solution. For example, when trying to understand the effect of some policy on radicalism or terrorism, it is possible that the effects are indirect, but searching through a model can help us better define what the important components are to the problem, and then help us to better address the issue. Subsequently, we can then search through the space of all possible outcomes, allowing us to potentially choose a decision (or policy) that is optimal for our time, place, budget, and other feasibility concerns.

8

The Future of Religion

In this final chapter, in addition to a summary of the past chapters, I also wish to give an overview of what the state of the art can be when applying AI to the study of religion and how the study of religion today can be greatly improved by a reframing of how it approaches its subject. From the beginning, this work set out to provide a better understanding of how groups maintain social cohesion. To narrow its focus to a high impact and highly misunderstood subset of groups, I aimed to synthesize multiple theories about religion, cognition, social cohesion, and group alignment that can explain a wider range of observations and address phenomena that are problematic for earlier theories that have attempted to create a similar theoretical foundation (namely, in the persistence of contemporary Pentecostal and Charismatic Christian churches, new religious movement formation, schism, consensus, and extremism). Some of these aspects are extremely problematic for earlier theories that have been widely applied in the research literature and are increasingly being refocused for applications in real-world and policy-relevant domains. For example, Pentecostal and Charismatic traditions are problematic for the DMR theory because it predicts that emotionally intense rituals in doctrinal religions will die out. However, Pentecostal and Charismatic Christians represent a large percentage of the world's largest doctrinal religion and demographic models and surveys suggest that they are growing in many regions, particularly in the Global South (D. E. Miller & Yamamori, 2007; Pew Research Center, 2011), which has a history of poorly implemented policy interventions rooted in cultural misunderstandings at best and histories (and anthropologies) of colonialism at worst. Yet, Pentecostal and Charismatic Christian traditions rely on high frequencies of in-group ritual attendance at low-arousal rituals as well as rare emotionally intense experiences; therefore, the inability of any theory to capture the key cultural dynamics is an important aspect of validation that should be discussed—and if needed, amended—prior to its use in any larger suggestion beyond the basic research community. Overall, the theoretical integration, studies, and semantic network mapping method presented here can contribute to the current literature on social cohesion and takes a more quantitative approach that can allow future implementations and policy applications to be checked empirically by subject-matter experts and local stakeholders prior to a policy being adopted in another culture.

To better address how emotionally intense events can facilitate social cohesion in large groups, the IIS built upon earlier research and contemporary data science techniques (such as semantic networks and network analytics) to define how schemas of information are constructed over time and how reflection on emotionally intense events can significantly impact one's schemas and therefore alignment to their group as well as the stability of beliefs within their schema. In this way, it provides a powerful approach to social cohesion and its dynamics. In addition, the IIS builds a clear bridge between the DMR theory on the one hand, and social identity theory and fusion theory on the other hand by extending the recent proposal connecting the three theories presented by Whitehouse & Lanman (2014) and clarifying many of the key empirical issues with fusion theory to date. It extends Whitehouse and Lanman's theoretical synthesis by proposing a new form of tie that underlies extended fusion called a conceptual tie. The IIS proposes that conceptual ties result from an individual having an emotionally intense experience that prompts reflection on the event. As a result, the event becomes more central to their identity as the individual uses the social schema of their doctrinal religion to interpret the experience. This reflection results in links between an individual's personal schema and essential beliefs in the group's social schema. This tie between one's personal schema, from which they derive their personal identity, and essential beliefs that define the group can create a porous boundary between one's personal and social identity, which we can call extended fusion.

This work set out to make several contributions to the literature. One of its most unique contributions to the literature is how to quantify within-group consensus using data-mining algorithms to analyze unstructured text data drawn from a field interview to construct computational approximations of an individual's schema; this is also discussed further in the next section. In the past, researchers have often relied on a participant's similarity to group responses on likert scales (e.g., Atran et al., 2002; Tastle & Wierman, 2007) or other ordinal measures in order to attempt to quantify within-group consensus (such calculations are often used in the literature on group decision making; e.g., Chiclana, Tapia García, del Moral, & Herrera-Viedma, 2013; Tapia Garcı́a, del Moral, Martínez, & Herrera-

Viedma, 2012). The cultural cybernetic approach presented in this book takes a more information-centric approach by applying a method previously unused (to my knowledge) in anthropology by analyzing semi-structured interviews to create semantic network representations of socially held information and then approximating within-group consensus using a lossy intersection distance metric to measure the within-group consensus (Carley, 1997; V. Hill & Carley, 1999). In the past, semi-structured interviews have been used by clinical psychologists and anthropologists in order to get freely offered information from individuals in a more controlled fashion than unstructured interviews. At the same time, semi-structured interviews are also not bound by a set of predetermined questions in the way that survey measures are. However, the quantification of semi-structured interviews has largely been done through coding schemes and human coders in the past. By introducing data analysis techniques that are compatible with modern big-data and AI methods, it not only provides a method for quantifying the structure of information in a semi-structured interview, it also builds a bridge that stretches from traditional qualitative fieldwork methods to the forefront of modern AI. In doing so it provides a powerfully integrated platform with theoretical continuity that stretches from the highly quantifiable and testable realm of computer modeling all the way back to textual studies, demonstrating the use of this technique for answering anthropological questions and opening up many future directions that were previously relegated to areas outside of the domain of the quantitative social sciences because of their data and scope—not because of their topic.

However, the information processing approach that I advocate here is not the only approach, and I believe that discussing another key competing approach warrants a small detour here. A great deal of ink has been spent on the idea of "cultural evolution."

Cultural evolution is, in effect, a resurgence of the application of Darwinian principles toward studying—and at times prescribing guidance concerning—a variety of human cultural (and religious) phenomena. This idea, that nonbiological systems can be Darwinian, is not unfamiliar. In fact, there are some who have purported that all systems, anything from physics, to psychology, to religion can be viewed as Darwinian systems; a position referred to as "universal Darwinism."

While I will delve into the ethical implications of the current research more fully in later sections, I believe a quick note is warranted about what the key difference here is between cultural evolution and a more cybernetic approach and how that implicates ethics. This is particularly important given that both approaches have been described as problematic in the past[1] and both approaches—I believe—can be (and to an extent—are being) used unethically today. One of the key differences between the two is that whereas cybernetics is focused specifically on an information processing approach that algorithmically approximates ways of manipulating information that is close to the way we do so in the human mind, cultural evolution relies on an analogy to biological evolution related to variation and selection. In addition, cultural evolution does not specifically define the units of selection or its mechanisms clearly enough to promote specific predictions from period to period, and thus cultural evolution cannot offer specific predictions about what beliefs will be selected for in a specific context. As such it provides an interesting interpretive framework for ultimate explanations of cultural phenomena (those things that are explained by over-reaching principles over evolutionary time periods), but it often fails to offer proximate explanations of cultural phenomena (such as those things explained by immediate cause and effect within a specific context or environment). Instead, cultural evolution offers an elegant description of how it is that populations can come to hold a specific belief (or trait) through analogy to evolution. In this way, cultural evolution provides an interesting—and potentially useful—description of how cultures and religions change, but it does not yet offer a sufficient explanation. On the other hand, the reliance of cultural cybernetics on human information processing capacities as the key mechanisms driving cultural change (as opposed to selection on uncontrolled variations)—in principle—offers a more clear set of algorithmic processes that should be able to predict which beliefs will be adopted, rejected, changed, recontextualized, etc. within the grand frameworks of the world's cultures. As such, cybernetics can offer theoretically grounded explanations of cultural and religious changes through complex interactions of different information mechanisms in a way that cultural evolution cannot. In this way, cultural evolution could be said to provide an interesting ideological framework for description and interpretation of some cultural and religious phenomena, while cybernetics offers an explanatory framework for the same phenomena that can offer far more promise in its ability to produce predictions that can be validated by real-world data in both its output (as is done in some models of cultural evolution) and its psychological mechanisms (which are almost always neglected by cultural evolution). Now, returning to my earlier point on the dangers of employing the cybernetic approach, its power also makes cybernetics more dangerous in my opinion. Because cultural evolution offers more of an ideological and interpretive framework, it would largely be employed post hoc and has little power to actually offer tangible predictions. However, using an approach that could produce psychologically realistic systems for prediction has a wide range of applications that—(again) in principle—could be accurate in its ability to allow for the control and manipulation of cultural and religious systems on multiple levels. In this way, a cybernetic or information processing approach to culture and religion is like a gun or a hammer; guns and hammers are tools that can provide food or build great town halls—but the same tool can also kill and create prisons. For myself, the question comes down to which framework is most open and empirically viable, and therefore correctable through scientific consensus. This discussion is further complicated by the ethical considerations of the power of modern computation and data analytics, which will be addressed in the discussion on future methodological directions and subsequent ethical considerations in a subsequent section.

8.1 Future Directions in Cultural Cybernetics and the IIS

Future directions fall into two categories: (1) methodological—future research can embrace and extend the use of data-mining techniques; (2) theoretical—future research can use the empirical findings to generate new research hypotheses that can serve to create a more accurate scientific understanding of social cohesion. What follows is a discussion of these future directions, addressing the status of any current research that is employing aspects of the framework outlined here.

8.2 Methodological Directions

The tools used and developed to quantify unstructured text data in the cultural cybernetic approach presented earlier can be expanded upon to incorporate larger datasets from digitized sources. Like other forms of computer-based text analytics, semantic network mapping is scalable. The analyses performed here were the result of analyzing networks created from the interview transcripts of a relatively small sample of individuals. However, in other venues, I have presented how we can utilize the technique to analyze the networks drawn from a corpus of over 500 digitized historical religious texts and sermons by employing parallel computing algorithms run on a high-performance computing system (Lane, 2015b). This demonstrated that the technique can be used to answer questions of interest to anthropologists by scaling the analysis onto larger computational architectures; for example, those available to academic (and private) research institutions such as the ARCUS (University of Oxford Advanced Research Computing, 2015), NOTUR (UNINETT Sigma AS, 2015), or private cloud computing services offered by Amazon (referred to as AWS; Amazon Web Services Incorporated, 2015), Google (referred to as Google Cloud or Google Compute; Google LLC, 2018), and Microsoft (referred to as Microsoft Azure; Microsoft Corporation, 2016).

An additional example of the use of this technique to study semantic networks drawn from doctrinal religious communities is currently being completed using the same collection of sermons discussed to create the AIwaken system discussed in Chapter 6. This represents the largest digitized collection of religious sermons for research purposes. The texts of the sermons included in this dataset have been analyzed the semantic network mapping techniques discussed in Chapter 4. A corpus of this kind can facilitate many additional avenues for future research. For instance, social schemas between churches, denominations, and geographic locations can be compared over time. These social schemas can also be analyzed in relation to other socio-demographic variables such as census data, political affiliation, or variations in social norms (Gelfand et al., 2011; Harrington & Gelfand, 2014).

Currently, the semantic network mapping technique is being employed to analyze data available on online social networks such as Twitter and Reddit. Online social networks store massive amounts of texts in the form of shared web pages, posts, responses, and status updates. Currently, Facebook has 1.44 billion active users, 936 million of which are daily users, and 82.8 percent of these users are outside the United States and Canada (Facebook, 2016). This potentially provides a research sample that includes many doctrinal religions (not just the Christian traditions discussed in earlier) as well as new and emerging religious traditions. In addition, the large population of users outside of the United States and Canada can help address the bias of using subjects from Western-educated industrialized rich and democratic countries noted in the psychological literature (Henrich, Heine, & Norenzayan, 2010). Online social networks represent a great research opportunity because they provide cross-cultural data from social groups that can be quantified both in terms of their conceptual output (i.e., user provided updates and data in the form of updates, comments, and replies to other users) and their social context (i.e., the network of contacts the individual has as well as their physical locations). Analyzing the data from online social networks provides both the social network and conceptual information needed to perform more robust studies of within-group consensus and cultural epidemiology and is being applied to better understand emergency response in Norway to the COVID-19 pandemic[2] as well as the rise of nationalism and populism in Europe[3] and how we can better understand the development of the field of religious studies and theology.[4]

Computational techniques for quantifying text data can also be used to understand social cohesion from a historical perspective. Despite the fact that texts have become digitized for computational analysis only relatively recently, efforts to digitize all of the world's books are currently underway (Aiden & Michel, 2014) and millions of books have already been digitized (Michel et al., 2010). Digital corpora provide a massive opportunity to employ the methods used in this research to study the information produced in relation to doctrinal religions over longer periods of time. In the future, research could employ semantic network mapping to study how it is that essential beliefs of doctrinal religions are presented over time using this massive CORPUS of texts.

There are many exciting prospects for future research using the computational methods discussed here. The cost of the computational systems needed to realize the expansions into ever-increasing data sources proposed earlier are steadily decreasing. Meanwhile, the amount of data stored in digitized archives, databases, and online social networks is increasing. This trend couples well with the fact that there are many questions in the field of anthropology that address important contemporary social issues, where the data provided earlier could provide valuable insight that can result in clear, causal, and computationally tractable solutions. Often, anthropologists study questions of great importance, such as how different contexts affect the beliefs and social cohesion of different groups throughout the world. The techniques developed here can allow for the traditionally qualitative comparisons of anthropologists to be supplemented with quantitative analyses that can support—or refute—their qualitative understandings.

Many questions of interest to anthropologists often focus on a particular group in a particular time and the researchers might not be interested in general models of explanation, but instead are interested in ways to better describe some cultural phenomena. Here too, I believe that semantic network mapping can be useful, even though it would fall outside of the scope of cultural cybernetics or MAAI as I've defined it here, as it can structure field data collected by anthropologists in a way that can distill and provide structure to material such as field notes and interviews (that would otherwise take days or weeks to read or listen to) and represent it as a searchable and analyzable structure that can help to provide a deeper understanding. In this way, the same algorithms from big data can be applied to smaller social groups to answer questions by looking deeper into a relatively smaller dataset.

One of the more interesting promises of cultural cybernetics is the possibility for *vertical research integration*. Typically, research in the social sciences progresses through painstaking stepwise motions. Researchers will use a preexisting theory, gather data, code and clean the data, analyze the data, and then report results. Recall that, from the perspective of cultural cybernetics, model *is* theory. So, if a well-validated and verified model exists, then it can represent the framework of the theory independent of being in the mind of any one researcher. Given the methods discussed in this book, data gathering for studies in the field of religion can be (and are being) automated to scrape the web for data on websites, social networks, and other sources. The coding and cleaning of data can be built into this pipeline using best practices and automated decision making for different parts of a model or variable. From this dataset, analysis can be scheduled or automated through preset triggers so that the data is analyzed in an efficient but relevant manner. Using the resulting data and analysis, data can be automatically ported into graphs or entire data dashboards for visualization and done in real-time or near-real-time. This data can then be put back into the model to parameterize it and update it so that the model (i.e., theory) becomes better over time and it can produce predictions (i.e., hypotheses) that can be further tested in the pipeline discussed earlier. In this way, research is not so much a lengthy activity yielding minimal results publication by publication. Rather, research becomes a semiautomated pipeline where insights are drawn almost continuously and in conjunction with the fast-paced changes that exist in the real-world social systems that it is designed to study.

While this may sound fantastical to many, these automated data pipelines for research integration already exist in many industries from manufacturing to finance. The control of many factory processes today follows a similar process as that described earlier. In my own experience, building data analysis systems for online social networks (mainly Twitter and Reddit), this approach to research is a powerful way to gain insight and quickly generate research results. However, this approach to research is not without its dangers. In my opinion, the most pressing dangers and concerns surrounding this approach are related to ethics and data privacy.

8.2.1 Ethical Concerns

In most fields, ethics play a central role in governing research. However, in the cognitive science of religion, the "field" is not so much a field in its own right so much as it is an interdisciplinary endeavor that has one foot in religious studies and anthropology and another foot in cognitive science—particularly cognitive psychology. In the research presented here, this duality still stands—and if anything is further complicated by incorporating the AI aspect of cognitive science in addition to cognitive and evolutionary psychology. When utilizing big-data and web-scraping, this does not necessarily place the research in a less controversial space.

Computational studies of online and offline social networks using the methods discussed in this volume might (and I would suggest that they should) raise ethical concerns among anthropologists, who traditionally put extreme emphasis on data and informant protection. The issue of ethics is complex and multifaceted. However, I believe there are two clear points that can serve to begin the discussion of the ethical implications of the research discussed earlier, particularly focusing on the ability to quantify religious and cultural beliefs and measures of within-group consensus.

The first is data protection and ensuring that participant data is not leaked or made vulnerable to individuals who would steal or seek to gain unauthorized access to the data. Modern data security practices, such as splitting the dataset across multiple locations and utilizing multi-factor authentication systems, can be used to ensure that the intimate details of a study which would probe one's personal religious experiences would be treated appropriately and with the utmost care (see Lane, 2015a for further discussion of data protection concerns for anthropologists).

The second is ethical misuse of the algorithms used to process the text data and create measures of within-group consensus. In contemporary society, our lives are increasingly lived "online," particularly with online social networks such as Facebook, Reddit, and Twitter having billions of daily users posting about their daily lives and discussing their beliefs and values. In countries such as China, new online social networks have been increasing in popularity; for example, WeChat and Sina Wiebo have approximately 1 billion and 340 million active monthly users, respectively (BBC News, 2017; Culpan, 2018). On both platforms, Chinese government authorities have played a role in censoring speech that is considered dissident or problematic for the Communist party, such as speech about corruption, and users have attempted to circumvent these censorship policies (Whitmarsh et al., 2013). In addition, WeChat's terms of service clearly state that they provide data access at the request of the government (Tencent Holdings Limited, 2019) and in the past, private communications from WeChat has been allegedly used as evidence in the prosecution of people labeled "political dissidents" by the Chinese authorities (see Davison, 2012). As such, it is logistically possible that governments such as China could use algorithms, such as those used to construct the semantic networks in Chapter 6, to process the data and target individuals with beliefs on the basis of their within-group consensus. Although this idea may seem dystopian, reports from the Xīnjiāng area of China (including satellite images; see Doman, Hutcheon, Welch, & Taylor, 2018; Sudworth, 2018) suggest that up to 1 million Uighurs (a Turkish Muslim minority in China) and other ethnic minorities are being put in concentration camps for "re-education" and forced labor in response to differences in their identities (both religiously and culturally) with the Communist ruling party (Buckley & Ramzy, 2019; Kuo, 2019). This practice is expanding and allegedly reliant on surveillance to decide potential targets for detention, causing many, including the United Nations, to condemn this behavior as it may lead to genocide of the Uighurs (Cronin-Furman, 2018; Eve, 2018; Staff agencies in Geneva and Beijing, 2019). While this news is disturbing, in its own right, it is exacerbated by news of China's new—and often misunderstood—"social credit system," which uses AI and big-data techniques to monitor and rate citizens based on their behaviors. While the system is not as centralized or advanced as is often believed (Horsley, 2018; Kobie, 2019), it does force us to ask hard questions about the potential misuse of research methods like those used here, particularly when deployed on the massive scales that online social networking platforms could provide. The example of China may be a particularly immediate one due to the suggestion that it may be a massive human rights abuse. However, the idea of collecting data on a massive scale where text analysis algorithms could be misused is not unique to China and indeed, European and North American defense and intelligence agencies have been known to share data for defense and security reasons (Ball, 2013).

On their own these two ethical issues are quite daunting, and there are other ethical issues in the field of data analytics regarding the field of AI that also go beyond the scope of the current research. Thankfully, there is an active debate among scholars from many fields on the ways that we can utilize different positions from philosophy of morality and ethics combined with regulation, oversight, knowledge of best practices and standards to help address these issues and—ideally—preempt possible misuse of technologies that use data mining to infringe on civil liberties (Bryson, 2018; Bryson & Winfield, 2017; Floridi & Taddeo, 2016; Gilbert et al., 2018; Pentland, 2014; Schneider, 2009). While this debate has been largely overlooked in anthropology, arguments have been put forward that, because of the new research contexts that big-data platforms like online social networks provide as a supplement to traditional fieldwork, anthropologists need to be engaging in these debates as well (Lane, 2015a).

So far, I believe that such ethical concerns highlight the need for far-reaching ethical frameworks to govern these systems and that such systems should always be created with the values of liberty and then safety as fundamental motivators and guiding principles. From a research perspective, many fields already have their own ethical guidelines. However, as computational approaches become more common in the social sciences, ethical frameworks will need to be updated to account for the scope and nature of data collection in digital environments. Also, as scientific fields (such as psychology), which push for distance between researcher and subject, begin to address questions from the field of anthropology, which has historically pushed for a closeness between researcher and subject, new methodologically based guidelines should be devised that can guide researchers regarding the most appropriate and beneficial stances to take in general, so that new research can push forward in this interdisciplinary space, with a parsimonious outlook on the ethical guidelines underlying the research.

8.3 Theoretical Directions

There are multiple ways in which the research discussed in this volume can be extended to better understand social cohesion in doctrinal religions. One direction involves further investigation of doctrinal religions from the perspective of the DMR theory. The second is by extending the DMR theory to address other theories, namely, devoted actor theory, which is a combination of fusion theory and sacred values theory (Atran et al., 2014a; Gómez et al., 2017; Sheikh et al., 2014; Sheikh, Ginges, & Atran, 2013; Sheikh et al., 2016). A third direction of future research involves producing a better understanding of social schisms.

8.3.1 Future Directions for the DMR Theory

The empirical and theoretical advancements discussed in this work can be built upon to address other aspects of the DMR theory, which largely go unaddressed in this volume because they are beyond its scope. For example, this volume focuses on the psychological aspects of the IIS insofar as they implicate doctrinal religions; the work only addresses imagistic religions insofar as they provide a basis for contextualizing some of the empirical and ethnographic observations regarding rare and emotionally intense experiences. However, in developing the IIS in such a way that it can address rare and emotionally intense experiences in the context of doctrinal religions, it opens the possibility to address imagistic religions as well. This could help researchers better understand historical transitions from imagistic to doctrinal systems (or vice versa).

Some researchers have proposed that the transition from imagistic to doctrinal religions was a major force during the Neolithic transition, which is the point in human history where humans transitioned from small-scale tribal arrangements largely reliant on hunting and gathering to large-scale polities that leveraged complex social hierarchies and agriculture to manage larger and denser populations (Whitehouse & Hodder, 2010; Whitehouse, Mazzucato, Hodder, & Atkinson, 2013). This transition is an extremely important aspect of human history and has been addressed by researchers using other theories, such as cultural evolution (e.g., Henrich, 2016; Norenzayan, 2013; Turchin, 2016) and resource management (e.g., Hayden, 1990, 1995). The IIS's extension to the DMR theory incorporates aspects of both the doctrinal and imagistic mode and could therefore provide a new explanation for how societies transitioned from one mode of social organization to another when previous accounts have held that they are divergent (see Whitehouse, 2000, 2004). Future research could instantiate the IIS into a computational model that could then be validated with future psychological and field research (gathered using the methods described in Chapters 3–5) as well as the large longitudinal datasets drawn from historical and archaeological records such as the World Religion Database (2016), Database for Religious History (2015), and SESHAT Databank (2017). This data could be used to test the predictions of a model that used the IIS as an architecture for explaining how different social and biological (i.e., environmental) conditions may have affected social cohesion in different historical contexts. Currently, a large research project at the Center for Mind and Culture has already worked to implement the IIS as an agent-based model to address religious violence (discussed in Section 6.2.2), however, future research could utilize agent-based models of the IIS in order to study large-scale religious transitions, such as the Neolithic transition discussed earlier.

The IIS's extension to the DMR theory makes a clear theoretical space for the ongoing performance of emotionally intense rituals in doctrinal religions. This not only implicates potential transitions from imagistic to doctrinal religions, as described earlier, but also why emotionally intense rituals may be found in doctrinal religions, which implicates the evolutionary argument put forth by the DMR theory in ways that suggest future directions for research of doctrinal religions. For example, the DMR theory posits that the frequent and low-arousal rituals eventually result in tedium, and that some traditions will utilize renewals in order to combat that tedium. The IIS's extension to the DMR theory suggests that the reinvigorations that are recorded in doctrinal traditions (such as those described in Whitehouse, 1995, 2000) will result in fused members of the group. So, even though the emotional intensity of renewal rituals might not afford the quick spread of low-arousal rituals that are frequently attended, they will result in highly committed members. This point presents a research question regarding the relationship between fusion and tedium; namely, if extended fusion is based on conceptual ties, are individuals who are fused to an essential belief of the group (like God; see Chapter 4) as affected by the tedium effect as others? In principle, if an individual has internalized an essential belief of their group's social schema into their personal schema, it may be that tedium does not affect that concept, because it has been linked with an emotionally intense and central aspect of their personal schema. Alternatively, if conceptual ties are also affected by tedium, it could be detrimental to group alignment because individuals could grow bored of the group's essential beliefs. Growing bored of a conceptual tie may cause them to abandon the group as it no longer allows them to facilitate a positive self-image, despite their previous extended fusion to the group, because they are no longer motivated by a belief that represent both the group, and a critical connection linking their personal schema to the social schema. Therefore, one research question of interest for the IIS's extension of the DMR theory should be to what extent are fused beliefs susceptible to the tedium effect and if so, whether this could be a possible path to de-fusion[5] or via viable approach toward deradicalization.

The fact that both frequent low-arousal rituals and rare emotionally intense experiences foster social cohesion in doctrinal religions appears to fit well with the DMR theory's selection argument. Having multiple ritual arrangements can serve different purposes. Frequently attending low-arousal rituals would be effective for spreading the beliefs of a group to a large population, thus creating the possibility for many potential cooperation partners as the in-group grows. Meanwhile, rare but emotionally intense experiences could facilitate intense social cohesion and self-sacrifice among smaller groups (such as military units) which could serve to defend the group against potential threats from out-groups. As such, the different formations of doctrinal rituals could often be found together due to the different evolutionary pressures that they can help address. This can help explain why doctrinal religious traditions perform multiple types of rituals. For example, Christians will likely perform weekly ceremonies at a church but will also undergo more emotionally intense ritual experiences, such as marriage, confirmation, or an evangelical retreat. The results of the studies presented in Chapters 3–5 suggest that the frequent low-arousal rituals can help to codify the group's beliefs and spread the group's schema to recruit more individuals to socially identify with the group while the rare and emotionally intense experiences can serve to bond some of the individuals to the essential beliefs of the group in ways that make them more willing to self-sacrifice for the group.

Recent research has observed that Pentecostal and Charismatic Christianity is growing in areas like Africa and South America (D. E. Miller & Yamamori, 2007; Pew Research Center, 2011). In comparison to areas like Northern and Western Europe, where atheism seems to be more prevalent and traditional religion seems to be in decline (Pew Research Center, 2012, 2015), Africa and South America also appear to have less economic development by some indicators (Welzel, Inglehart, & Klingemann, 2003) and those living in Africa and South America typically have less potable water, higher death rates, and less resource security (The World Bank, 2016). As such, it could be hypothesized that emotionally intense experiences occurring in these religious traditions are facilitating intense social cohesion in order to increase coordination efforts and increase access the necessary resources for survival. Similar rituals would not be required in Northern Europe due to higher levels of economic development and secular political institutions that provide resources to those in need. Future research can therefore seek to investigate the effects of relative resource scarcity on the possible prevalence of high-arousal rituals in doctrinal religions.

8.3.2 Future Directions for Devoted Actor Theory

The IIS's reconciliation between the DMR theory, social identity theory, and fusion theory has also opened up a new direction for future research that may impact on our understanding of religious extremism. The theory of sacred values predicts that, under certain conditions, individuals will be willing to fight and die for a set of beliefs (Atran, Axelrod, & Davis, 2007; Atran & Ginges, 2012). Sacred values are said to represent nonnegotiable beliefs that people do not think about rationally. One study has even found that reasoning about sacred values utilizes brain regions associated with semantic rule retrieval and moral evaluations but not with utilitarian reasoning (Berns et al., 2012). It has been noted that the extreme behavior of individuals who hold sacred values is often similar to the predicted (and observed) behavioral outputs of highly fused individuals; including a greater endorsement of extreme sacrifices for one's in-group and endorsement of extreme behaviors toward out-groups. Recently, researchers focusing on fusion theory and sacred values theory have come together to investigate a new theory that combines the two that is referred to as devoted actor theory (e.g., Atran et al., 2014a; Gómez et al., 2017; Sheikh et al., 2016). Devoted actor theory hypothesizes that people will protect sacred values, even being willing to kill or die or those values, when the values are embedded in or fused with a social identity (Sheikh et al., 2014). In previous publications, sacred values have been defined as "a value that incorporates moral and ethical beliefs that can motivate action independently of its prospect of success" (Atran, 2006a, p. 2, also see 2006b).

Given the similarities in behavioral responses between fused individuals and individuals confronted with a threat to a sacred value (i.e., devoted actors), it is possible that these two phenomena are closely related. One avenue for future research could investigate the extent to which extended fusion and sacred values are both built upon conceptual ties. In principle, conceptual ties make good potential targets for sacred values because they both are related to a socially shared idea that is essential to a group and both can motivate extreme responses, such as endorsing violent attacks against out-groups. For example, the personal histories of many terrorists include autobiographically salient events that informed not only their personal schema, but also the way they aligned with a particular social group (Jensen, Atwell Seate, & James, 2018; Lane et al., 2018). Prima facie, the relationship between intense autobiographically relevant experiences and extremism appears to align with the IIS's predictions for how conceptual ties are formed. Because of the fact that conceptual ties make connections between the social schema and personal schema that result in one's self being inseparable from a group (since both are defined by the same "essential" information), outside threats to the group's sacred values that have been internalized as conceptual ties would be akin to an attack on the self. As such, it may seem reasonable to a fused individual to endorse or enact extreme actions in light of the threat.

As suggestive as the literature may be for the links above, future research should directly investigate the extent to which those with conceptual ties also show patterns of endorsing self-sacrifice or extreme parochial altruism in the ways that devoted actors appear to. In addition, future fieldwork should aim to replicate the studies presented in Chapters 4 and 5 with large groups of devoted actors in order to (1) check if the results of Chapter 4 can be replicated in other cultures with larger samples and (2) examine if devoted actors are also fused to beliefs that are essential to their group. Currently, I have begun working in collaboration with a group of scholars in Central and Eastern Europe deploy surveys in conjunction with semi-structured interviews conducted with members of militia groups in the region. While the research is not focusing on a doctrinal religion, the frequency of participation with the militia group's regular trainings appears to be an appropriate variable to be analyzed in the model instead of frequency of in-group ritual attendance.

In addition, the relationship between sacred values and the conceptual ties is currently being investigated through computational modeling and simulation techniques. A recent computational model has incorporated the theoretical propositions of the IIS into an agent-based model of the effects of threat perception mechanisms described in the terror management and hazard precaution literature on religion (Shults, Lane, et al., 2017)[6] to produce an agent-based model that can allow researchers to study the effects of sacred values and fusion on patterns of mutually escalating religious violence (Shults, Toft, et al., 2017).[7] The model defines sacred values as conceptual ties held by an agent, which are codified by being associated with previous "intense" experiences in the simulation—such as an act of violence. In the model, fused agents can choose to "attack" an out-group member if their anxiety is above a specific threshold. Their anxiety is manipulated by perceptions of hazards in the environment and rises and falls using the associative mechanisms proposed by Joshua Epstein's (2014) Agent_Zero architecture. By investigating data collected by a parameter sweep of the model it was found that the most probable conditions for mutually escalating religious violence were when two nearly equal populations of different religious groups are found in environments with relatively high social and contagion hazards. These findings appear congruent with other findings in the literature. For example, previous research has found that contagion prevalence in a society is associated with predictors of out-group violence and xenophobia (Cashdan, 2001; Cashdan & Steele, 2013; Fincher & Thornhill, 2012; Schaller & Murray, 2008). In addition, the finding that group sizes are roughly matched in intense sustained conflicts appears to be convergent with a previous model of intergroup violence that models the probability of violence using data from the conflict in the former Yugoslav region (M. Lim, Metzler, & Bar-Yam, 2007).

8.3.4 Future Directions for Understanding Social Schisms

The approach to social schisms outlined here could also be tested using data drawn from online social networks, such as Twitter or Facebook, where data between individuals who are engaging in debates about beliefs essential to a social identity are often recorded in detail along with social network links. For example, debates about the allowance of homosexuality in the Anglican community, or the ordination of women in the Catholic community could be useful potential research targets. Examples of this effect might be found outside of doctrinal religions as well. Debates about controversial topics associated with political identities (such as Brexit in the United Kingdom or gun rights in the United States) might also show similar effects. Using the semantic network mapping techniques to analyze the posts on online social networks to measure within-group consensus and the "friends" or "follows" already present in the data of online social networks can present a powerful opportunity to study these effects and presents a target for future longitudinal studies that can test the claims of the IIS.

To conclude, this work allows for a range of future directions that would potentially clarify many theoretical issues, such as the role of fused individuals in introducing new idiosyncratic beliefs into a group, and potentially be used to address contemporary social and political issues such as schisms, radicalization, and extremism.

8.4 Reframing and Reflections

The cognitive cybernetic approach discussed throughout this work looks at religions as definable *cybernetic assemblages* (as opposed to the ultimately ineffable—and impenetrable—assemblages of post modernism). Beyond this work and in other scientific research programs that have operationalized religion in a similar way, definitions of religion have been scarce and largely focused on heuristics or groups, falling into the trappings (and associated misgivings) of group-level approaches and heuristic definitions. This leaves us with an issue: if defining religious heuristically or as groups (i.e., entitatively) is fundamentally problematic, what does it mean for the field which has primarily done both for decades? I believe it means that the field has created a great deal of ethnographic and historical knowledge but lacked in its contributions to theorizing about religion. This has resulted in a general approach that has—at times deliberately—been incompatible with scientific knowledge (particularly in the approaches embraced by the more extreme postmodernist and critical theorists), where instead of a scientific or objective approach, some have favored personal revelation and armchair anthropology, which cannot generalize outside of specific contexts and are of extremely limited utility to actually address the extremely important and pressing needs of the modern world. This has led to the field of religious studies largely neglecting (or rejecting) explanatory theorizing about religion as a human phenomenon in exchange for a focus on knowledge about hyper-contextualized and isolated historical and cultural instantiations of a religious tradition typically bounded by political geographies. We see this clearly in course offerings at most religious studies departments, who compartmentalize topics into "Religions of Africa," "Religions of Asia," "American Religions," etc. This shift toward geopolitical foci builds on the previous approach, where compartmentalization was intrinsically tied with the theological leanings of religious studies, and clergy or seminarians from the "world religions" would be hired to teach those religions (Lawson, 1967). In this way, religious studies has taken the "zoo approach"[8] where each religion is presented in its own little habitat, to be observed and enjoyed primarily for the delight of the scholar; regrettably failing to produce as much useful real-world knowledge that could be used to address relevant issues as it produces enjoyment and fulfillment of the spectator.

This pattern is also implicated in deeper institutional issues for the study of religion (and AI). In recent years, universities and funding agencies have focused on science and technology (or STEM) fields, often to the neglect and underfunding of the humanities and social sciences. This is obviously not because the humanities and social sciences are no longer important. To the contrary, I would argue that the humanities and social sciences have never been more important. Monica Toft, for example, has written at length about how religion will be an extremely prominent subject in the coming century and will play an increasingly important role in global geopolitics (see Toft et al., 2011).

Religion's impact on the everyday lives of billions of people is an example of the subject's importance to the contemporary world. However, those who have been studying religion, particularly since the post-modern turn in the latter half of the 1900s have rendered themselves useless to those outside of academia. By adopting frameworks that do not allow them to fruitfully address religious phenomena outside of a limited subtopic within the study of religion, they may find it difficult to effectively formulate how their research is valuable to the world today. While some defend that knowledge for knowledge sake is itself valuable, I find this argument to be unconvincing to say the least and generally the result of the privilege of academic life. The history and philosophy that they have committed to memory is not something that can help the average policy maker solve the problems of today that intersect with religion unless their focus happens to be related. Otherwise, there is no overarching framework to facilitate generalization as interpretation is reliant entirely on the application of a specific theory to a specific context. This approach is limited, when compared to a scientific approach that aims to produce falsifiable and generalizable frameworks that can be applied and contextualized to better understand (and even predict) the causes and effects that surround religious phenomena.

To be clear, my statements earlier are not to suggest that the study of religion is a useless endeavor. Rather, my suggestion is—to put it bluntly—that the people who are studying religion are all too often making themselves useless. Religion is an important topic with wide ranging implications, and to study something such as a single ritual centuries ago in a culture that no longer exists, and then suggest that such knowledge cannot bear on the issues of today (as an anecdotal example), is to relegate oneself to uselessness. It is not the subject itself, in my opinion, that is the problem; rituals and cultures of the past tell us a great deal about religion and human nature and do so in a way that is comparable to today, but to make the relevant comparisons we have to abandon frameworks that cannot support or outright deny the possibility of generalization. Decisions are made throughout the world about how to address religious extremists, how to stop terrorism, how to best integrate minorities from different religious communities as they immigrate or seek asylum, and how to stop genocides; in many of these examples the subject of religion is a life or death subject. However, when we relegate ourselves to obscurity in the ivory tower and are unable to quickly and succinctly defend why our work produces value to our wider community, we give up our seat at the table. To address these issues, we need scholars of religion who can create useful knowledge about and help to participate in its critical discussions; not in the form of virtue signaling and vocal support, which rarely ever echo beyond the halls in the Ivory Tower, but in the form of viable, realistic, and well-thought-out policy proposals. To do so, I argue, we need to embrace a study of religion that is naturalistic in its assumptions and able to be falsified (i.e., scientific). This does not preclude nonscientific studies, but it does suggest that the field, as a whole, should seriously reconsider the role of a scientific study of religion, which today is either ignored or being pushed away, despite its impact in the wider academic context.

In this reframing, I suggest that a cybernetic study of religion is one of the approaches that should be embraced. I believe that its level of analysis is appropriate, its empirical methods make it reliable, and its compatibility with computational modeling make it extremely powerful and applicable to many domains ranging from defense and intelligence to social policy and immigration planning. I also believe that the field of cultural evolution, when it is able to address the issues I've discussed earlier—and elsewhere (Lane, 2017b)—can produce useful knowledge that can help inform our understanding of religion and its effects on human societies throughout history. Sociology, psychology, and archaeology are also regularly producing knowledge that is helping us to better understand religion.

This line of reasoning is not suggesting that the scientific study of religion is without issue. Even at its best, the scientific study of religion has at least one issue that needs to be addressed. In the past, scholars of religion have argued that the scientific study of religion is too reductionistic. At times, this claim has been a defense of a sui generis approach to religion, which I argue is incompatible with the idea that religion is not a natural kind—and this claim is sometimes implicit in some work on cultural evolution (Lane, 2017b). Regardless, there is merit to the claims that the scientific approach's focus on reductionism is problematic.

Effectively, in the study of any complex system, multiple parts are interrelated and many of these parts interact in ways that produce their own unique effects on other variables and subsequent interactions in the system; recall from Chapter 1, that complex interactions are explicitly assumed in the cultural cybernetic approach. So, when researchers reduce a complex phenomenon and focus on just the interaction of a few variables in isolation, we are missing part of the picture. Scholars of religion have mentioned this in the past as a critique against the cognitive science of religion in particular and few scholars using a scientific approach would deny it; however, the issue is often misunderstood, and might be worse than some critics realize. This is because to isolate a small fraction of the relevant variables and test for causal relationships between them in isolation not only limits the view of religion in that study to just those variables, it neglects any effect that external variables might have on that system. From the epistemological perspective, this is the sacrifice that experimental methods make in order to increase controllability and interpretability of results. It is, on the whole, a powerful—if problematic—decision to make, but this kind of rampant reductionism is increasingly hard to defend as the cognitive science of religion moves away from experimental methods and is more reliant on online survey methods, where controllability is scarified to increase sample sizes. This reductionist tendency is particularly problematic given the empirical evidence suggesting that the causes and effects of religious beliefs and behaviors are both broad and complex. So, when we look at a subset of the cause-effect relationships in isolation, we are not just seeing part of the story, we are seeing part of the story that is not as accurate as it could be given the potentiality for other (external) effects on the reduced system of variables included in the study. With complex social phenomena such as religions, we have to ask ourselves, how many variables are important and how many interactions can we define in the assemblage of the religious system. From there, mapping those relationships is increasingly difficult as there is not a single experimental method that could facilitate the investigation of all of these variables in real-world contexts (either in reduced pairs of cause and effect relationships or holistically as a system).

This issue, I believe, calls for us to rethink how we approach the study of complex social systems generally, religion included. In my opinion this does not call for us to reject the sound findings that we have and start over, or to be any more skeptical about specific studies than we should be as scientists to begin with. Rather, we should employ ways to incorporate multiple causal effects and interactions simultaneously using methods that can allow us to make specific, quantifiable, testable predictions about religious beliefs and behaviors at both the individual and group level in the real world.

One powerful way of doing this today is through the use of MAAI systems. When I first presented the idea of multi-agent AI to the field of religious studies (Lane, 2013), I promoted the method as a way to deal with complex social phenomena because, by putting many variables and interactions into a simulation, we can use it to test for predicted effects in ways that are unavailable to other methods. In addition, MAAI systems can model group-level religious phenomena as the result from the complex interactions of individuals and their environment.

I believe the cultural cybernetic approach, complex as it may be, is a useful tool because it allows for us to be specific in our claims, precise in our models, and it allows us to validate our models more directly. It also allows us to admit one of the most powerful critiques against a reductionistic study of religion: that religion is complex and by reducing it you lose your ability to understand it holistically. Cultural cybernetics, I contend, embraces the premise that religions are complex to the full extent, but offers a response to the conclusion that this suggests that we cannot fruitfully study religions and other complex social systems scientifically; indeed, I go as far as to suggest that we can use the cultural cybernetic approach, rooted in the cognitive science of religion, to predict—at least in the near term (see Lane, 2017a)—religious systems and their probable paths for the future.

Looking back through the pages of this book, there are many passages that I can see being construed to suggest that I would hold the scientific study of religion in a supreme position. However, from an epistemological perspective, we can look at the framework that discussed throughout this book as one that is critically interdisciplinary and reliant upon scholars from across disciplines to function. This is evidenced by how, in the critical phase of model validation, empirical studies can work hand in hand with ethnographic and historical observations to determine if a model works. In this way, the critical scientific notion of falsification is one in which humanities and social science scholars play a critical role. The scientists studying religion could come up with models such as those outlined here, but these models would need to engage with scholars outside of the cognitive science of religion in order to ensure their validity; quite simply, there aren't enough scientific scholars of religion (much less those who have the ability to program computational models) with a viable knowledge base of key ethnographic and historical religions to facilitate that kind of validation without engaging teams of other religious scholars. In this way, scholars who do not have a background in the cognitive or computational sciences ultimately stand on level footing with those who do during model validation (Lane, 2019c). This can allow for truly interdisciplinary work in the scientific study of religion, which has all the rigor, precision, and (to be honest) funding appeal of the sciences but engages a topic, scope, and set of disciplines that have not enjoyed the attention of the sciences. In this way, I believe it help to bring scholars from many backgrounds into a single "big tent" interdisciplinary framework that is built upon three legs: computer modeling, psychology, and history.[9]

In recent years, top scholars in both religious studies and computer modeling and simulation have proposed that computer modeling could serve as a "lingua franca" for the computational social sciences (Tolk & Wildman, 2018), and this is a position that I generally agree with. I think that this "lingua franca" can have the effect of broadening the base of the social sciences to both strengthen its foundations epistemologically and engage a wider range of scholars. In the past, there has been a demarcation in the academic world, rooted in the German demarcation between *Geisteswißenschaften* (generally the humanities) and *Naturwißenschaften* (generally the natural sciences). The work of many scholars in the social sciences today is defining a trend toward integration of the two, where the questions and themes of the humanities are being addressed with the rigor and tools of scientific disciplines. The possible value of this trend for our understanding of complex social systems like religion, culture, economics, and politics is hard to estimate currently, although almost every stakeholder engaged today knows that it is a step forward from our current understanding of these subjects. In the field of religious studies, there has been a trend that looks generally at the study of religion from a naturalistic perspective, which is well captured—I believe—by the Czech and Slovak term "*religionistika*," which can be juxtaposed with *teologicka* (or theology) as an approach to religion that is not bound by naturalistic assumptions. In this new emergent study of religion, it allows for scholars with many backgrounds to come together on a single set of foundational assumptions rather than topics or methods. In the framework of cultural cybernetics outlined here, the current assumptions rest on the idea that the mind, as an organ that performs information processing and has been shaped by evolutionary pressures, plays a critical role in mediating the input of all our interactions with our biological and social environment and the outputs of our behaviors beliefs, and their subsequent effects in the "real" and "mental" worlds that we inhabit.

If nothing else, I hope this work—in the very least—challenges beliefs about how we can study the most important topics of today. By bringing together the study of religion and AI, I believe we can build a fruitful and interdisciplinary framework for the study of religion that makes progress in both the scientific and (traditionally) nonscientific approach to the topic. Ideally, I hope that the discussions and themes inspire engagement and further exploration into both the use of computer modeling by religious scholars and the investigation of critical topics from the humanities and social sciences by data scientists and AI experts. The complex problems that we face today as a civilization of many societies and cultures are too important to address in the ways that we have before. Recent work has shown how important a well-founded scientific approach that understands how we can contextualize human cognition within an appropriate evolutionary framework can be in addressing issues in society (e.g., Boyer, 2018; Diamond, 2012). With the rise of AI as an important and world-changing technology that affects so much of our daily life, it would appear to be a shame to miss out on the opportunity to apply this technology to aid our exploration and development regarding the most important topics to our own humanity.

Notes

Chapter 1

1 While there is some debate about how this translates to deep learning (Leshno, Lin, Pinkus, & Schocken, 1993) and what specifically the role of the activation function plays (Chen, Chen, & Liu, 1995), this is beyond our current point. Suffice to say here that basically any mathematical function that you provide that is directly relevant to religion is likely able to be approximated reliably by an artificial neural network.

2 Mereology is the study of how parts become wholes and the interaction between something and its constituent parts.

3 Here I am using the term in a way that is similar to, but a revision of, DeLanda's conception of an assemblage (2006, 2015, 2016); the obvious difference being that I am more open to assemblages as cognitive systems that are definable and more structured.

   Some readers may recognize this term as that coined by Deleuze and Guattari (1987) for the study of social complexity, which was later a key topic of discussion in the book *Fashionable Nonsense: Postmodern Intellectuals' Abuse of Science* (1998) because of its nonsensical phrasing and misuse of scientific terms. While the term does share lineage, I believe that the differences between its original use there and that of DeLanda, and now myself, are apparent.

4 In this way lessening the issue of "exteriority" in the conceptualization of an assemblage as traditionally construed.

5 I return to this point in the final chapter and discuss it more specifically in light of its repercussions for religious studies (also see Lane, 2018b, 2019c; Lane & Shults, 2018; Lane et al., 2019; Tolk & Wildman, 2018).

6 "Supernatural agent" is a term commonly used in the cognitive science of religion to describe nonnatural entities that people believe can have their own intentions and autonomous effects on the world, colloquially the supernatural agents of world religions are often referred to as a Gods or deities.

7 Personal and social identities are discussed in greater detail in later chapters. As a terminological note, I use the terms "personal schema," "personal identity," and "self-image." These are all discussed at length here and refer to slightly different things. A *personal schema* holds information that individuals have regarding their own personal experiences, knowledge about the world, beliefs, and values. As such, a personal schema holds the information from which individuals derive their

personal identity in a similar way to how a *social schema* holds the information one holds about their social identity. *Self-image* is used to refer to the attitudes we have toward our self and the attitudes others might have toward us; here it is used more selectively to refer to the emotional valence (positive or negative) one has for themselves regarding their group membership.

8 To clarify, "social identification" is not the same as "social identity." Social identity is used as a noun to refer to the group (or groups) that one feels is a part of one's self concept. Social identification is used as a verb to describe a way of aligning one's self to a group. Similarly, the term "social identity theory" is used in this book, but it only refers to the theory as found in the psychological literature. These concepts are discussed further in Chapter 2.

Chapter 2

1 For example, a particularly relevant example is the debate and defense of the SESHAT database findings (Whitehouse et al., 2019), which may have found evidence that the theological shifts to beliefs in "big gods" comes after a rise in social complexity—such as that seen in the Neolithic transition.

2 Long-term memory can be considered in terms of two additional forms: non-declarative and declarative. *Non-declarative* memory (sometimes called implicit memory) refers to memories that one does not have direct access to recall. For example, how to walk or ride a bike are non-declarative memories; those who can perform those tasks can remember how to perform these tasks but cannot fully describe how to perform them. *Declarative memory* (sometimes called explicit memory) is the information that we can express. This would include our cultural and religious beliefs, acquired knowledge, personal experiences, and personal histories. Therefore, when we refer to culturally transmitted beliefs that can serve as the basis for social cohesion, we are in fact referring to information stored in declarative memory.

3 Whitehouse writes:

> Schemas of this type form the cognitive underpinnings of universalistic ideology or, indeed, any conception of a community whose members are not individually specifiable. Religious identity, in the doctrinal mode, is primarily conferred on the basis of presumed commonalities in the thought and behavior of anonymous others, a state of affairs which is only conceivable with reference to semantic knowledge. (Whitehouse, 2000, p. 10)

4 This distribution is common throughout nature as well as the distributions of many natural phenomena follow this distribution (Mandlebrot, 1982) as do patterns in

economic markets (Mandlebrot & Hudson, 2008; Taleb, 2010, 2012) and in many aspects of social and cultural life (Lansing, 2003).

5 In the fusion literature, the terms "shared essence" and "core characteristics" are often used. Their definitions are extremely similar and for the sake of clarity, I use the term "essential beliefs" as the literature would suggest that essential beliefs are possible targets for perceived shared essences or core concepts. In this way, essential beliefs are a subset of shared essences or core characteristics (although some possible shared essences or core characteristics, such as race, might not qualify as essential beliefs). In the literature, *shared essences* are "qualities of a group that capture its very nature, without which the group would be fundamentally altered, and differentiate it from outgroups" (Buhrmester, Newson, et al., 2018, p. 5). Buhrmester et al. propose that shared essences can be "*symbolically represented* by physical objects, people, places, and events" (2018, p. 5; emphasis in origional) and are expanding on what Swann, Buhrmester et al. (2014) referred to as *core characteristics*.

6 In the text, Vázquez, Gómez, and Swann use the term "collective ties" but it is clear that this term is functionally equivalent to categorical ties. They state, "collective ties are based on sentiments toward the group category as a whole, independent of one's interpersonal relationships" (Vázquez et al., 2017, p. 481), citing Brewer and Gardner's (1996) seminal paper where the term "categorical ties" was outlined as the source for their definition.

7 Cronbach's α (or Cronbach's alpha) is a statistic used to test for scale reliability. It measures the internal consistency between items in a measure (such as the individual likert scale responses in the multi-item measures of social identification presented later).

8 The 15M protest is similar in motivation to the "Occupy Wall Street" movement but started in May of 2011, a few months before the earliest gatherings of the "Occupy" protesters in New York's Financial District began in September (Páez et al., 2015, p. 10).

Chapter 3

1 These map generally onto the schemas which would hold relevant information for personal and social identities respectively, discussed in Chapter 2.

2 The sign of the cross is a hand movement made by some Christians where they trace the outline of a cross in front of their body as a form of blessing; it is sometimes also used in times where safety, protection, or good luck is needed by the person making the sign. Salawat is a short prayer commonly translated as "peace be upon him" or abbreviated as PBUH.*

3 Semantic information can be represented as a schema or even interacting sets of schemas (Quillian, 1966). There have been extensive proposals concerning how

to best represent the schemas in human memory. This includes lists, hierarchies, and networks (or frames, discussed later) of information. This is not to say that the mind represents information as a computer might represent a list, hierarchy, or network, but that these are useful theoretical tools for abstraction that have real-world examples. For example, lists are often held by adherents of doctrinal religions, such as Islam's five pillars, Buddhism's eightfold path, and Judaism and Christianity's Ten Commandments. Furthermore, some types of information appear to be hierarchically formed. These include how humans construct categories of the natural world. While we may have a high-level category for "TREE," this category might include EVER-GREEN and DECIDUOUS. Within the category of EVER-GREEN, one might include PINE, REDWOOD, and CEDAR. Meanwhile, their category of DECIDUOUS can include ASH, BEACH, and BIRCH. While some researchers, such as Atran and Medin (2008) appear to suggest that this hierarchical storage has some cognitive realism, this is beyond the scope of this book, and the research here does not require such strong assumptions.

4   To be clear, *schemas* are structured sets of information that stores the relationships between representations. A *representation* is a concept or "a system of symbols isomorphic to some aspect of the environment" (Gallistel, 2001). The approach advocated here holds that it is unnecessary to believe that a specific representation has a schema that can adequately describe it. Rather, a schema is always a higher-level abstraction built upon representations. A frame is a representation of a schema. As such, representations are signified by nodes in the frame. The structure of information in the frame is defined by links between these nodes. In addition, there is no reason to believe that the information that is part of one schema cannot be part of another schema. In this way, multiple schemas could be viewed as a hyper-graph of representations, however, doing so is beyond the scope of the current research.

5   Although Quillian proposes that links represent ontological types of relationships between nodes (Quillian, 1988) this goes beyond the scope of the current research. It is addressed in the final chapter's discussion regarding the future directions for cultural cybernetics.

6   As such, this network approach does represent a form of hierarchical organization. However, this is a complex network hierarchy rather than one based on lateral classification of entities into different levels based on some property. Complex network-based hierarchies are often utilized and well-studied in network science (see Ravasz & Barabási, 2003).

7   This approach to computationally representing meaning for concepts has become standard due to the development of large computational systems such as the WordNet lexical database (G. A. Miller, 1995).

8   This single network, which allows for latent hierarchical formation by means of complex network links has also been suggested as a plausible way to model the changes in cultural representations and schemas over time (Whitehouse, 2013).

9 It should be noted that no claim is being made concerning the realism of these representations, they are only meant to be useful abstractions that can be efficiently represented and analyzed using modern computational techniques. In addition, Carley notes that they are not as complete as other structures that represent schemas, such as frames, which represent schemas as a hierarchical set of interrelated definitions (Minsky, 1974, p. 1). As it was originally formulated, a frame organizes information into two levels: the first level holds information which is always true for the schema (axioms); and the second level includes places where information is held (called "terminals") as well as the constraints on what that information can take (called "markers"). The information in one frame can reference information in another frame. For example, a frame for the concept JESUS can reference the frame for the concept HUMAN. Furthermore, HUMAN will include information such as age, a quality which all instances of HUMAN possess. A semantic network map is more simplified, and can include some definitions, but not all. For example, if the idea that the concept HUMAN can be defined by a numerical age is not relevant to a specific application, this definitional aspect of HUMAN does not need to be included in the semantic network map.
10 This prayer is frequently spoken by Christian communities. Many denominations recite it in unison on a weekly basis and others encourage or require it to be recited more frequently. The text for churches changes on tradition, but the version I refer to in this example is as follows: "Our Father who art in heaven, Hallowed be thy name. Thy kingdom come. Thy will be done, on earth as it is in heaven. Give us this day our daily bread, and forgive us our trespasses, as we forgive those who trespass against us, and lead us not into temptation, but deliver us from evil. For thine is the kingdom, and the power, and the glory, for ever and ever. Amen."
11 For those who are unfamiliar, this works in the same way as a multiplication table. You have some number on the top–for example, 5—and some number along the side—for example, 9—the value where column 5 and row 9 intersect holds the product of 5 and 9.

Chapter 4

1 Specifically, Jn 3:3-5 and 1 Pet. 1:22-23, which, in the original Greek, used to the term "ἀναγεγεννημένοι" (anagegennēmenoi) to refer to being "born again."
2 Singapore's independence came approximately two years after Singapore was emancipated from British control and federated with Malaysia in 1963.
3 In Singapore, this term refers to those individuals born into working class families with low educational attainment in the previous generation, who are better educated (i.e., university or college educated) and have higher paying jobs than their parents.

4   This phenomenon, called glossolalia, is considered by Pentecostal Christians to be a blessing of the Holy Spirit and is common in Singapore's Charismatic churches (Adam, 2003); however, glossolalia is uncommon in many mainline denominations such as Methodism, Lutheranism, Presbyterianism, or Anglicanism.
5   Signs and wonders also include being unburnt when touching fire and the handling of snakes. To my knowledge both of these phenomena are undocumented in the history of Singaporean Christianity. To this day, it is rare for any leader to perform exorcisms, but this was reported to have happened at home-based prayer groups during the period following the Clock Tower Revival (M. Tan, 2014).
6   The only notable exceptions in these churches being "youth services," which are services that utilize contemporary Christian music instead of traditional hymns, but such services do not encourage signs and wonders and I am unaware of any Singaporean church in the main Presbyterian or Lutheran tradition which have reported signs and wonders in a youth service.
7   "Lah" is a ubiquitous term in the dialect and speech of Singapore. It has no inherent meaning and is in many ways akin to the overuse of the word "like" by Americans. It is generally used as an interjection (Wee, 2011).
8   A *RMSEA* > .06 suggests that the model may be significant, but it is not a high-quality fit (see Westland, 2010; Wolf, Harrington, Clark, & Miller, 2013). In addition, future research should also check that the CFI, which is a fit index of an SEM that compares the specified model to a baseline model with the same structure but assumes no correlations between variables (Fan, Thompson, & Wang, 1999), improves with larger samples.

Chapter 5

1   It should be noted that scholars like Rodney Stark and William S. Bainbridge were engaged in both theorizing about religion (Stark & Bainbridge, 1987) and simulation of cultural change (Bainbridge, 1984) since the 1980s, but I'm unaware of any publications that aimed to engage directly with simulation of religion during this period. However, it is quite clear that the same modality of careful thinking and interactions that are required for building computer models are reflected in the precision presented by Stark and Bainbridge's key works.
2   NetLogo is a popular open source tool for agent-based modeling. It is freely available online for download, and it uses a language that is easy to learn, making it accessible for novices and those who are not trained in computer science. The BehaviorComposer is a tool developed by Ken Kahn at the University of Oxford that allows for individuals to quickly develop and prototype agent-based models within the NetLogo platform with even less coding on the part of the

researcher than NetLogo normally requires. As such, it represents a powerful tool for researchers who wish to develop computational models but may not have experience coding computer models. New alternatives for this technology are also being developed by colleagues at Old Dominion University and can be found at https://beta.cloudes.me/about

The original code for the DMR1 model can be found at the following URL: http://m.modelling4all.org/m/?frozen=MVCJ1KiGf59OARDR8vds6g&MforAllModel=1

3 Although code was developed to address the effects of dysphoric and euphoric emotional arousal, the functions were not included in the published version of the model.
4 This is done using the die command in NetLogo.
5 These anchors are mind-body dualism, promiscuous teleology, immanent justice, and hazard precaution.
6 Within the field of modelling and simulation, the terms "validation" and "verification" have a substantial literature for which there is not space to address in this book; therefore, I only focus on the most relevant aspects here. However, within the field, verification is the process of model development which addresses the extent to which the model represents the propositions or theory being addressed in the model—a sort of theoretical consistency check of sorts. Validation is the process by which one checks the model against the real-world system. This can be done in a number of ways—only a few are discussed in this book (for a review of validation and verification in modelling and simulation, see Sargent, 2013).
7 MATLAB is a software program with its own language that is often used for engineering and finance. Its efficient use of matrices as a key variable made it a common and flexible choice for analysis that historically was difficult or impossible to do with other analytics software such as SPSS. However, many of MATLAB's key functionality can also be done in R or Python, which are freely available (MATLAB requires a costly license, which, although available at most research universities and departments, limits its practicality for many in the social sciences).
8 This is a common practice in modeling and simulation. Although published code does not always include the commented functions of a model that are not active or depreciated, most models developed to investigate phenomena in the social sciences include a great deal of functionality that is taken out of the model in order to simplify it. This is done because simplifying the model can help you to better understand causal patterns, provide clarity in an already complex system, or simple for theoretical or other epistemological reasons. I believe that it should be considered best practice to publish code with functions commented that were part of the research, but not published or investigated. This can fast-track critiques and replication from other research groups, which are imperative to the scientific investigation of any phenomenon.

9 The use of evolutionary analogies is beyond the scope of this book, but is discussed at length in recent work by Knudt (2015) and in my subsequent response (Lane, 2017b). Among the key issues are the validity of simplifying assumptions made by such models. For example, the fusion model here assumes that humans reproduce as sexual haploids (Whitehouse et al., 2017b, p. 7), when in fact, humans are sexual diploids. This, however, is not necessarily an assumption with significant impact on the processes of cooperation or self-sacrifice, as such, the critique here will focus on more substantial issues with the model's assumptions and oversights.

10 Each of these variables are weighted and their weights can vary within the model depending on the target group one attempts to simulate. Recall that these variables reflect the empirical findings discussed in Chapters 3 and 4, which provided evidence that these are key variables to understanding social cohesion within doctrinal religious groups.

11 This question, noted by Barrett (2005) as one of the crucial empirical questions for the doctrinal mode, has never been systematically investigated. However, the variation analysis of the model here can provide at least a bearing for which to start with subsequent field studies in the future.

Chapter 6

1 A name coined by F. LeRon Shults.
2 For example, simulations of the Spanish Flu pandemic have been able to shed light on different historical debates (Kahn, 2012) by testing counterfactuals. In addition, the work of the GEHIR project at Masaryk University also pushed the field of modeling and simulation in this direction focusing on classical religions in the Greco-Roman Mediterranean (Fousek, Kaše, Mertel, Výtvarová, & Chalupa, 2018; Glomb, Mertel, Pospíšil, Stachoň, & Chalupa, 2018; Kaše, Hampejs, & Pospíšil, 2018).
3 You can find one here for example: http://www.gutenberg.org/ebooks/10
4 Web-spiders are programs that are designed to go to a website and follow link after link in order to download or copy a targeted set of information. In this case, the web-spider was set to find church websites that had links to sermons and download them. Then, web-scrapers, which are programs that harvest a specific kind of data from the internet, would download only the relevant information from the website, including the text of the website, and associated "meta-data" about it, such as the location, the date of the sermon, the name of the church, and its denomination. Naturally, all of this data cannot be found for every church either because the data isn't available on the website, or because it was in a format that the web-scrapers couldn't recognize.

5 While other organizations, such as the PEW Research Forum, have attempted to create similar databases, their methods are largely outdated and their focus on converting audio and video to text, which is very error prone, computationally burdensome, financially costly, and generally inefficient; this makes it more appropriate for very basic analyses as opposed to kind of high-quality research that could inform our understanding of religion in a more impactful way.

6 A video recording can be found here: https://www.youtube.com/watch?v=ELuIrk790pk

7 Although it may be a tertiary point, the same can be said for the field of social psychology. Although intergroup relations are still an important topic in social psychology, of the many questions and new directions in the field, computational modeling is rarely—if ever—included in the discussion. For example, a paper published by Jetten and Branscombe (2016) outlines the current state and directions of intergroup relations in social psychology, and the use of computational tools is not mentioned, likely because it is so rarely used in the field.

8 It is reasonable to list access to computational resources such as those used in this study as a potential limitation to the study. However, given the prevalence of HPC resources such as those in many universities as well as offered through Amazon (Amazon Web Services Incorporated, 2015) and Microsoft (Microsoft Corporation, 2016), these resources are becoming more available. It is more likely that learning how to use such tools will be the more significant barrier to entry for the use of HPC systems in the near future.

9 A "flash crash" is when the price of a stock or market plummets unnaturally quickly because of algorithmic anomalies. In May of 2010, high-frequency trading algorithms were associated with a 5 percent crash in the US stock markets, and it was then recovered in less than an hour. The only times a daily loss of 5 percent of more has been recorded in the US markets were due to the economic losses in the stock market associated with the economic slowdown caused by the Coronavirus.

10 As the topic is likely foreign to many readers, it is worth noting that there are very accessible resources on this topic, including a TED talk by Sean Gourley (Gourley, 2012), who has a different estimate on the volume of automated trades, as well as the easy-to-read book *Flash Boys* by Michael Lewis (2014).

Chapter 8

1 With cultural evolution, this was seen most clearly in programs of eugenics and social Darwinism while with cybernetics, it was through many discussions about control related to cold war concerns (Pickering, 2010).

2 Through a grant funded by the Norwegian Research Council titled "Emotional Contagion (EmotiCon): Predicting and Preventing the Spread of Anxiety, Stigma, and Misinformation during a Pandemic" in conjunction with the NORCE Center for Modeling Social Systems.
3 Through private research funded by Kingston University being led in collaboration with Josh Bullock.
4 Through research funded by the Center for Mind and Culture.
5 De-fusion is currently a hypothetical proposal where a fused individual would no longer be fused to their group (Fredman et al., 2015; Gómez & Vázquez, 2015).
6 This model was developed as part of the Modeling Religion Project at the Center for Mind and Culture. On this project, my role was to aid in model development and the programming of the simulation. I also aided in the validation, verification, analysis of the model, and the writing of the paper cited here. The Modeling Religion Project was funded by the John Templeton Foundation.
7 This model was developed as part of a joint effort between the Modeling Religion Project at the Center for Mind and Culture and the MODRN project at the Center for Modeling Social Systems.
8 This term was originally coined by Lawson in regards to how religion is taught in public universities decades ago (Lawson, 1967), but is still just as relevant to the treatment of religion in the twenty-first century (see essays in Light & Wilson, 2004).
9 Here it may be important to reiterate that by history I not only mean archaeology and the study of the past, but also the study of historical texts and the study of recent history through many paradigms including anthropology, sociology, political science, etc.

References

Adam, V. (2003). *The psychological aspects of Singaporean Glossolalia: A qualitative study*. UMI, Ann Arbor, MI: Saybrook University.

Adamczyk, A., LaFree, G., & Barrera-Vilert, M. (2019). Using google and twitter to measure, validate and understand views about religion across Africa. *Society, 56*, 231–240. https://doi.org/10.1007/s12115-019-00359-4

Ahn, Y. Y., Han, S., Kwak, H., Moon, S., & Jeong, H. (2007). Analysis of topological characteristics of huge online social networking services. WWW 2007, 835–844. Retrieved from http://dl.acm.org/citation.cfm?id=1242685

Ahrweiler, P., Schilperoord, M., Pyka, A., & Gilbert, N. (2015). Modelling research policy: Ex-ante evaluation of complex policy instruments. *Journal of Artificial Societies and Social Simulation, 18*(4), 1–30. https://doi.org/10.18564/jasss.2927

Aiden, E., & Michel, J.-B. (2014). *Uncharted: Big-data as a lens on human culture*. New York: Riverhead Books.

Albanese, C. L. (2008). *A republic of mind and spirit: A cultural history of American metaphysical religion*. New Haven, CT: Yale University Press.

Aldridge, J. W., & Crisp, T. (1982). Maintenance rehearsal and long-term recall with a minimal number of items. *The American Journal of Psychology, 95*(4), 565–570.

Alesina, A., & Perotti, R. (1993). Income distribution, political instability, and investment (Working Paper No. 4486). Retrieved from https://www.nber.org/papers/w4486

Amazon Web Services Incorporated. (2015). AWS | Amazon elastic compute cloud (EC2)—scalable cloud hosting. Retrieved June 21, 2015, from Amazon Web Services website: http://aws.amazon.com/ec2/

Anderson, B. (2006). *Imagined Communities* (4th ed.). London and New York: Verso.

Aron, A., Aron, E. N., Tudor, M., & Nelson, G. (1991). Close relationships as including other in the self. *Journal of Personality and Social Psychology, 60*(2), 241–253.

Ashmore, R. D., Deaux, K., & McLaughlin-Volpe, T. (2004). An organizing framework for collective identity: Articulation and significance of multidimensionality. *Psychological Bulletin, 130*(1), 80–114. https://doi.org/10.1037/0033-2909.130.1.80

Atkinson, Q. D., & Whitehouse, H. (2011). The cultural morphospace of ritual form. *Evolution and Human Behavior, 32*(1), 50–62. https://doi.org/10.1016/j.evolhumbehav.2010.09.002

Atran, S. (2006a). Sacred values, terrorism, and the limits of rational choice. U.S. Interagency Meeting, Department of Homeland Security. Retrieved from https://www.researchgate.net/publication/265069924_SACRED_VALUES_TERRORISM_AND_THE_LIMITS_OF_RATIONAL_CHOICE

Atran, S. (2006b). Sacred values and the limits of rational choice: Conflicting cultural frameworks in the struggle against terrorism. In J. McMillan (Ed.), *"In the same light as slavery": Building a global antiterrorist consensus* (pp. 151–177). Washington, DC: Institute for National Strategic Studies, National Defense University Press.

Atran, S. (2016). The devoted actor: Unconditional commitment and intractable conflict across cultures. *Current Anthropology, 57*(S13), S192–S203. https://doi.org/10.1086/685495

Atran, S., Axelrod, R., & Davis, R. (2007). Sacred barriers to conflict resolution. *Science, 317*(5841), 1039–1040. https://doi.org/10.1126/science.1144241

Atran, S., & Ginges, J. (2012). Religious and sacred imperatives in human conflict. *Science, 336*(6083), 855–857. https://doi.org/10.1126/science.1216902

Atran, S., & Medin, D. (2008). *The native mind and the cultural construction of nature*. Boston, MA: MIT Press.

Atran, S., Medin, D., Ross, N., Lynch, E., Vapnarsky, V., Ek', E. U., . . . Baran, M. (2002). Folkecology, cultural epidemiology, and the spirit of the commons. *Current Anthropology, 43*(3), 421–450. https://doi.org/10.1086/339528

Atran, S., Sheikh, H., & Gómez, Á. (2014a). Devoted actors sacrifice for close comrades and sacred cause. *Proceedings of the National Academy of Sciences of the United States of America, 111*(50), 17702–17703. https://doi.org/10.1073/pnas.1420474111

Atran, S., Sheikh, H., & Gómez, Á. (2014b). For cause and comrade: Devoted actors and willingness to fight. *Cliodynamics, 5*(1), 41–57. Retrieved from https://escholarship.org/uc/item/6n09f7gr

Axelrod, R. (1984). *The evolution of cooperation*. New York: Basic Books.

Axelrod, R., & Hamilton, W. D. (1981). The evolution of cooperation. *Science, 211*(4489), 1390–1396. https://doi.org/10.1126/science.7466396

Bainbridge, W. S. (1984). Computer simulation of cultural drift—limitations on interstellar colonisation. *British Interplanetary Society, Journal (Interstellar Studies), 37*, 420–429. Retrieved from http://labs.adsabs.harvard.edu/adsabsadsabs/abs/1984JBIS...37..420B/

Bainbridge, W. S. (2006). *God from the machine: Artificial intelligence models of religious cognition*. Lanham, MD: AltaMira Press.

Ball, J. (2013, November 20). US And UK struck secret deal to allow NSA to "Unmask" Britons' personal data. *The Guardian*. Retrieved from https://www.theguardian.com/world/2013/nov/20/us-uk-secret-deal-surveillance-personal-data

Bar-Yosef, O. (2001). The chronology of the Levantine Middle Paleolithic. *Zephyrus, 53–54*, 15–26.

Bar-Yosef Mayer, D. E., Vandermeersch, B., & Bar-Yosef, O. (2009). Shells and ochre in Middle Paleolithic Qafzeh Cave, Israel: Indications for modern behavior. *Journal of Human Evolution, 56*(3), 307–314. https://doi.org/10.1016/j.jhevol.2008.10.005

Barker, G. (2009). *The agricultural revolution in prehistory: Why did foragers become farmers?* Oxford: Oxford University Press.

Barkow, J. H., Cosmides, L., & Tooby, J. (Eds.). (1992). *The adapted mind: Evolutionary psychology and the generation of culture*. New York: Oxford University Press.

Barrett, J. L. (2005). In the empirical mode: Evidence needed for the modes of religiosity theory. In H. Whitehouse & R. N. McCauley (Eds.), *Mind and religion: Psychological and cognitive foundations of religiosity* (pp. 109–126). Walnut Creek, CA: AltaMira Press.

Bartlett, F. C. (1932). *Remembering: A study in experimental and social psychology* (1995 Reprint). New York and Cambridge: Cambridge University Press.

Bateson, G. (1972). *Steps to an ecology of mind: Collected essays in anthropology, psychiatry, evolution, and epistemology* (2nd ed.). Northvale, NJ and London: Jason Aronson Inc.

Baumard, N., & Boyer, P. (2013). Explaining moral religions. *Trends in Cognitive Sciences, 17*(6), 272–280. https://doi.org/10.1016/j.tics.2013.04.003

Baumard, N., Hyafil, A., Morris, I., & Boyer, P. (2014). Increased affluence explains the emergence of ascetic wisdoms and moralizing religions. *Current Biology, 25*(1), 10–15. https://doi.org/10.1016/j.cub.2014.10.063

BBC News. (2017, May 17). Twitter user numbers overtaken by China's Sina Weibo. *BBC News*: Technology. Retrieved from https://www.bbc.com/news/technology-39947442

BBC News. (2018, July 6). *Aum Shinrikyo: The Japanese cult behind the Tokyo Sarin attack*. Retrieved from https://www.bbc.com/news/world-asia-35975069

Bellah, R. N. (2011). *Religion in human evolution: From the paleolithic to the axial age*. Cambridge, MA: Belknap Press of Harvard University Press.

Benjamin, O. N. (2012). Foreign direct investment in Sub-Saharan Africa. *African Journal of Economic and Sustainable Development, 1*(1), 49–66.

Berns, G. S., Bell, E., Capra, C. M., Prietula, M. J., Moore, S., Anderson, B., . . . Atran, S. (2012). The price of your soul: Neural evidence for the non-utilitarian representation of sacred values. *Philosophical Transactions of the Royal Society of London. Series B, Biological Sciences, 367*(1589), 754–762. https://doi.org/10.1098/rstb.2011.0262

Berntsen, D. (2001). Involuntary memories of emotional events: Do memories of traumas and extremely happy events differ? *Applied Cognitive Psychology, 15*(7), 135–158. https://doi.org/10.1002/acp.838

Berntsen, D., & Rubin, D. C. (2006). The centrality of event scale: A measure of integrating a trauma into one's identity and its relation to post-traumatic stress disorder symptoms. *Behavior Research and Therapy, 44*(2), 219–231. https://doi.org/10.1016/j.biotechadv.2011.08.021.Secreted

Berntsen, D., & Thomsen, D. K. (2005). Personal memories for remote historical events: Accuracy and clarity of flashbulb memories related to World War II. *Journal of Experimental Psychology: General, 134*(2), 242–257. https://doi.org/10.1037/0096-3445.134.2.242

Berntsen, D., Willert, M., & Rubin, D. C. (2003). Splintered memories or vivid landmarks? Qualities and organization of traumatic memories with and without PTSD. *Applied Cognitive Psychology*, *17*(6), 675–693. https://doi.org/10.1002/acp.894

Besta, T., Szulc, M., & Jaśkiewicz, M. (2015). Political extremism, group membership and personality traits: Who accepts violence? / Extremismo político, pertenencia al grupo y rasgos de personalidad: ¿Quién acepta la violencia? *Revista de Psicología Social*, *30*(3), 563–585. https://doi.org/10.1080/02134748.2015.1065085

Bew, L. P. A. E., & Gillespie, G. (1999). *Northern Ireland: A chronology of the troubles 1968–1999*. Dublin: Gill & MacMillan.

Bhattacharya, C. B., & Elsbach, K. D. (2002). Us versus them: The roles of organizational identification and disidentification in social marketing initiatives. *Journal of Public Policy & Marketing*, *21*(1), 26–36. https://doi.org/10.1509/jppm.21.1.26.17608

Bigiotti, A., & Navarra, A. (2019). Optimizing automated trading systems. In T. Antipova & A. Rocha (Eds.), *Digital Science* (pp. 254–261). Berlin: Springer. https://doi.org/10.1007/978-3-030-02351-5

Billig, M., & Tajfel, H. (1973). Social categorization and similarity in intergroup behaviour. *European Journal of Social Psychology*, *3*(1), 27–52. https://doi.org/10.1002/ejsp.2420030103

Binder, J. R., Desai, R. H., Graves, W. W., & Conant, L. L. (2009). Where is the semantic system? A critical review and meta-analysis of 120 functional neuroimaging studies. *Cerebral Cortex*, *19*(12), 2767–2796. https://doi.org/10.1093/cercor/bhp055

Bird, A., & Tobin, E. (2017). Natural kinds. In *Stanford encyclopedia of philosophy*. The Metaphysics Research Lab, Center for the Study of Language and Information (CSLI), Stanford University.

Bohorquez, J. C., Gourley, S., Dixon, A. R., Spagat, M., & Johnson, N. F. (2009). Common ecology quantifies human insurgency. *Nature*, *462*(7275), 911–914. https://doi.org/10.1038/nature08631

Bonin, K., & Lane, J. E. (n.d.). Identity fusion, devoted actor theory, and extremism. In *Routledge handbook of evolution and religion*. New York: Routledge.

Bortolini, T., Newson, M., Natividade, J. C., Vázquez, A., & Gómez, Á. (2018, January). Identity fusion predicts endorsement of pro-group behaviours targeting nationality, religion, or football in Brazilian samples. *British Journal of Social Psychology*. https://doi.org/10.1111/bjso.12235

Boyd, R., & Richerson, P. J. (2005). *The origin and evolution of cultures*. New York: Oxford University Press.

Boyer, P. (2018). *Minds make societies: How cognition explains the world humans create*. New Haven, CT: Yale University Press.

Boyer, P., & Liénard, P. (2006). Why ritualized behavior? Precaution Systems and action parsing in developmental, pathological and cultural rituals. *Behavioral and Brain Sciences*, *29*(6), 595–613; discussion 613–50. Retrieved from http://www.ncbi.nlm.nih.gov/pubmed/17918647

Boyer, P., & Ramble, C. (2001). Cognitive templates for religious concepts: Cross-cultural evidence for recall of counter-intuitive representations. *Cognitive Science, 25*, 535–564.

Braxton, D. M., Upal, M. A., & Nielbo, K. L. (2012). Computing religion: A new tool in the multilevel analysis of religion. *Method & Theory in the Study of Religion, 24*(3), 267–290. https://doi.org/10.1163/157006812X635709

Brewer, M. B. (1991). The social self: On being the same and different at the same time. *Personality and Social Psychology Bulletin, 17*(5), 475–482. https://doi.org/10.1177/0146167291175001

Brewer, M. B., & Gardner, W. (1996). Who is this "we"? Levels of collective identity and self representations. *Journal of Personality and Social Psychology, 71*(1), 83–93. https://doi.org/10.1037//0022-3514.71.1.83

Brewer, M. B., & Pierce, K. P. (2005). Social identity complexity and outgroup tolerance. *Personality and Social Psychology Bulletin, 31*(3), 428–437. https://doi.org/10.1177/0146167204271710

Brubaker, R. (2002). Ethnicity without groups. *European Journal of Sociology, 43*(2), 163–189.

Bruce, S. (1993). Religion and rational choice atiocritique of economic explanations of religious behavior. *Sociology of Religion, 54*(2), 193–205.

Bryson, J. J. (2018). Patiency is not a virtue: The design of intelligent systems and systems of ethics. *Ethics and Information Technology, 20*(1), 15–26. https://doi.org/10.1007/s10676-018-9448-6

Bryson, J. J., & Winfield, A. (2017). Standardizing ethical design for artificial intelligence and autonomous systems. *Computer, 50*(5), 116–119. https://doi.org/10.1109/MC.2017.154

Buck, C., Bulian, J., Ciaramita, M., Gajewski, W., Gesmundo, A., Houlsby, N., & Wang, W. (2018). Ask the right questions: Active question reformulation with reinforcement learning. In *Proceedings of the 6th international conference on learning representations (ICLR 2018)*. Retrieved from https://storage.googleapis.com/pub-tools-public-publication-data/pdf/75e359c2883f4d287a8753d32e2c5e22bfbfb55f.pdf

Buckley, B. C., & Ramzy, A. (2019, December 16). China's detention camps for muslims turn to forced labor. *The New York Times*, pp. 1–7. Retrieved from https://www.nytimes.com/2018/12/16/world/asia/xinjiang-china-forced-labor-camps-uighurs.html

Buhrmester, M. D., Burnham, D., Johnson, D. D. P., Curry, O. S., Macdonald, D. W., & Whitehouse, H. (2018, May). How moments become movements: Shared outrage, group cohesion, and the lion that went viral. *Frontiers in Ecology and Evolution, 6*, 1–7. https://doi.org/10.3389/fevo.2018.00054

Buhrmester, M. D., Fraser, W. T., Lanman, J. A., Whitehouse, H., & Swann, W. B. (2014). When terror hits home: Fused Americans saw Boston bombing victims as "family" and rushed to their aid. *Self and Identity, 14*(3), 253–270. https://doi.org/10.1080/15298868.2014.992465

Buhrmester, M. D., Gómez, Á., Brooks, M. L., Morales, J. F., Fernández, S., & Swann, W. B. (2012). My group's fate is my fate: Identity-fused Americans and Spaniards link personal life quality to outcome of 2008 elections. *Basic and Applied Social Psychology*, *34*(6), 527–533. https://doi.org/10.1080/01973533.2012.732825

Buhrmester, M. D., Newson, M., Vázquez, A., Hattori, W. T., & Whitehouse, H. (2018). Winning at any cost: Identity fusion, group essence, and maximizing ingroup advantage. *Self and Identity*, *17*(5), 500–516.

Bulbulia, J., Geertz, A. W., Atkinson, Q. D., Cohen, E., Evans, N., François, P., . . . Wilson, D. S. (2013). The cultural evolution of religion. In P. J. Richerson & M. H. Christiansen (Eds.), *Cultural evolution: Society, technology, language, and religion* (pp. 381–404). https://doi.org/10.7551/mitpress/9780262019750.003.0020

Bunge, M. (2011). Knowledge: Genuine and bogus. *Science and Education*, *20*(5–6), 411–438. https://doi.org/10.1007/s11191-009-9225-3

Burgess, S. (2005). Introduction. In Stanley M. Burgess (Ed.), *Encyclopedia of Pentecostal and charismatic Christianity* (pp. xiii–xiv). New York: Routledge.

Byrne, C. A., Hyman, I. E., & Scott, K. L. (2001). Comparisons of memories for traumatic events and other experiences. *Applied Cognitive Psychology*, *15*(7), 119–133. https://doi.org/10.1002/acp.837

Carley, K. M. (1986). An approach for relating social structure to cognitive structure. *The Journal of Mathematical Sociology*, *12*(2), 137–189. https://doi.org/10.1080/0022250X.1986.9990010

Carley, K. M. (1987). *Increasing consensus through shared social position and interaction*. Retrieved from http://www.casos.cs.cmu.edu/publications/papers/carley_1987_increasingconsensus.PDF

Carley, K. M. (1997). Extracting team mental models through textual analysis. *Journal of Organizational Behavior*, *18*, 533–558. https://doi.org/10.1002/(SICI)1099-1379(199711)18:1+<533::AID-JOB906>3.3.CO;2-V

Carley, K. M., & Kaufer, D. S. (1993). Semantic connectivity: An approach for analyzing symbols in semantic networks. *Communication Theory*, *3*(3), 183–213.

Carley, K. M., Pfeffer, J., Reminga, J., Storrick, J., & Columbus, D. (2012). *ORA user's guide 2012*. Retrieved from http://www.casos.cs.cmu.edu/publications/papers/CMU-ISR-13-108.pdf

Cashdan, E. (2001). Ethnocentrism and xenophobia: A cross-cultural study. *Current Anthropology*, *42*(5), 760–765. https://doi.org/10.1086/323821

Cashdan, E., & Steele, M. (2013). Pathogen prevalence, group bias, and collectivism in the standard cross-cultural sample. *Human Nature*, *24*(1), 59–75. https://doi.org/10.1007/s12110-012-9159-3

Cassotti, M., Agogue, M., Camarda, A., Houde, O., & Borst, G. (2016). Inhibitory control as a core process of creative problem solving and idea generation from childhood to adulthood. In B. Barbot (Ed.), *Perspectives on creativity development. New directions for child and adolescent development* (pp. 61–72). https://doi.org/10.1002/cad

Chen, T., Chen, H., & wen Liu, R.(1995). Approximation capability in C(Rn) by multilayer feedforward networks and related problems. *IEEE Transactions on Neural Networks, 6*(1), 25–30. https://doi.org/10.1109/72.363453

Chiclana, F., Tapia García, J. M., del Moral, M. J., & Herrera-Viedma, E. (2013). A statistical comparative study of different similarity measures of consensus in group decision making. *Information Sciences, 221,* 110–123. https://doi.org/10.1016/j.ins.2012.09.014

Chong, T., & Yew-Foong, H. (2013). *Different under God: A survey of church-going protestants in Singapore.* Singapore: Institute of Southeast Asian Studies.

Christian, D. (2005). *Maps of time: An introduction to big history.* Berkely, CA: University of California Press.

Clark, A. (2004). Testing the two modes theory: Christian practice in the later middle ages. In H. Whitehouse & L. H. Martin (Eds.), *Theorizing religions past: Archaeology, history, and cognition.* Walnut Creek, CA: AltaMira Press.

Clauset, A., & Young, M. (2005). Scale invariance in global terrorism. *ArXiv Preprint,* 1–6.

Collins, D. J., & Shanks, D. R. (2006). Summation in causal learning: Elemental processing or configural generalization? *Quarterly Journal of Experimental Psychology, 59*(9), 1524–1534. https://doi.org/10.1080/17470210600639389

Conte, R., Gilbert, N., Bonelli, G., Coiffi-Revilla, C., Deffuant, G., Kertesz, J., ... Helbing, D. (2012). Manifesto of computational social science. *The European Physical Journal Special Topics, 214,* 325–346. https://doi.org/10.1140/epjst/e2012-01697-8

Conti, M., Passarella, A., & Pezzoni, F. (2011). A model for the generation of social network graphs. Paper presented at the IEEE International Symposium on a World of Wireless, Mobile and Multimedia Networks, WoWMoM 2011—*Digital Proceedings* (January 2016). https://doi.org/10.1109/WoWMoM.2011.5986141

Conway, A. R. A., Skitka, L. J., Hemmerich, J. A., & Kershaw, T. C. (2009). Flashbulb memory for 11 September 2001. *Applied Cognitive Psychology, 23,* 605–623. https://doi.org/10.1002/acp

Cronin-Furman, K. (2018, September 19). China has chosen cultural genocide in Xinjiang—for now. *Foreign Policy.* Retrieved from https://foreignpolicy.com/2018/09/19/china-has-chosen-cultural-genocide-in-xinjiang-for-now/

Culpan, T. (2018, November 14). Tencent's wechat giant is still quick on its feet. *Bloomberg.* Retrieved from https://www.bloomberg.com/opinion/articles/2018-11-14/tencent-s-wechat-giant-is-still-quick-on-its-feet

Curci, A., & Luminet, O. (2009). Flashbulb memories for expected events: A test of the emotional-integrative model. *Applied Cognitive Psychology, 23,* 98–114. https://doi.org/10.1002/acp

Dávid-Barrett, T., & Carney, J. (2015, April). The deification of historical figures and the emergence of priesthoods as a solution to a network coordination problem. *Religion, Brain & Behavior, 5981.* https://doi.org/10.1080/2153599X.2015.1063001

Dávid-Barrett, T., & Dunbar, R. I. M. (2013). Processing power limits social group size: Computational evidence for the cognitive costs of sociality. *Proceedings of the Royal Society B, 280*, 1–8.

Davis, J. A., & Smith, T. W. (2004). *General social survey, 2004*. Retrieved from http://www.thearda.com/Archive/Files/Descriptions/GSS2004.asp

Davison, N. (2012, December 7). WeChat: The Chinese social media app that has dissidents worried. *The Guardian*. Retrieved from https://www.theguardian.com/world/2012/dec/07/wechat-chinese-social-media-app

Dawson, M. R. W., & Spetch, M. L. (2005). Traditional perceptrons do not produce the overexpectation effect. *Neural Information Processing, 7*(1), 11–17.

de Gelder, B., & Hortensius, R. (2014). New frontiers in social neuroscience. *Research and Perspectives in Neurosciences, 21*(1), 153–164. https://doi.org/10.1007/978-3-319-02904-7

DeLanda, M. (2006). *A new philosophy of society: Assemblage theory and social complexity*. London: Bloomsbury Academic.

DeLanda, M. (2015). *Philosophy and simulation: The emergence of synthetic reason*. London: Bloomsbury Academic.

DeLanda, M. (2016). *Assemblage theory*. Edinburgh: Edinburgh University Press.

Deleuze, G., & Guattari, F. (1987). *A thousand plateaus: Capitalism and schizophrenia*. Minneapolis: University of Minnesota Press.

Diamond, J. (2012). *The world until yesterday*. London: Penguin Books.

DiAngelo, R. (2007). *Beyond human mind: The soul evolution of heaven's gate*. Beverly Hills, CA: Rio DiAngelo.

DiFonzo, N., Bourgeois, M. J., Suls, J., Homan, C., Stupak, N., Brooks, B. P., . . . Bordia, P. (2013). Rumor clustering, consensus, and polarization: Dynamic social impact and self-organization of hearsay. *Journal of Experimental Social Psychology, 49*(3), 378–399. https://doi.org/10.1016/j.jesp.2012.12.010

Doman, M., Hutcheon, S., Welch, D., & Taylor, K. (2018, October 31). China's frontier of fear. *ABC News*. Retrieved from https://www.abc.net.au/news/2018-11-01/satellite-images-expose-chinas-network-of-re-education-camps/10432924

Dunbar, R. I. M. (1992). Neocortex size as a constraint size in primates. *Journal of Human Evolution, 20*, 469–493.

Dunbar, R. I. M., Gamble, C., & Gowlett, J. A. (Eds.). (2014). *Lucy to language: The benchmark papers*. Oxford: Oxford University Press.

Dunbar, R. I. M., & Sosis, R. (2018). Optimising human community sizes. *Evolution and Human Behavior, 39*(1), 106–111. https://doi.org/10.1016/j.evolhumbehav.2017.11.001

Durkheim, E. (1915). *The elementary forms of the religious life: A study in religious sociology* (1st English; J. W. Trans., Swain, Ed.). Retrieved from https://archive.org/details/elementaryformso00durk/page/n5

Ehrman, B. D. (2008). *The new testament: A historical introduction to the early Christian writings*. New York: Oxford University Press.

Eisenman, R. (1998). *James, the brother of Jesus: The key to unlocking the secrets of Early Christianity and the Dead Sea Scrolls.* New York: Penguin Books.

Ellemers, N., Spears, R., & Doosje, B. (2002). Self and social identity. *Annual Review of Psychology, 53,* 161–186. https://doi.org/10.1146/annurev.psych.53.100901.135228

Elsbach, K. D., & Bhattacharya, C. B. (2001). Defining who you are by what you're not. *Organization Science, 12*(4), 393–413. https://doi.org/10.1287/orsc.12.4.393.10638

Epstein, J. M. (1999). Agent-based computational models and generative social science. *Complexity, 4*(5), 41–60. https://doi.org/10.1002/(SICI)1099-0526(199905/06)4:5<41::AID-CPLX9>3.3.CO;2-6

Epstein, J. M. (Ed.). (2006). *Generative social science: Studies in agent-based computational modeling (Princeton Studies in Complexity).* Princeton, NJ: Princeton University Press.

Epstein, J. M. (2014). *Agent_Zero: Toward neurocognitive foundations for generative social science.* Princeton, NJ: Princeton University Press.

Epstein, J. M., & Axtell, R. L. (1996). *Growing artificial societies: Social science from the bottom up.* Washington, DC: Brookings Institution Press.

Eve, F. (2018, November 3). China is committing ethnic cleansing in Xinjiang it's time for the world to stand up. *The Guardian.* Retrieved from www.theguardian.com/world/2018/nov/03/china-is-committing-ethnic-cleansing-in-xinjiang-its-time-for-the-world-to-stand-up

Facebook. (2016). Company Info | Facebook. Retrieved May 22, 2016, from Facebook Newsroom website: http://newsroom.fb.com/company-info/

Fan, X., Thompson, B., & Wang, L. (1999). Effects of sample size, estimation methods, and model specification on structural equation modeling fit indexes. *Structural Equation Modeling, 6*(1), 56–83. https://doi.org/10.1080/10705519909540119

Ferdinand, V., Kirby, S., & Smith, K. (2017, February). The cognitive roots of regularization in language. *Cognition, 184,* 53–68. https://doi.org/10.1016/j.cognition.2018.12.002

Festinger, L., Riecken, H. W., & Schachter, S. (2008). *When prophecy fails* (2nd ed.). London: Pinter & Martin.

Fincher, C. L., & Thornhill, R. (2012). Parasite-stress promotes in-group assortative sociality: The cases of strong family ties and heightened religiosity. *Behavioral and Brain Sciences, 35*(2), 61–79. https://doi.org/10.1017/S0140525X11000021

Fivush, R., Habermas, T., Waters, T. E. A., & Zaman, W. (2011). The making of autobiographical memory: Intersections of culture, narratives and identity. *International Journal of Psychology, 46*(5), 321–345. https://doi.org/10.1080/00207594.2011.596541

Flores Kanter, P. E., Medrano, L., & Conn, H. (2015). Does mood affect self-concept? Analysis through a natural semantic networks based approach. *International Journal of Behavioral Research & Psychology, 3,* 114–120. https://doi.org/10.19070/2332-3000-1500022

Floridi, L., & Taddeo, M. (2016). What is data ethics? *Philosophical Transactions of the Royal Society of London. Series A*, *374*(20160360). http://doi.org/10.1098/rsta.2016.0360

Fodor, J. A. (1985). Precis of the modularity of mind. *Behavioral and Brain Sciences*, *8*, 1–42.

Fousek, J., Kaše, V., Mertel, A., Výtvarová, E., & Chalupa, A. (2018). Spatial constraints on the diffusion of religious innovations: The case of early Christianity in the Roman Empire. *PLoS One*, *13*(12), 1–14. https://doi.org/10.1371/journal.pone.0208744

Fredman, L. A., Buhrmester, M. D., Gómez, Á., Fraser, W. T., Talaifar, S., Brannon, S. M., & Swann, W. B. (2015). Identity fusion, extreme pro-group behavior, and the path to defusion. *Social and Personality Psychology Compass*, *9*(9), 468–480. https://doi.org/10.1111/spc3.12193

Friedkin, N. E. (2004). Social cohesion. *Annual Review of Sociology*, *30*(1), 409–425. https://doi.org/10.1146/annurev.soc.30.012703.110625

Gallistel, C. R. (2001). Mental representations; psychology of. In Neil Smelser and Paul Baltes (Eds.), *Encyclopedia of the Social and Behavioral Sciences* (Vol. 1, p. 8). Amsterdam: Elsevier Science Ltd.

Gardiner, J. M., Gawlik, B., & Richardson-Klavehn, A. (1994). Maintenance rehearsal affects knowing, not remembering; elaborative rehearsal affects remembering, not knowing. *Psychonomic Bulletin & Review*, *1*(1), 107–110. https://doi.org/10.3758/BF03200764

Gelfand, M. J., Nishii, L. H., & Raver, J. L. (2006). On the nature and importance of cultural tightness-looseness. *The Journal of Applied Psychology*, *91*(6), 1225–1244. https://doi.org/10.1037/0021-9010.91.6.1225

Gelfand, M. J., Raver, J. L., Nishii, L., Leslie, L. M., Lun, J., Lim, B. C., . . . Yamaguchi, S. (2011). Differences between tight and loose cultures: A 33-nation study. *Science*, *332*(6033), 1100–1104. https://doi.org/10.1126/science.1197754

Gilbert, N., Ahrweiler, P., Barbrook-Johnson, P., Narasimhan, K. P., & Wilkinson, H. (2018). Computational modelling of public policy: Reflections on practice. *Journal of Artificial Societies and Social Simulation*, *21*(1). https://doi.org/10.18564/jasss.3669

Ginges, J., & Atran, S. (2009). What motivates participation in violent political action. *Annals of the New York Academy of Sciences*, *1167*, 115.

Ginges, J., Atran, S., Medin, D., & Shikaki, K. (2007). Sacred bounds on rational resolution of violent political conflict. *Proceedings of the National Academy of Sciences of the United States of America*, *104*(18), 7357–7360.

Ginges, J., Atran, S., Sachdeva, S., & Medin, D. (2011). Psychology out of the laboratory: The challenge of violent extremism. *The American Psychologist*, *66*(6), 507–519. https://doi.org/10.1037/a0024715

Gleick, J. (2012). *The information: A history, a theory, a flood*. New York: Vintage Books.

Glomb, T., Mertel, A., Pospíšil, Z., Stachoň, Z., & Chalupa, A. (2018). Ptolemaic military operations were a dominant factor in the spread of Egyptian cults across the early

Hellenistic Aegean Sea. *PLoS One, 13*(3), e0193786. https://doi.org/10.1371/journal.pone.0193786

Goh, D. P. S. (2010). State and social Christianity in post-colonial Singapore. *SOJOURN: Journal of Social Issues in Souteast Asia, 25*(1), 54–89. https://doi.org/10.1355/s

Goh, R. B. H. (2005). *Christianity in Southeast Asia.* Singapore: ISEAS Publications.

Gómez, Á., Brooks, M. L., Buhrmester, M. D., Vázquez, A., Jetten, J., & Swann, W. B. (2011). On the nature of identity fusion: Insights into the construct and a new measure. *Journal of Personality and Social Psychology, 100*(5), 918–933. https://doi.org/10.1037/a0022642

Gómez, Á., López-Rodríguez, L., Sheikh, H., Ginges, J., Wilson, L., Waziri, H., . . . Atran, S. (2017). The devoted actor's will to fight and the spiritual dimension of human conflict. *Nature Human Behaviour, 1*(9), 673–679. https://doi.org/10.1038/s41562-017-0193-3

Gómez, Á., Morales, J. F., Hart, S., Vázquez, A., & Swann, W. B. (2011). Rejected and excluded forevermore, but even more devoted: Irrevocable ostracism intensifies loyalty to the group among identity-fused persons. *Personality & Social Psychology Bulletin, 37*(12), 1574–1586. https://doi.org/10.1177/0146167211424580

Gómez, Á., & Vázquez, A. (2015). The power of "feeling one" with a group: Identity fusion and extreme pro-group behaviours / El poder de "sentirse uno" con un grupo: fusión de la identidad y conductas progrupales extremas. *Revista de Psicología Social, 30*(3), 481–511. https://doi.org/10.1080/02134748.2015.1065089

Gonçalves, B., Perra, N., & Vespignani, A. (2011). Modeling users' activity on twitter networks: Validation of Dunbar's number. *PLoS One, 6*(8), e22656. https://doi.org/10.1371/journal.pone.0022656

González-Val, R. (2015). War size distribution: Empirical regularities behind conflicts. *Defence and Peace Economics, 2694*(April), 1–16. https://doi.org/10.1080/10242694.2015.1025486

Goodall, J. (2005). Primate spirituality. In *The encyclopedia of religion and nature* (pp. 1303–1306). New York: Bloomsbury Continuum.

Goodwin, J. (2009). *Commentary on Mark Juergensmeyer, terror in the mind of God: The global rise of religious violence.* Berkeley: University of California Press, 3rd ed., 2003. (*Critical Studies on Terrorism, 2*(2), 335–337). https://doi.org/10.1080/17539150903024880

Google LLC. (2018). *Google cloud.* Retrieved February 18, 2019, from Documentation website: https://cloud.google.com/docs/

Gore, R., Lemos, C., Shults, F. L., & Wildman, W. J. (2018). Forecasting changes in religiosity and existential security with an agent-based model. *Journal of Artificial Societies and Social Simulation, 21*(1), 1–31. https://doi.org/10.18564/jasss.3596

Gore, R. J., Lynch, C. J., & Kavak, H. (2017). Applying statistical debugging for enhanced trace validation of agent-based models. *Simulation, 93*(4), 273–284. https://doi.org/10.1177/0037549716659707

Gourley, S. (2012). High frequency trading and the new algorithmic ecosystem. *TEDxNewWallStreet*. Retrieved from https://www.youtube.com/watch?v=V43a-KxLFcg

Granovetter, M. S. (1983). The strength of weak ties: A network theory revisited. *Sociological Theory*, *1*, 201–233. https://doi.org/10.2307/202051

Gsell, M. (2008). Assessing the impact of algorithmic trading on markets: A simulation approach. In *16th European conference on information systems, ECIS*.

Gunning, J., & Jackson, R. (2011). What's so "religious" about "religious terrorism"? *Critical Studies on Terrorism*, *4*(3), 369–388. https://doi.org/10.1080/17539153.2011.623405

Gyimah-Brempong, K. (1999). Political instability, investment and economic growth in sub-Saharan Africa. *Journal of African Economics*, *8*(1), 52–86. https://doi.org/10.1093/jae/8.1.52

Hamid, N., Pretus, C., Atran, S., Crockett, M. J., Ginges, J., Sheikh, H., . . . Vilarroya, O. (2019). Neuroimaging "will to fight" for sacred values: An empirical case study with supporters of an Al Qaeda associate. *Royal Society Open Science*, *6*(181585). https://doi.org/10.1098/rsos.181585

Hamming, R. W. (1950). Error detecting and error correcting codes. *The Bell System Technical Journal*, *29*(2), 147–160.

Harrington, J. R., & Gelfand, M. J. (2014). Tightness–looseness across the 50 united states. *Proceedings of the National Academy of Sciences*, *111*(22), 7990–7995. https://doi.org/10.1073/pnas.1317937111

Haslam, C., Jetten, J., Haslam, S. A., Pugliese, C., & Tonks, J. (2011). "I remember therefore I am, and I am therefore I remember": Exploring the contributions of episodic and semantic self-knowledge to strength of identity. *British Journal of Psychology*, *102*(2), 184–203. https://doi.org/10.1348/000712610X508091

Hayden, B. (1990). Nimrods, piscators, pluckers, and planters: The emergence of food production. *Journal of Anthropological Archaeology*, *9*. https://doi.org/10.1016/0278-4165(90)90005-X

Hayden, B. (1995). A new overview of domestication. In T. D. Price & A. B. Gebauer (Eds.), *Last hunters, first farmers: New perspectives on the prehistoric transition to agriculture* (pp. 273–299). Santa Fe: School of American Reserach Press.

Hayden, B. (2009). The proof is in the pudding: Feasting and the origins of domestication. *Current Anthropology*, *50*(5), 597–601. https://doi.org/10.1086/605110

Henrich, J. (2016). *The secret of our success: How culture is driving human evolution, domesticating our species, and making us smarter*. Princeton, NJ: Princeton University Press.

Henrich, J., Heine, S. J., & Norenzayan, A. (2010). The weirdest people in the world? *The Behavioral and Brain Sciences*, *33*(2–3), 61–83; discussion 83–135. https://doi.org/10.1017/S0140525X0999152X

Hill, R. A., Bentley, R. A., & Dunbar, R. I. M. (2008). Network scaling reveals consistent fractal pattern in hierarchical mammalian societies. *Biology Letters*, *4*(6), 748–751. https://doi.org/10.1098/rsbl.2008.0393

Hill, R. A., & Dunbar, R. I. M. (2003). Social network size in humans. *Human Nature*, *14*(1), 53–72.

Hill, V., & Carley, K. M. (1999). An approach to identifying consensus in a subfield: The case of organizational culture. *Poetics*, *27*(1), 1–30.

Hinton, K. (1985). *Growing churches Singapore style: Ministry in an urban context*. Singapore: Overseas Missionary Fellowship (IHQ) Ltd.

Hodges, S. D., Sharp, C. A., Gibson, N. J. S., & Tipsord, J. M. (2013). Nearer my God to thee: Self-God overlap and believers' relationships with God. *Self and Identity*, *12*(3), 337–356. https://doi.org/10.1080/15298868.2012.674212

Hogg, M. A. (2001). From prototypicality to power: A social identity analysis of leadership. In S. R. Thye & E. Lawler (Eds.), *Advances in group processes* (Vol. 18, pp. 1–30). Bradford: Emerald Group Publishing Limited.

Hogg, M. A., & Abrams, D. (1988). The social identity approach: Context and content. In D. Abrams & M. A. Hogg (Eds.), *Social identifications: A social psychology of intergroup relations and group processes* (pp. 6–30). New York: Routledge.

Hogg, M. A., Abrams, D., Otten, S., & Hinkle, S. (2004). The social identity perspective: Intergroup relations, self-conception, and small groups. *Small Group Research*, *35*(3), 246–276. https://doi.org/10.1177/1046496404263424

Hogg, M. A., & Turner, J. C. (1985). Interpersonal-attraction, social identification and psychological group formation. *European Journal of Social Psychology*, *15*(1), 51–66. https://doi.org/10.1002/ejsp.2420150105

Holmes, E. A., Grey, N., & Young, K. A. D. (2005). Intrusive images and "hotspots" of trauma memories in posttraumatic stress disorder: An exploratory investigation of emotions and cognitive themes. *Journal of Behavior Therapy and Experimental Psychiatry*, *36*(1), 3–17. https://doi.org/10.1016/j.jbtep.2004.11.002

Holmes, V. M., & McGregor, J. (2007). Rote memory and arithmetic fact processing. *Memory & Cognition*, *35*(8), 2041–2051. https://doi.org/10.3758/BF03192936

Hornik, K. (1991). Approximation capabilities of multilayer feedforward networks. *Neural Networks*, *4*(2), 251–257. https://doi.org/10.1016/0893-6080(91)90009-T

Horsley, J. (2018, November 16). China's Orwellian social credit score isn't real. *Foreign Policy*. Retrieved from https://foreignpolicy.com/2018/11/16/chinas-orwellian-social-credit-score-isnt-real/

Hoyt, S. F. (1912). The etymology of religion. *Journal of the American Oriental Society*, *32*(2), 126–129. Retrieved from https://www.jstor.org/stable/3087765

Humphries, M. D., & Gurney, K. (2008). Network "small-world-ness": A quantitative method for determining canonical network equivalence. *PLoS One*, *3*(4), 10. https://doi.org/10.1371/journal.pone.0002051

Iannaccone, L. R., & Makowsky, M. D. (2007). Accidental atheists? Agent-based explanations for the persistence of religious regionalism. *Journal for the Scientific Study of Religion*, *46*(1), 1–16. https://doi.org/10.1111/j.1468-5906.2007.00337.x

Intel IT Center. (2012). Big data analytics: Intel's IT manager survey on how organizations are using big data. In *Peer Research* (Vol. 62). https://doi.org/10.5206/uwomj.v87i2.1149

Jaccard, P. (1912). The distribution of flora in the Alpine Zone. *The New Phytologist*, *11*(2), 37–50. https://doi.org/10.1111/j.1469-8137.1912.tb05611.x

Jackson, M. O. (2008). Average distance, diameter, and clustering in social networks with homophily. In C. Papadimitriou & S. Zhang (Eds.), *Internet and network economics: Lecture notes in computer science*. 4th International Workshop, *WINE 2008* (Vol. 5385, pp. 4–11). Retrieved from http://link.springer.com/chapter/10.1007%2F978-3-540-92185-1_3

James, W. (1890). *The principles of psychology* (Vol. 1). https://doi.org/10.1037/11059-000

James, W. (1902). *The varieties of religious experience: A study in human nature*. New York: Longmans, Green, and Co.

Jans, L., Postmes, T., & Van der Zee, K. I. (2011). The induction of shared identity: The positive role of individual distinctiveness for groups. *Personality & Social Psychology Bulletin*, *37*(8), 1130–1141. https://doi.org/10.1177/0146167211407342

Jensen, M. A., Atwell Seate, A., & James, P. A. (2018). Radicalization to violence: A pathway approach to studying extremism. *Terrorism and Political Violence*, *32*(5), 1067–1090. https://doi.org/10.1080/09546553.2018.1442330

Jetten, J., & Branscombe, N. R. (2016). Editorial overview: Current issues and new directions in intergroup relations. *Current Opinion in Psychology*, *11*. https://doi.org/10.1016/j.copsyc.2016.09.001

Jimenez, J., Gómez, Á., Buhrmester, M. D., Vazquez, A., Whitehouse, H., & Swann, W. B. (2015). The dynamic identity fusion index: A new continuous measure of identity fusion for web-based questionnaires. *Social Science Computer Review* (Online preprint), 1–14. https://doi.org/10.1177/0894439314566178

Johnson, D. D. P. (2015). *God is watching you: How the fear of God makes us human*. Oxford: Oxford University Press.

Johnson, N., Carran, S., Botner, J., Fontaine, K., Laxague, N., Nuetzel, P., . . . Tivnan, B. (2011, July). Pattern in escalations in insurgent and terrorist activity. *Science*, *333*, 81–84.

Jong, J., Philip, T., Chang, S.-H., & Halberstadt, J. (2015). The religious correlates of death anxiety: A systematic review and meta-analysis. *Religion, Brain & Behavior*, *8*(1), 4–20.

Jong, J., Whitehouse, H., Kavanagh, C., & Lane, J. E. (2016). Shared Trauma Leads to Identity Fusion via Personal Reflection. *PLoS One*, *10*(12), e0145611. https://doi.org/10.1371/journal.pone.0145611

Juergensmeyer, M. (2000). *Terror in the mind of God: The global rise of religious violence*. Berkeley: University of California Press.

Kahn, K. (2012). *The "Spanish" influenza pandemic and its relation to World War I*. Retrieved May 14, 2015, from World War I Centenary: Continuations and Beginnings website: http://ww1centenary.oucs.ox.ac.uk/?p=2190

Kahn, K. (2013). *Behaviour composer: Modelling4all project*. Retrieved from http://m.modelling4all.org/

Kahn, K., & Noble, H. (2010). The BehaviourComposer 2.0: A web-based tool for composing NetLogo code fragments. *Constructionism 2010*, 1–14. Retrieved from https://docs.google.com/viewer?a=v&pid=sites&srcid=ZGVmYXVsdGRvbWFpbnxtb2RlbGxpbmc0YWxscHJvamVjdHxneDoxZDhmOGI5NjViMzhkZjA

Kaplan, D., & Marshall, A. (1996). *The cult at the end of the world: The terrifying story of the Aum Doomsday Cult, from the subways of Tokyo to the nuclear arsenals of Russia*. New York: Crown Publishers.

Kaše, V., Hampejs, T., & Pospíšil, Z. (2018). Modeling cultural transmission of rituals in Silico: The advantages and pitfalls of agent-based vs. system dynamics models modeling. *Journal of Cognition & Culture*, *18*(5), 483–507. https://doi.org/10.1163/15685373-12340041

Kavanagh, C., Jong, J., Mckay, R., & Whitehouse, H. (2018). Positive experiences of high arousal martial arts rituals are linked to identity fusion and costly progroup actions. *European Journal of Social Psychology*. https://doi.org/10.1002/ejsp.02514

Kehoe, E. J., & White, N. E. (2004). Overexpectation: Response loss during sustained stimulus compounding in the rabbit nictitating membrane preparation. *Learning and Memory*, *11*(4), 476–483. https://doi.org/10.1101/lm.77604

Keren, H., Boyer, P., Mort, J., & Eilam, D. (2013). The impact of precaution and practice on the performance of a risky motor task. *Behavioral Sciences*, *3*(3), 316–329. https://doi.org/10.3390/bs3030316

Knudt, R. (2015). *Contemporary evolutionary theories of culture and the study of religion*. London: Bloomsbury Academic.

Kobie, N. (2019, January 3). The complicated truth about China's social credit system. *Wired UK*. Retrieved from https://www.wired.co.uk/article/china-social-credit-system-explained

Koziol, M. (2015, July 3). Hillsong conference at Sydney Olympic Park: 30,000 flock for enlightenment. *The Sydney Morning Herald*. Retrieved from http://www.smh.com.au/nsw/hillsong-conference-at-sydney-olympic-park-30000-flock-for-enlightenment-20150701-gi2hd1.html

Kühl, H. S., Kalan, A. K., Arandjelovic, M., Aubert, F., D'Auvergne, L., Goedmakers, A., . . . Boesch, C. (2016). Chimpanzee accumulative stone throwing. *Scientific Reports*, *6*(November 2015), 1–8. https://doi.org/10.1038/srep22219

Kuo, L. (2019, January 11). "If you enter a camp, you never come out": Inside China's war on Islam. *The Guardian*, pp. 1–6. Retrieved from https://www.theguardian.com/world/2019/jan/11/if-you-enter-a-camp-you-never-come-out-inside-chinas-war-on-islam

Kvavilashvili, L., Mirani, J., Schlagman, S., Foley, K., & Kornbrot, D. E. (2009). Consistency of flashbulb memories of September 11 over long delays: Implications for consolidation and wrong time slice hypotheses. *Journal of Memory and Language*, *61*(4), 556–572. https://doi.org/10.1016/j.jml.2009.07.004

Lai, A. E. (Ed.). (2008). *Religious diversity in Singapore*. Singapore: Institute of Southeast Asian Studies.

Lane, J. E. (2009). Potential causes of ritual instability in doctrinal new religious movements: A cognitive hypothesis. *Sacra*, 7(2), 82–92.

Lane, J. E. (2011). Cognition in context: New approaches to new Islamist movements in the Middle East. *Sacra*, 9(1), 22–33.

Lane, J. E. (2013). Method, theory, and multi-agent artificial intelligence: Creating computer models of complex social interaction. *Journal for the Cognitive Science of Religion*, 1(2), 161–180. https://doi.org/10.1558/jcsr.v1i2.161

Lane, J. E. (2014). *Digital records of TRAC methodist church archives*. Retrieved from archives.methodist.org.sg

Lane, J. E. (2015a). Big Data and Anthropology: Concerns for data collection in a new research context. *Journal for the Anthropological Society of Oxford*, 8(1), 74–88 .

Lane, J. E. (2015b). Semantic network mapping of religious material. *Journal for Cognitive Processing*, 16(4), 333–341. https://doi.org/10.1007/s10339-015-0649-1

Lane, J. E. (2016). Analyzing sermons across the world: Opening the study of religion to the world of "big-data." Paper presented at the Meeting of the International Association for the Cognitive Science of Religion. Vancouver, BC.

Lane, J. E. (2017a). Can we predict religious extremism? *Religion, Brain & Behavior*, 7(4), 299–304. https://doi.org/10.1080/2153599X.2016.1249923

Lane, J. E. (2017b). Contemporary evolutionary theories of culture and the study of religion. *Journal for the Cognitive Science of Religion*, 3(2), 210–221. https://doi.org/10.1558/jcsr.30498

Lane, J. E. (2018a). Big data, deep data: Studying culture through texts using data mining. In *Invited Lecture to University of Plzen*. https://doi.org/10.13140/RG.2.2.12715.08480

Lane, J. E. (2018b). Bridging qualitative and quantitative approaches to religion. *Religion, Brain & Behavior*, 9(3), 301–307. https://doi.org/10.1080/2153599X.2018.1429008

Lane, J. E. (2018c). The emergence of social schemas and lossy conceptual information networks: How information transmission can lead to the apparent "emergence" of culture. In S. Mittal, S. Y. Diallo, & A. Tolk (Eds.), *Emergent behavior in complex systems engineering: A modeling and simulation approach* (1st ed., pp. 329–256). New York: John Wiley & Sons, Inc.

Lane, J. E. (2019a). *The evolution of doctrinal religions: Using semantic network analysis and computational models to examine the evolutionary dynamics of large religions*. Oxford: University of Oxford.

Lane, J. E. (2019b). Understanding epistemological debates in the humanities and social sciences can aid in model development: Modeling interpretive and explanatory theories. In S. Y. Diallo, W. J. Wildman, F. L. Shults, & A. Tolk (Eds.), *Human simulation*. Berlin: Springer.

Lane, J. E. (2019c). Understanding epistemological debates in the humanities and social sciences can aid in model development: Modeling interpretive and explanatory theories. In S. Y. Diallo, W. J. Wildman, F. L. Shults, & A. Tolk (Eds.), *Human *simulation: Perspectives, insights, and applications* (pp. 67–79). Cham, Switzerland: Springer Nature.

Lane, J. E. (2019d, October). The promise of reincarnation in the Grundtvig AI. The Religious Studies Project. Retrieved from https://www.religiousstudiesproject.com/2019/10/18/the-promise-of-reincarnation-in-the-grundtvig-ai/

Lane, J. E., & Shults, F. L. (2018). Cognition, culture, and social simulation. *Journal of Cognition & Culture, 18*(5), 451–461. https://doi.org/10.1163/15685373-12340039

Lane, J. E., & Shults, F. L. (2019). Can we model religious behavior using computer simulation? In W. W. M. J. D. Jason Slone, D. Wiebe, L. H. Martin, & R. Kundt (Ed.), *The cognitive science of religion and its philosophical implications* (pp. 123–132). London: Bloomsbury Academic.

Lane, J. E., Shults, F. L., & McCauley, R. N. (2019). Modeling and simulation as a pedagogical and heuristic tool for developing theories in cognitive science: An example from ritual competence theory. In S. Y. Diallo, W. J. Wildman, F. L. Shults, & A. Tolk (Eds.), *Human simulation: Perspectives, insights, and applications* (pp. 143–154). Cham, Switzerland: Springer Nature.

Lane, J. E., Shults, F. L., & Wildman, W. J. (2018). A potential explanation for self-radicalisation. *Behavioral and Brain Sciences, 41*, e207. Retrieved from https://www.cambridge.org/core/journals/behavioral-and-brain-sciences/article/potential-explanation-for-selfradicalisation/46180567213843B94D217E50C7F1193E

Lansing, J. S. (2003). Complex adaptive systems. *Annual Review of Anthropology, 32*, 183–204.

Lawson, E. T. (1967). The study of religion in public universities: A panel presentation. In M. McLean (Ed.), *Religious studies in public Universities* (pp. 45–54). Carbondale, IL: Southern Illinois University Press.

Lawson, E. T., & McCauley, R. N. (1990). *Rethinking religion: Connecting cognition and culture*. New York: Cambridge University Press.

Layton, D. (1999). *Seductive poison: A Jonestown survivor's story of life and death in the people's temple*. New York: Anchor Books.

Lee, J. K., & Kim, E. (2017). Incidental exposure to news: Predictors in the social media setting and effects on information gain online. *Computers in Human Behavior, 75*, 1008–1015. https://doi.org/10.1016/j.chb.2017.02.018

Lentz, C., & Sturm, H.-J. (2001). Of trees and earth shrines: An interdisciplinary approach to settlement histories in the West African savanna. *History in Africa, 28*, 139–168. https://doi.org/10.2307/3172212

Leshno, M., Lin, V. Y., Pinkus, A., & Schocken, S. (1993). Multilayer feedforward networks with a nonpolynomial activation function can approximate any function. *Neural Networks, 6*(6), 861–867. https://doi.org/10.1016/S0893-6080(05)80131-5

Lewis, M. (2014). *Flash boys: A Wall Street revolt*. New York: W.W. Norton & Co.

Liénard, P., & Lawson, E. T. (2008). Evoked culture, ritualization and religious rituals. *Religion, 38*(March), 157–171. https://doi.org/10.1016/j.religion.2008.01.004

Light, T., & Wilson, B. C. (Eds.). (2004). *Religion as a human capacity: A festschrift in honor of E. Thomas Lawson*. Leiden, Netherlands: Brill.

Lim, J. (2012, February 22). NUS orders Christian group to stop all activities on campus. *The Straits Times*, p. A9.

Lim, M., Metzler, R., & Bar-Yam, Y. (2007). Global pattern formation and ethnic/cultural violence. *Science, 317*, 1540–1544. https://doi.org/10.1126/science.1142734

Lincoln, B. (2006). *Holy terrors: Thinking about religion after september 11* (2nd ed.). Chicago: The University of Chicago Press.

Luhrmann, T. M. (2012). *When God talks back: Understanding the American evangelical relationship with God*. New York: Vintage Books.

Macdonald, D. W., Jacobsen, K. S., Burnham, D., Johnson, P. J., & Loveridge, A. J. (2016). Cecil: A moment or a movement? Analysis of media coverage of the death of a lion, Panthera Leo. *Animals, 6*(5). https://doi.org/10.3390/ani6050026

Malley, B. (2004). The doctrinal mode and evangelical Christianity in the United States. In H. Whitehouse & J. Laidlaw (Eds.), *Ritual and memory: Toward a comparative anthropology of religion* (pp. 79–87). Walnut Creek, CA: AltaMira Press.

Mandlebrot, B. B. (1982). *The fractal geometry of nature*. San Francisco: W.H. Freeman.

Mandlebrot, B. B., & Hudson, R. (2008). *The (mis)behavior of markets: A fractal view of risk, ruin, and reward*. London: Profile Books.

Martin, L. H. (2005). The hellenisation of Judaeo-Christian faith or the Christianisation of Hellenic thought? *Religion & Theology, 12*(1), 2–19.

Martin, L. H., & Wiebe, D. (2012). Religious studies as a scientific discipline: The persistence of a delusion? *Religion, 20*(1), 39–42.

Mashek, D. J., Aron, A., & Boncimino, M. (2003). Confusions of self with close others. *Personality and Social Psychology Bulletin, 29*(3), 382–392. https://doi.org/10.1177/0146167202250220

Mathworks. (2014). *pdist function: Matlab*. Retrieved from http://uk.mathworks.com/help/stats/pdist.html

Matthews, K. E. (2014). [Personal communication]. Singapore.

McCants, W. (2015). *The ISIS Apocalypse: The history, strategy, and doomsday vision of the Islamic State*. New York: St. Martin's Press.

Mccauley, C. (2006). Group identification under conditions of threat dentificatstudents' attachment to country, family, ethnicity, religion, and university before and after September 11, 2001. *Political Psychology, 27*(1), 77–98.

McCauley, R. N., & Lawson, E. T. (1993). Connecting the cognitive and the cultural: Artificial minds as methodological devices in the study of socio-cultural. In R. G. Burton (Ed.), *Minds: Natural and artifical* (pp. 121–145). Albany, NY: State University of New York Press.

McCauley, R. N., & Lawson, E. T. (2002). *Bringing ritual to mind: Psychological foundations of cultural forms*. New York: Cambridge University Press.

McComb, K., Baker, L., & Moss, C. (2006). African elephants show high levels of interest in the skulls and ivory of their own species. *Biology Letters, 2*(1), 26–28. https://doi.org/10.1098/rsbl.2005.0400

McCorkle, W. W., & Lane, J. E. (2012). Ancestors in the simulation machine: Measuring the transmission and oscillation of religiosity in computer modeling. *Religion, Brain & Behavior, 2*(3), 215–218. https://doi.org/10.1080/2153599X.2012.703454

McFarlane, K. A., & Humphreys, M. S. (2012). Maintenance rehearsal: The key to the role attention plays in storage and forgetting. *Journal of Experimental Psychology: Learning, Memory, and Cognition, 38*(4), 1001–1018. https://doi.org/10.1037/a0026783

McLeod, J., & Von Treuer, K. (2013). Towards a cohesive theory of cohesion. *International Journal of Business and Social Research, 3*(12), 1–11. Retrieved from http://dro.deakin.edu.au/view/DU:30059957

McPherson, M., Smith-Lovin, L., & Cook, J. M. (2001). Birds of a feather: Homophily in social networks. *Annual Review of Sociology, 27*, 415–444. Retrieved from http://www.jstor.org/stable/2678628

Meeter, M., & Murre, J. M. J. (2004). Consolidation of long-term memory: Evidence and alternatives. *Psychological Bulletin, 130*(6), 843–857. https://doi.org/10.1037/0033-2909.130.6.843

Meeter, M., & Murre, J. M. J. (2005). Tracelink: A model of consolidation and amnesia. *Cognitive Neuropsychology, 22*(5), 559–587. https://doi.org/10.1080/02643290442000194

Melton, J. G. (2009). *Melton's Encyclopedia of American religions* (8th ed.; J. Bevereley, C. Jones, & P. S. Nadell, Eds.). Farmington Hills, MI: Gale.

Melton, J. G. (2018). Branch Davidian. In *Encyclopaedia Britannica*. Retrieved from https://www.britannica.com/topic/Branch-Davidian

Melton, J. G., & Bromley, D. G. (2009). Violence and new religions: An assessment of problems, progress, and prospects in understanding the NRM-violence connection. In M. Al-Rasheed & M. Shterin (Eds.), *Dying for faith: Religiously motivated violence in the contemporary world* (pp. 27–41). London and New York: I.B.Tauris & Co. Ltd.

Michel, J.-B., Shen, Y. K., Aiden, A. P., Veres, A., Gray, M. K., The Google Books Team, ... Aiden, E. L. (2010). Quantitative analysis of culture using millions of digitized books. *Science, 331*(January), 176–183. https://doi.org/10.1126/science.1199644

Microsoft Corporation. (2016). *Microsoft Azure*. Retrieved from https://azure.microsoft.com

Miller, D. E., & Yamamori, T. (2007). *Global pentecostalism: The new face of Christian social engagement*. Berkeley, CA: University of California Press.

Miller, G. A. (1995). WordNet: A lexical database for english. *Communications of the ACM, 38*(11), 39–41. Retrieved from https://wordnet.princeton.edu/

Minsky, M. (1974). A framework for representing knowledge. In *The psychology of computer vision* (No. 306). Retrieved from https://web.media.mit.edu/~minsky/papers/Frames/frames.html

Mitchell, C. (2006). *Religion, identity and politics in Northern Ireland: Boundaries of belonging and belief*. Burlington, VT: Ashgate.

Mithen, S. (2006). *After the ice: A global human history 20,000–5,000 BC*. Cambridge, MA: Harvard University Press.

Moscovitch, M., Nadel, L., Winocur, G., Gilboa, A., & Rosenbaum, R. S. (2006). The cognitive neuroscience of remote episodic, semantic and spatial memory. *Current Opinion in Neurobiology, 16*(2), 179–190. https://doi.org/10.1016/j.conb.2006.03.013

Müller, F. M. (1882). *Introduction to the science of religion* (New ed.). London: Longmans, Green, and Co.

Newport, K. G. C. (2006). *The branch Davidians of Waco: The history and beliefs of an apocalyptic sect*. Oxford: Oxford University Press.

Newson, M., Buhrmester, M., & Whitehouse, H. (2016). Explaining lifelong loyalty: The role of identity fusion and self-shaping group events. *PLos One, 11*(8), e0160427. https://doi.org/10.1371/journal.pone.0160427

Norenzayan, A. (2013). *Big Gods: How religion transformed cooperation and conflict*. Princeton, NJ: Princeton University Press.

Nowak, M. A., Tarnita, C. E., & Wilson, E. O. (2010). The evolution of eusociality. *Nature, 466*(7310), 1057–1062. https://doi.org/10.1038/nature09205

Otten, S. (2016). The Minimal Group Paradigm and its maximal impact in research on social categorization. *Current Opinion in Psychology, 11*, 85–89. https://doi.org/10.1016/j.copsyc.2016.06.010

Páez, D., Rimé, B., Basabe, N., Wlodarczyk, A., Zumeta, L., Páez, D., ... Wlodarczyk, A. (2015). Psychosocial effects of perceived emotional synchrony in collective gatherings. *Journal of Personality and Social Psychology, 108*(5), 711–729. https://doi.org/10.1037/pspi0000014

Paskelian, O. G. (2010). The impact of algorithmic trading models on the stock market. In G. N. Gregoriu (Ed.), *The Handbook of trading: Strategies for navigating and profiting from currency, bond, and stock markets* (pp. 275–285). New York: McGraw-Hill Finance & Investing.

Pavlov, I. P. (1906). The scientific investigation of the psychical faculties or processes in the higher animals. *Science, 24*(620).

Pavlov, I. P. (2010). Conditioned reflexes: An investigation of the physiological activity of the cerebral cortex (G. V. Anrep, Trans.). *Annals of Neurosciences, 17*(3), 136–141. https://doi.org/10.2307/1134737

Pennebaker, J. W., Booth, R. J., & Francis, M. E. (2007). *Linguistic inquiry and word count*. Retrieved from http://www.liwc.net/

Pentland, A. (2014). *Social physics: How good ideas spread-the lessons from a new science*. London: Scribe.

Pew Research Center. (2006). Spirit and power: A 10-country survey of pentecostals. In *The PEW Forum on Religion & Public Life*. Retrieved from http://www.pewforum.org/2006/10/05/spirit-and-power/

Pew Research Center. (2009a). Many Americans mix multiple faiths: Easter, new age beliefs widespread. In *Pew Forum on Religion & Public Life*. Retrieved from http://assets.pewresearch.org/wp-content/uploads/sites/11/2009/12/multiplefaiths.pdf

Pew Research Center. (2009b). Mapping the global muslim population: A report on the size and distribution of the world's muslim population. In *Pew Research Center: Religion and public life*. Retrieved from http://pewforum.org/docs/?DocID=450

Pew Research Center. (2011). *Global Christianity: A report on the size and distribution of the world's Christian population.* Retrieved from http://www.pewforum.org/files/2011/12/Christianity-fullreport-web.pdf

Pew Research Center. (2012). *The global religious landscape.* Retrieved from http://www.pewforum.org/files/2012/12/globalReligion-full.pdf

Pew Research Center. (2015). *The future of world religions uture of worlgrowth projections, 2010–2050.* Retrieved from http://www.pewforum.org/2015/04/02/religious-projections-2010-2050/

Pickering, A. (2010). *The cybernetic brain: Sketches of another future.* Chicago and London: The University of Chicago Press.

Picoli, S., & Mendes, R. S. (2008). Universal features in the growth dynamics of religious activities. *Physical Review E - Statistical, Nonlinear, and Soft Matter Physics, 77*(3), 1–6. https://doi.org/10.1103/PhysRevE.77.036105

Pomeroy, E., Bennett, P., Hunt, C. O., Reynolds, T., Farr, L., Frouin, M., . . . Barker, G. (2020). New Neanderthal remains associated with the "flower burial" at Shanidar Cave. *Antiquity, 94*(373), 11–26. https://doi.org/10.15184/aqy.2019.207

Poon, M., & Tan, M. (Eds.). (2012). *The clock tower story: The beginnings of the charismatic renewals in Singapore* (Revised Ed.). Singapore: Trinity Theological College.

Prebble, S. C., Addis, D. R., & Tippett, L. J. (2012). Autobiographical memory and sense of self. *Psychological Bulletin, 139*(4), 815–840. https://doi.org/10.1037/a0030146

Purzycki, B. G., & Willard, A. K. (2015). MCI theory: A critical discussion. *Religion, Brain & Behavior,* 1–42. https://doi.org/10.1080/2153599X.2015.1024915

Pyysiäinen, I. (2004). Corrupt doctrine and doctrinal revival: On the nature and limits of the modes theory. In H. Whitehouse & L. H. Martin (Eds.), *Theorizing religions past: Archaeology, history, and cognition* (pp. 173–194). Walnut Creek, CA: AltaMira Press.

Pyysiäinen, I. (2005). Religious conversion and modes of religiosity. In H. Whitehouse & R. N. McCauley (Eds.), *Mind and religion: Psychological and cognitive foundations of religiosity* (pp. 149–166). Walnut Creek, CA: AltaMira Press.

Quillian, M. R. (1966). *Semantic memory* (No. 2). Cambridge, MA: Bolt Beranek and Newman .

Quillian, M. R. (1988). Semantic memory. In A. Collins & E. E. Smith (Eds.), *Readings in cognitive science: A perspective from psychology and artificial intelligence* (pp. 80–101). San Mateo, CA: Morgan Kaufmann Publishers, Inc.

Radford, A., Wu, J., Child, R., Luan, D., Amodei, D., & Sutskever, I. (2018). *Language models are unsupervised multitask learners.* https://github.com/openai/gpt-2

Ravasz, E., & Barabási, A.-L. (2003). Hierarchical organization in complex networks. *Physical Review. E, Statistical, Nonlinear, and Soft Matter Physics, 67*(2), 026112-1-026112–026117. https://doi.org/10.1103/PhysRevE.67.026112

Reicher, S. D., Spears, R., & Postmes, T. (1995). A social identity model of deindividuation phenomena. *European Review of Social Psychology*, 6(1), 161–198. https://doi.org/10.1080/14792779443000049

Reiterman, T. (1982). *Raven: The untold story of the Rev. Jim Jones and his people*. New York: Dutton.

Rendu, W., Beauval, C., Crevecoeur, I., Bayle, P., Balzeau, A., Bismuth, T., . . . Maureille, B. (2014). Evidence supporting an intentional Neandertal burial at La Chapelle-aux-Saints. *Proceedings of the National Academy of Sciences of the United States of America*, 111(1), 81–86. https://doi.org/10.1073/pnas.1316780110

Renoult, L., Davidson, P. S. R., Palombo, D. J., Moscovitch, M., & Levine, B. (2012). Personal semantics: At the crossroads of semantic and episodic memory. *Trends in Cognitive Sciences*, 16(11), 550–558. https://doi.org/10.1016/j.tics.2012.09.003

Rescorla, M. (2015). The computational theory of mind. In E. N. Zalta (Ed.), *Stanford encyclopedia of philosophy* (Spring 2017). Retrieved from https://plato.stanford.edu/archives/spr2017/entries/computational-mind/

Rescorla, R. A., & Wagner, A. R. (1972). A theory of Pavlovian conditioning: Variations in the effectiveness of reinforcement and nonreinforcement. In A. H. Black & W. F. Prokasy (Eds.), *Classical conditioning II: Current research and theory* (pp. 64–99). New York: Appleton-Century-Crofts.

Reuters. (2019, September 27). Pope urges silicon valley to avoid a new "barbarism" with tech like artificial intelligence. *Nbcnews.Com*. Retrieved from https://www.nbcnews.com/news/pope-francis/pope-urges-silicon-valley-avoid-new-barbarism-tech-artificial-intelligence-n1059441

Richert, R. A., Whitehouse, H., & Stewart, E. E. A. (2005). Memory and analogical thinking in high-arousal rituals. In H. Whitehouse & L. H. Martin (Eds.), *Mind and religion: Psychological and cognitive foundations of religiosity*. Walnut Creek, CA: AltaMira Press.

Ritter, R. S., Preston, J. L., & Hernandez, I. (2013). Happy tweets: Christians are happier, more socially connected, and less analytical than atheists on twitter. *Social Psychological and Personality Science*. https://doi.org/10.1177/1948550613492345

Roberts, D. C., & Turcotte, D. L. (1998). Fractality and self-organised criticality of wars. *Fractals*, 6(4), 351–357.

Russell, S., & Norvig, P. (2003). *Artificial intelligence: A modern approach* (International ed.). Upper Saddle River, NJ: Prentice Hall/Pearson Education.

Rybanska, V. (2020). *The impact of ritual on child cognition*. Retrieved from https://www.bloomsbury.com/us/the-impact-of-ritual-on-child-cognition-9781350108912/

Rybanska, V., Mckay, R., Jong, J., & Whitehouse, H. (2018). Rituals improve children's ability to delay gratification. *Child Development*, 89(2), 349–359. https://doi.org/10.1111/cdev.12762

Saramäki, J., Leicht, E. a, López, E., Roberts, S. G. B., Reed-Tsochas, F., & Dunbar, R. I. M. (2014). Persistence of social signatures in human communication. *Proceedings of the National Academy of Sciences of the United States of America*, 111(3), 942–947. https://doi.org/10.1073/pnas.1308540110

Sargent, R. G. (2013). Verification and validation of simulation models. *Journal of Simulation, 7*, 12–24. https://doi.org/10.1057/jos.2012.20

Schaller, M., & Murray, D. R. (2008). Pathogens, personality, and culture: Disease prevalence predicts worldwide variability in sociosexuality, extraversion, and openness to experience. *Journal of Personality and Social Psychology, 95*(1), 212–221. https://doi.org/10.1037/0022-3514.95.1.212

Schiffman, L. H. (1991). *From text to tradition: A history of Second Temple and Rabbinic Judaism.* Hoboken, NJ: Ktav Pub Inc.

Schneider, S. (Ed.). (2009). *Science fiction and philosophy: From time travel to superintelligence.* Hoboken, NJ: Wiley.

Schonmann, R. H., Vicente, R., & Caticha, N. (2011). Two-level Fisher-Wright framework with selection and migration: An approach to studying evolution in group structured populations. *ArXiv: 1106.4783*(55), 1–71. Retrieved from http://arxiv.org/abs/1106.4783%5Cnhttp://www.arxiv.org/pdf/1106.4783.pdf

Seshat Databank. (2017). *Seshat: Global history databank.* Retrieved February 13, 2017, from Seshat: Global History Databank website: http://seshatdatabank.info/

Settles, I. H. (2004). When multiple identities interfere: The role of identity centrality. *Personality & Social Psychology Bulletin, 30*(4), 487–500. https://doi.org/10.1177/0146167203261885

Shank, R., & Abelson, R. (1977). *Scripts, plans, goals, and understanding: An inquiry into human knowledge structures.* New York: Halsted.

Sharp, C. A., Rentfrow, P. J., & Gibson, N. J. S. (2015). One God but three concepts: Complexity in Christians' representations of God. *Psychology of Religion and Spirituality, 9*(1), 95–105. https://doi.org/10.1037/rel0000053

Sheikh, H., Atran, S., Ginges, J., Wilson, L., Obeid, N., & Davis, R. (2014). The devoted actor as parochial altruist: Sectarian morality, identity fusion, and support for costly sacrifices. *Cliodynamics, 5*(1), 23–40.

Sheikh, H., Ginges, J., & Atran, S. (2013). Sacred values in the Israeli–Palestinian conflict: Resistance to social influence, temporal discounting, and exit strategies. *Annals of the New York Academy of Sciences, 12991*(1), 11–24. https://doi.org/10.1111/nyas.12275

Sheikh, H., Gómez, Á., & Atran, S. (2016). Empirical evidence for the devoted actor model. *Current Anthropology, 57*(13), S204–S209. https://doi.org/10.1086/686221

Shults, F. L., Gore, R., Wildman, W. J., Christopher, J., Lane, J. E., & Toft, M. D. (2018). A generative model of the mutual escalation of anxiety between religious groups. *Journal of Artificial Societies and Social Simulation, 21*(4). https://doi.org/10.18564/jasss.3840

Shults, F. L., Lane, J. E., Wildman, W. J., Diallo, S., Lynch, C. J., & Gore, R. (2017). Modeling terror management theory: A computer simulation of the impact of mortality salience on religiosity. *Religion, Brain & Behavior, 8*(1), 77–100. https://doi.org/10.1080/2153599X.2016.1238846

Shults, F. L., Toft, M. D., Gore, R., Wildman, W. J., Lynch, C. J., & Lane, J. E. (2017). Mutually escalating religious violence: A generative model. In *Proceedings of the Social Simulation Conference* (pp. 1–12). Dublin, Ireland: European Social Simulation Association.

Shults, F. L., Wildman, W. J., Lane, J. E., Lynch, C. J., & Diallo, S. (2018). Multiple axialities: A computational model of the axial age. *Journal of Cognition & Culture, 18*(5), 537–564. https://doi.org/10.1163/15685373-12340043

Small, M., & Singer, J. D. (1982). *Resort to arms: International and civil wars, 1816-1980*. Beverly Hills, CA: Sage Publications.

Smith, E. R., Coats, S., & Walling, D. (1999). Overlapping mental representations of self, in-group, and partner: Further response time evidence and a connectionist model. *Personality and Social Psychology Bulletin, 25*(7), 873–882. https://doi.org/10.1177/0146167299025007009

Smith, T. W. (2006). The national spiritual transformation study. *Journal for the Scientific Study of Religion, 45*(2), 283–296. https://doi.org/10.1111/j.1468-5906.2006.00306.x

Sng, B. E. K. (2003). *In his good time: The story of the Church in Singapore 1819–2003* (3rd ed.). Singapore: Bible Society of Singapore and the Graduates' Christian Fellowship.

Sokal, A. D., & Bricmont, J. (1998). *Fashionable nonsense: Postmodern intellectuals' abuse of science*. New York: Picador USA.

Spiro, M. E. (1966). Religion: Problems of definition and explanation. In M. Banton (Ed.), *Anthropological approaches to the study of religion* (2004 Reprint, pp. 85–126). New York, Oxford: Routledge.

Staff agencies in Geneva and Beijing. (2019, August 31). Detention of Uighurs must end, UN tells China, amid claims of prison camps. *The Guardian*, pp. 2018–2020. Retrieved from www.theguardian.com/world/2018/aug/31/detention-of-uighurs-must-end-un-tells-china-amid-claims-of-mass-prison-camps

Stark, R. (1996). Why religious movements succeed or fail: A revised general model. *Journal of Contemporary Religion, 11*(2), 133–146. https://doi.org/10.1080/13537909608580764

Stark, R., & Bainbridge, W. S. (1985). *The future of religion: Secularization, revival, and cult formation*. Berkeley: University of California Press.

Stark, R., & Bainbridge, W. S. (1987). *A theory of religion* (1987 Paper). New Brunswick, NJ: Rutgers University Press.

Steffens, N. K., Jetten, J., Haslam, C., Cruwys, T., & Haslam, S. A. (2016, October). Multiple social identities enhance health post-retirement because they are a basis for giving social support. *Frontiers in Psychology*. https://doi.org/10.3389/fpsyg.2016.01519

Stewart, P. (1963). *Jacobellis V. Ohio*. Retrieved from https://cdn.loc.gov/service/ll/usrep/usrep378/usrep378184/usrep378184.pdf

Steyvers, M., & Tenenbaum, J. B. (2005). The large-scale structure of semantic networks: Statistical analyses and a model of semantic growth. *Cognitive Science, 29*(1), 41–78. https://doi.org/10.1207/s15516709cog2901_3

Stiller, J., Nettle, D., & Dunbar, R. I. M. (2003). The small world of Shakespeare's plays. *Human Nature, 14*(4), 397–408. https://doi.org/10.1007/s12110-003-1013-1

Sudworth, J. (2018, October 24). China's hidden camps: What's happened to the vanished uighurs of Xinjiang? *BBC News*. Retrieved from https://www.bbc.co.uk/news/resources/idt-sh/China_hidden_camps

Sun, R. (2001). Cognitive science meets multi-agent systems: A prolegomenon. *Philosophical Psychology, 14*(1), 5–28. https://doi.org/10.1080/09515080120033599

Sun, R. (2006). Prolegomena to integrating cognitive modelling and social simulation. In R. Sun (Ed.), *Cognition and Multi Agent Interaction*. Cambridge: Cambridge University Press.

Sun, R., & Hélie, S. (2013). Psychologically realistic cognitive agents: Taking human cognition seriously. *Journal of Experimental & Theoretical Artificial Intelligence, 25*(1), 65–92. https://doi.org/10.1080/0952813X.2012.661236

Svoboda, E., & Levine, B. (2009). The effects of rehearsal on the functional neuroanatomy of episodic autobiographical and semantic remembering: A functional magnetic resonance imaging study. *The Journal of Neuroscience: The Official Journal of the Society for Neuroscience, 29*(10), 3073–3082. https://doi.org/10.1523/JNEUROSCI.3452-08.2009

Swann, W. B., & Buhrmester, M. D. (2015). Identity fusion. *Current Directions in Psychological Science, 24*(1), 52–57. https://doi.org/10.1177/0963721414551363

Swann, W. B., Buhrmester, M. D., Gómez, Á., Jetten, J., Bastian, B., Vázquez, A., . . . Zhang, A. (2014). What makes a group worth dying for? Identity fusion fosters perception of familial ties, promoting self-sacrifice. *Journal of Personality and Social Psychology, 106*(6), 912–926. https://doi.org/10.1037/a0036089

Swann, W. B., Gómez, Á., Buhrmester, M. D., López-Rodríguez, L., Jiménez, J., & Vázquez, A. (2014). Contemplating the ultimate sacrifice: Identity fusion channels pro-group affect, cognition, and moral decision making. *Journal of Personality and Social Psychology, 106*(5), 713–727. https://doi.org/10.1037/a0035809

Swann, W. B., Gómez, Á., Dovidio, J. F., Hart, S., & Jetten, J. (2010). Dying and killing for one's group: Identity fusion moderates responses to intergroup versions of the trolley problem. *Psychological Science, 21*(8), 1176–1183. https://doi.org/10.1177/0956797610376656

Swann, W. B., Gómez, Á., Seyle, D. C., Morales, J. F., & Huici, C. (2009). Identity fusion: The interplay of personal and social identities in extreme group behavior. *Journal of Personality and Social Psychology, 96*(5), 995–1011. https://doi.org/10.1037/a0013668

Swann, W. B., Jetten, J., Gómez, Á., Whitehouse, H., & Bastian, B. (2012). When group membership gets personal: A theory of identity fusion. *Psychological Review, 119*(3), 441–456. https://doi.org/10.1037/a0028589

Tabor, J. D., & Gallagher, E. (1997). *Why Waco? Cults and the battle for religious freedom in America*. Berkeley: University of California Press.

Tajfel, H. (1974). Social identity and intergroup behaviour. *Social Science Information*, *13*(2), 65–93.

Tajfel, H., & Turner, J. C. (1979). An integrative theory of intergroup conflict. In W. G. Austin & S. Worchel (Eds.), *The Social Psychology of Intergroup Relations* (pp. 33–47). Monterey, CA: Brooks-Cole.

Tajfel, H., & Turner, J. C. (1986). The social identity theory of intergroup behavior. In S. Worchel & W. G. Austin (Eds.), *Psychology of Intergroup Relations* (2nd ed., pp. 7–24). https://doi.org/10.1111/j.1751-9004.2007.00066.x

Taleb, N. N. (2010). *The black swan: The impact of the highly improbable* (2nd ed.). New York: Random House Trade Paperbacks.

Taleb, N. N. (2012). *Antifragile: Things that gain from disorder*. New York: Random House.

Tan, E. K. B. (2008). Keeping God in place: The management of religion in Singapore. In A. E. Lai (Ed.), *Religious diversity in Singapore*. Singapore: Institute of Southeast Asian Studies.

Tan, M. (2014, March 21). [Personal Communication].

Tapia García, J. M., del Moral, M. J., Martínez, M. A., & Herrera-Viedma, E. (2012). A consensus model for group decision making problems with linguistic interval fuzzy preference relations. *Expert Systems with Applications*, *39*(11), 10022–10030. https://doi.org/10.1016/j.eswa.2012.02.008

Tastle, W. J., & Wierman, M. J. (2007). Consensus and dissention: A measure of ordinal dispersion. *International Journal of Approximate Reasoning*, *45*(3), 531–545. https://doi.org/10.1016/j.ijar.2006.06.024

Taves, A. (2016). *Revelatory events: Three case studies of the emergence of new spiritual paths*. Princeton, NJ and Oxford: Princeton University Press.

Tencent Holdings Limited. (2019). *WeChat privacy policy*. Retrieved February 20, 2019, from WeChat website: https://www.wechat.com/en/privacy_policy.html

The Database of Religious History. (2015). *The database of religious history*. Retrieved April 22, 2015, from The University of British Columbia [website] website: http://www.religiondatabase.arts.ubc.ca/

The National Council of Churches of Singapore. (2004). *Many faces, one faith*. Singapore: The National Council of Churches of Singapore.

The National Council of Churches of Singapore. (2013). *A guide to Churches & Christian organizations in Singapore 2013–2014*. Singapore: The Bible Society of Singapore.

The World Bank. (2016). Data. Retrieved May 22, 2016, from World Development Indicators website: http://data.worldbank.org/

Toft, M. D., Philpott, D., & Shah, T. S. (2011). *God's century: Resurgent religion and global politics*. Retrieved from https://wwnorton.com/books/9780393932737

Tolk, A., & Wildman, W. J. (2018). Human simulation as the Lingua Franca for computational social sciences and humanities: Potential and pitfalls. *Journal of Cognition & Culture*, *18*(5), 462–482. https://doi.org/10.1163/15685373-12340040

Tooby, J., & Cosmides, L. (1992). The psychological foundations of culture. In J. H. Barkow, L. Cosmides, & J. Tooby (Eds.), *The adapted mind: Evolutionary psychology and the generation of culture* (pp. 19–136). Oxford and New York: Oxford University Press.

Travers, J., & Milgram, S. (1969). An experimental study of the small world problem. *Sociometry, 32*(4), 425–443. Retrieved from http://www.jstor.org/stable/2786545

Turchin, P. (2016). *Ultrasociety: How 10,000 years of war made humans the greatest cooperators on Earth*. Chaplin, CT: Beresta Books.

Turchin, P., Whitehouse, H., Francois, P., Slingerland, E., & Collard, M. (2012). A historical database of sociocultural evolution. *Cliodynamics: The Journal of Theoretical and Mathematical History, 3*(2), 271–293. Retrieved from http://www.escholarship.org/uc/item/2v8119hf

Turner, J. C., Reynolds, K. J., Haslam, S. A., & Veenstra, K. E. (2006). Reconceptualizing personality: Producing individuality by defining the personal self. In T. Postmes & J. Jetten (Eds.), *Individuality and the group: Advances in social identity* (pp. 11–36). London: SAGE.

Turner-Zwinkels, F. M., Postmes, T., & Van Zomeren, M. (2015). Achieving harmony among different social identities within the self-concept: The consequences of internalising a group-based philosophy of life. *PLoS One, 10*(11), 1–31. https://doi.org/10.1371/journal.pone.0137879

UNINETT Sigma AS. (2015). NOTUR | The Norwegian Metacentre for computational science. Retrieved June 21, 2015, from NOTUR website: https://www.notur.no/

United States Department of Justice. (1993). *Report to the Deputy Attourney general on the events at Waco, Texas: February 18 to April 19, 1993*. Retrieved from https://www.justice.gov/archives/publications/waco/evaluation-handling-branch-davidian-stand-waco-texas-february-28-april-19-1993

University of Oxford Advanced Research Computing. (2015). *Services*. Retrieved June 21, 2015, from Advanced Research Computing website: http://www.arc.ox.ac.uk/content/services

Upal, M. A. (2005a). Role of context in memorability of intuitive and counterintuitive concepts. In *Proceedings of the 27th Annual Meeting of the Cognitive Science Society* (pp. 2224–2229). Retrieved from http://faculty.oxy.edu/aupal/res/05/css.pdf

Upal, M. A. (2005b). Simulating the emergence of new religious movements. *Journal of Artificial Societies and Social Simulation, 8*(1). Retrieved from http://jasss.soc.surrey.ac.uk/8/1/6.html

Upal, M. A. (2005c). Towards a cognitive science of new religious movements. *Journal of Cognition and Culture, 5*(1), 214–239. https://doi.org/10.1163/1568537054068598

Upal, M. A. (2010). An alternative account of the minimal counterintuitiveness effect. *Cognitive Systems Research*. https://doi.org/10.1016/j.cogsys.2009.08.003

Upal, M. A. (2011). From individual to social counterintuitiveness: How layers of innovation weave together to form multilayered tapestries of human cultures. *Mind & Society, 10*(1), 79–96. https://doi.org/10.1007/s11299-011-0083-8

Upal, M. A. (2015). A framework for agent-based social simulations of social identity dynamics. In P. V. Fellman, Y. Bar-Yam, & A. A. Minai (Eds.), *Conflict and complexity: Countering terrorism, insurgency, ethnic and regional violence* (pp. 89–109). https://doi.org/10.1007/978-1-4939-1705-1

Upal, M. A. (2017). Moderate fundamentalists. In *Moderate fundamentalists*. https://doi.org/10.1515/9783110556643

Upal, M. A., & Gibbon, S. (2015). Agent-based system for simulating the dynamics of social identity beliefs. In *Proceedings of the 48th annual simulation symposium* (pp. 94–101). San Diego: Society for Computer Simulation International.

Vail, K. E., Rothschild, Z. K., Weise, D. R., Solomon, S., Pyszczynski, T., & Greenberg, J. (2010). A terror management analysis of the psychological functions of religion. *Personality and Social Psychology Review, 14*(1), 84–94.

Vázquez, A., Gómez, Á., Ordoñana, J. R., & Paredes, B. (2015). From interpersonal to extended fusion: Relationships between fusion with siblings and fusion with the country. *Revista de Psicología Social, 30*(3), 512–530. https://doi.org/10.1080/02134748.2015.1093755

Vázquez, A., Gómez, Á., & Swann, W. B. (2017). Do historic threats to the group diminish identity fusion and its correlates? *Self and Identity, 16*(4), 480–503. https://doi.org/10.1080/15298868.2016.1272485

Verkuyten, M., & Yildiz, A. A. (2007). National (Dis)identification and ethnic and religious identity: A study among Turkish-Dutch muslims. *Personality and Social Psychology Bulletin, 33*(10), 1448–1462. https://doi.org/10.1177/0146167207304276

Wagoner, B. (2013). Bartlett's concept of schema in reconstruction. *Theory & Psychology, 23*(5), 553–575. https://doi.org/10.1177/0959354313500166

Wallis, R., & Bruce, S. (1984). The stark-bainbridge theory of religion: A critical and counter analysis. *Sociological Analysis, 45*(1), 11–27.

Ward, J. S., & Barker, A. (2013). Undefined by data: A survey of big data definitions. *ArXiv Preprint*.

Watts, D. J., & Strogatz, S. H. (1998). Collective dynamics of "small-world" networks. *Nature, 393*(6684), 440–442. https://doi.org/10.1038/30918

Wee, L. (2011). Metadiscursive convergence in the Singlish debate. *Language and Communication, 31*(1), 75–85. https://doi.org/10.1016/j.langcom.2010.04.001

Welzel, C., Inglehart, R., & Klingemann, H.-D. (2003). The theory of human development: A cross-cultural analysis. *European Journal of Political Research, 42*(3), 341–379. https://doi.org/10.1111/1475-6765.00086

Wessinger, C. (2000). *How the Millennium comes violently: From Jonestown to Heaven's Gate*. New York: Seven Bridges Press.

Westland, J. C. (2010). Lower bounds on sample size in structural equation modeling. *Electronic Commerce Research and Applications, 11*(4), 476–487. https://doi.org/10.1016/j.elerap.2010.07.003

Whitehouse, H. (1995). *Inside the cult: Religious innovation and transmission in Papua New Guinea*. Oxford and New York: Clarendon Press; Oxford University Press.

Whitehouse, H. (1996). Rites of terror: Emotion, metaphor and memory in Melanesian initiation cults. *The Journal of the Royal Anthropological Institute*, *2*(4), 703–715. Retrieved from http://www.jstor.org/stable/3034304

Whitehouse, H. (2000). *Arguments and icons: Divergent modes of religiosity*. Oxford: Oxford University Press.

Whitehouse, H. (2002). Modes of religiosity: Towards a cognitive explanation of the socioloplitical dynamics of religion. *Method & Theory in the Study of Religion*, *14*, 293–315.

Whitehouse, H. (2004). *Modes of religiosity: A cognitive theory of religious transmission*. In Luther H. Martin and Harvey Whitehouse (Eds.), *Cognitive Science of Religion*. Walnut Creek, CA: AltaMira Press.

Whitehouse, H. (2013). Rethinking proximate causation and development in religious evolution. In Peter J. Richerson and Morten H. Christiansen (Eds.), *Cultural Evolution: Society, Technology, Language, and Religion* (pp. 349–364). Cambridge, MA: MIT Press.

Whitehouse, H. (2018). Dying for the group: Towards a general theory of extreme self-sacrifice. *Behavioral and Brain Sciences*, *41*, 1–12. https://doi.org/10.1017/S0140525X 18000249

Whitehouse, H., François, P., Savage, P. E., Currie, T. E., Feeney, K. C., Cioni, E., ... Turchin, P. (2019). Complex societies precede moralizing Gods throughout world history. *Nature*, *568*, 226–229. https://doi.org/10.1038/s41586-019-1043-4

Whitehouse, H., & Hodder, I. (2010). Modes of religiosity at Çatalhöyük. In I. Hodder (Ed.), *Religion in the emergence of civilization: Çatalhöyük as a case study* (pp. 122–145). Cambridge: Cambridge University Press.

Whitehouse, H., Jong, J., Buhrmester, M. D., Bastian, B., Kavanagh, C. M., Newson, M., ... Gavrilets, S. (2017a). Supplementary materials: The evolution of identity fusion and extreme cooperation. *Nature Scientific Reports*, *7*(44292), 1–33.

Whitehouse, H., Jong, J., Buhrmester, M. D., Bastian, B., Kavanagh, C. M., Newson, M., ... Gavrilets, S. (2017b). The evolution of identity fusion and extreme cooperation. *Nature Scientific Reports*, *7*(44292), 1–10. https://doi.org/10.1038/srep44292

Whitehouse, H., Kahn, K., Hochberg, M. E., & Bryson, J. J. (2012). The role for simulations in theory construction for the social sciences: Case studies concerning divergent modes of religiosity. *Religion, Brain & Behavior*, *2*(3), 182–201. https://doi.org/10.1080/2153599X.2012.691033

Whitehouse, H., & Lanman, J. A. (2014). The ties that bind US: Ritual, fusion, and identification. *Current Anthropology*, *55*(6), 674–695.

Whitehouse, H., Mazzucato, C., Hodder, I., & Atkinson, Q. D. (2013). Modes of religiosity and the evolution of social complexity at Çatalhöyük. In I. Hodder (Ed.), *Religion at work in a neolithic society: Vital matters* (pp. 134–155). Cambridge: Cambridge University Press.

Whitehouse, H., McQuinn, B., Buhrmester, M. D., & Swann, W. B. (2014). Brothers in arms: Libyan revolutionaries bond like family. *Proceedings of the National Academy of Sciences of the United States of America, 111*(50), 17783–17785. https://doi.org/10.1073/pnas.1416284111

Whitmarsh, A., Walls, E., Papadaki, E., Ryoo, K., Zhuang, M., Kim, S., & Lee, M. (2013). *Methodological challenges and opportunities in studying corruption reposting on Sina Weibo* (pp. 1–5).

Wiebe, D. (1991). *The irony of theology and the nature of religious thought*. Montreal Que: McGill-Queen's University Press.

Wiebe, D. (1999). *The politics of religious studies: The continuing conflict with theology in the academy*. New York: Palgrave.

Wildman, W. J., & Sosis, R. (2011). Stability of groups with costly beliefs and practices. *Journal of Artificial Societies and Social Simulation, 14*(3), 6.

Wilensky, U. (1999). *Netlogo*. Retrieved from http://ccl.northwestern.edu/netlogo/

Wilson, A. E., & Ross, M. (2003). The identity function of autobiographical memory: Time is on our side. *Memory, 11*(2), 137–149. https://doi.org/10.1080/741938210

Wilson, D. S. (2002). *Darwin's Cathedral: Evolution, religion, and the nature of society*. Chicago: University of Chicago Press.

Winocur, G., & Moscovitch, M. (2011). Memory transformation and systems consolidation. *Journal of the International Neuropsychological Society: JINS, 17*(5), 766–780. https://doi.org/10.1017/S1355617711000683

Witnauer, J. E., & Miller, R. R. (2009). Contrasting the overexpectation and extinction effects. *Behavioural Processes, 81*(2), 322–327. https://doi.org/10.1016/j.beproc.2009.01.010

Wixted, J. T. (1991). Conditions and consequences of maintenance rehearsal. *Journal of Experimental Psychology. Learning, Memory, and Cognition, 17*(5), 963–973. https://doi.org/10.1037/0278-7393.17.5.963

Wolf, E. J., Harrington, K. M., Clark, S. L., & Miller, M. W. (2013). Sample size requirements for Structural Equation Models: An evaluation of power, bias, and solution propriety. *Educational and Psychological Measurement, 76*(6), 913–934. https://doi.org/10.1177/0013164413495237

World Religion Database. (2016). World religion database. In T. M. Johnson & B. J. Grim (Eds.), *World Religion Database*. Retrieved from http://www.worldreligiondatabase.org/

Xu, Y., & Reitter, D. (2018). Information density converges in dialogue: Towards an information-theoretic model. *Cognition, 170*, 147–163. https://doi.org/10.1016/j.cognition.2017.09.018

Xygalatas, D. (2012). *The burning saints: Cognition and culture in the fire-walking rituals of the Anastenaria*. Bristol, CT: Equinox Publishing Ltd.

Xygalatas, D. (2014). Ritual and cohesion: What is the place of euphoric arousal?. *Current Anthropology, 55*(6), 689–690.

Xygalatas, D., Schjoedt, U., Bulbulia, J., Konvalinka, I., Jegindo, M., Reddish, P., ... Roepstoff, A. (2013). *Autobiographical memory in a fire-walking ritual* (pp. 1–16).

Young, J.-G., Hébert-Dufresne, L., Allard, A., & Dubé, L. J. (2016). Growing networks of overlapping communities with internal structure. *Physical Review E, 94,* 1–14. https://doi.org/10.1103/PhysRevE.94.022317

Zeder, M. A. (2011). The origins of agriculture in the near east. *Current Anthropology, 54*(S4), s221–s235. https://doi.org/10.1086/659307

Zhou, W.-X., Sornette, D., Hill, R. A., & Dunbar, R. I. M. (2005). Discrete hierarchical organization of social group sizes. *Proceedings. Biological Sciences / The Royal Society, 272*(1561), 439–444. https://doi.org/10.1098/rspb.2004.2970

Index

AI guru   1, 153–9
AI sermon   154–7
alpha leaders   27, 172
artificial human intelligence   8–10
artificial neural networks   5–10, 154, 157, 199
assemblage theory   10–18, 22–5, 191–5

Bainbridge, William S.   106, 125, 169, 204
BehaviorComposer   107, 204
Bible   144
Bible study   49, 80, 98, 125
big data   142–6, 159, 181–4
Boston bombing   81–4
Boyer, Pascal   158
Branch Davidians (Waco, TX)   39, 171–2

Center for Mind and Culture   142, 144, 145, 186, 208
Center for Modeling Social Systems   208
centrality
  event   66–7, 77–8, 85–95, 114, 171
  network   114, 171
charasmatic leaders   41, 169–72
charasmatic leadership, human alphas   27, 172
Charismatic and Pentecostal Christianity   37–45, 79–80, 97–8
complex systems   15–16, 24–5, 99, 194
consensus   18, 26, 30, 33, 36–7, 57–60, 64–72, 94–5, 99–103, 122–3, 131–2, 163–7, 176–7, 183

cultural cybernetics   10–25, 59, 99, 135, 148–51, 177–85, 191–7
cultural epidemiology   19, 166, 181
cultural evolution   19–20, 23, 110, 140, 150, 168, 177–9, 194, 207

Darwinism   148, 177–9
data science   2, 74, 95, 99, 103, 105, 147, 176
Database of Religious History   186
Delanda, Manuel   13–14
devoted actor theory   129, 170–2, 185, 188–90
Divergent Modes of Religiosity Theory, failed predictions   42–4
Divergent Modes of Religiosity Theory, overview   33–8
Durkheim, Emile   21

early Christianity   163
emergence   13–16, 24, 60, 99, 131, 138–40
emotional intensity   34, 42–4, 59–65, 77–8, 81–5, 88–94, 187
  dysphoria   33–5, 40, 48, 53–4, 61, 67, 78, 81, 84–94, 118–21, 205
  euphoria   48, 53–4, 61, 81, 84–91, 93–4, 118–21
entropy   16–17, 121, 152–3
Epstein, Joshua   8, 14, 137–9, 190
ethics   50, 177–8, 182–5
evolution   23, 50, 60, 110, 139–41, 150–2, 177–9, 186–7
extremism   1–2, 6, 23, 26, 30, 55, 60, 69, 77–104, 164, 171–5, 188–91

extremism and identity 77–104, 164, 171–5, 188–91

Facebook 19, 144–6, 180, 183, 190
frame 56–9, 202, 203

game theory 118, 140–1
generative emergence 14–16, 23–5, 64, 125, 129–31, 138–40
GPT-2 154
group definition 23, 27
Gujarat Riots 141

humanities 21–2, 143, 160–1, 192–6

identity
  categorical ties 29, 35, 51–2, 63–4, 68–72, 129, 201
  conceptual ties 68–74, 78–9, 89–90, 92–4, 133–4, 139–40, 151, 165–7, 171, 176, 187–91
  fusion 28–30, 36–7, 46–54, 65–75, 77–9, 84–5, 91–4, 120–4, 129, 151, 187–9
  fusion, extended 29, 48–54, 66–75, 77–9, 85, 91–4, 124, 151, 187–9
  fusion, local 29, 48–51, 65, 71–3, 84–5, 92, 120–4, 129
  relational ties 36, 46–9, 50–4, 65–6, 71–4, 77–9, 92–4
  simulation, fusion 118–21, 123–6
  simulation, social identification 115–17, 123–6
  social identity theory 45–8
imagistic shift 111–12
information
  definition 16–17
  definition of information, Bateson 16
  definition of information, Shannon 16–17
  identity system 55–95
  identity system, simulation 68–72, 121–32

James (Apostle) 163
James, William 2–3, 38, 66, 80
Jesus 41, 67, 80, 163
Jonestown/Jim Jones 39–40
Judiasm 12, 37, 41, 163, 168

Lawson, E. Thomas 18
leadership 36–7, 80, 125, 151–2, 165, 169–72
lossy distance 99, 102, 177
lossy intersection matrix 99–101, 123

McCauley, Robert N. 18
machine learning 4–10, 137, 141, 143, 153–9
Melton's Encyclopedia of American Religions 41
memory
  consolidation 56, 61–5, 122
  episodic 35–6, 49–50, 60–5
  semantic 34–5, 42, 57–65, 71, 79, 89, 95, 151
mereology 11–12, 168, 199
Model of mutually escalating religious violence (MERV) 136–42
modeling theory 21–2
multi-agent artificial intelligence (MAAI) 7–10, 24–5, 105, 115, 141, 143, 153, 157, 170–3, 178–9, 195

natural language processing (NLP), see text analysis
natural sciences 17, 192–7
netlogo 107, 109, 204, 205
network distance 99–102, 123
  Euclidian 101
  hamming 101
  jaccard 101
networks and assemblages 15, 25, 27
networks and schemas 57–9, 61, 69–74, 112–14
New Religious Movements (NRMs) 30, 39–42, 125–6, 129–30, 146, 164, 168–74
Northern Ireland 81–2, 134–6, 141

online social networks   19, 74, 144, 146, 152, 180–5, 190–1

Paul (Apostle)   114, 163
personal schema   54, 59, 66–72, 74, 79, 84, 89, 91, 94, 100, 123, 124, 167, 171, 176, 187–9, 199
politics   27, 58, 82, 134–5, 141, 148–51, 172, 184–8, 191–2
Pope Francis   vii, 1, 144, 146
prediction   17, 59–60, 142–3, 177–82

Reddit   19, 146, 180, 182–3
reflection   33–7, 50, 59, 62–74, 77–95, 131, 151
  frequency   85–94
religion, definition of religion   12–14, 17–18, 134, 135, 142–3, 148–50, 164, 170, 173–4, 189, 193
religionistika   195–7
religious studies   2–3, 12, 144–5, 169–70, 181, 191–7
religious violence   134–42, 159, 164, 186, 190
Rescorla-Wagner   59, 137–8
retreat   44, 79–80, 93, 123–7, 188
revival   43, 97, 125, 129, 204
  Clock Tower   97, 204
ritual   31–44, 55–64, 67, 75, 77, 79–80, 97–9, 175, 187–9
  bonding   25–6, 33–8, 48–9, 120–4
  Charismatic Christianity   79–81, 97–8
  divergent modes of religiosity   32–45
  frequency   14, 34, 38–43, 59–64, 69, 75–8, 95, 99–102
  simulation   105–32

sacred values   129, 140–1, 163–74, 185, 188–90
scale free   113–14, 139

schemas   25, 34–5, 55–74, 77–81, 89, 91–5, 100, 114, 122–5, 165–7, 171, 176, 187, 199–203
scientific study of religion   2–3, 11–14, 18, 193–7
script   56–7, 99
self schema   56
semantic networks   7, 25, 68–72, 99–103, 107–8, 114, 128, 176–7, 179–82, 184, 191, 203
Sermon database   150–3
SESHAT Database   186
Shults, F. LeRon   206
signs and wonders   97, 204
Singapore, growth of Christianity in   95–8
Singapore, religion in   91–3, 95–8, 125
singularity   16–17, 27–8
social cohesion   25–8, 33–7, 48–9, 59–65, 86–95, 114–17, 121–34, 143–61, 167–8, 176–81, 185–8
social cohesion (definition)   25–6
social darwinism   148, 150, 177, 207
social networks   19, 23, 25, 65–6, 68, 71–2, 74, 96, 102, 125, 130, 138–40, 144–6, 165, 167, 180–5, 190–1
social schema   35, 56–7, 59–75, 78–81, 89, 94–5, 100–3, 123–4, 165–7, 171, 176, 180, 187, 189, 200
social schism   39–40, 60, 108–12, 115–17, 129, 163–74, 190–1
social stability   133–63
sophia (android)   153–7
structural equation model   102–3
Sun, Ron   8
supercomputers   137, 142, 145–6, 154, 159, 180, 189
surveillance   183–5

terrorism   30, 48–50, 55

terrorism, September 11, 2001   148–52
text analysis   4, 17, 69–72, 79, 99–102, 105, 113–15, 143–57, 159, 179–84
theology   2–3, 12–13, 80–1, 96, 133, 134, 153, 181, 192, 197
The Troubles   61–2, 134–5, 141
Twitter   144–6, 180, 182, 183, 190

Upal, M. Afzal   106, 116–19

validation   108, 123, 126, 141, 196
   mechanistic correspondence   24–5, 120–1, 170
   output correspondence   24–5, 108, 120, 123, 126, 134, 141, 170, 196

Whitehouse, Harvey   35–6, 38, 39, 41, 50, 86, 107, 111–12, 115, 120, 125–7, 176
Wildman, Wesley J.   145

www.ingramcontent.com/pod-product-compliance
Lightning Source LLC
Chambersburg PA
CBHW062137300426
44115CB00012BA/1963